AF694841

The Recognition and Enforcement of Punitive Damages Judgments Across the Globe

The Recognition and Enforcement of Punitive Damages Judgments Across the Globe

Insights from Various Continents

Cedric Vanleenhove and Lotte Meurkens

eleven

Published, sold and distributed by Eleven
P.O. Box 85576
2508 CG The Hague
The Netherlands
Tel.: +31 70 33 070 33
Fax: +31 70 33 070 30
e-mail: sales@elevenpub.nl
www.elevenpub.com

Sold and distributed in USA and Canada
Independent Publishers Group
814 N. Franklin Street
Chicago, IL 60610, USA
Order Placement: +1 800 888 4741
Fax: +1 312 337 5985
orders@ipgbook.com
www.ipgbook.com

M-EPLI
MAASTRICHT
EUROPEAN
PRIVATE LAW
INSTITUTE

Eleven is an imprint of Boom uitgevers Den Haag.
ISBN 978-90-4730-162-2
ISBN 978-94-0011-317-6 (e-book)

© 2023 The authors | Eleven

This publication is protected by international copyright law.
All rights reserved. No part of this publication may be reproduced, stored in a retrieval system, or transmitted in any form or by any means, electronic, mechanical, photocopying, recording or otherwise, without the prior permission of the publisher.

Prologue

Our interest in punitive damages grew when we chose this fascinating civil sanction as our PhD topic at Maastricht University and Ghent University respectively. Lotte Meurkens defended her dissertation concerning the question whether punitive damages have a future as a substantive law remedy in continental Europe from a general perspective in 2014. Cedric Vanleenhove defended his dissertation on the private international law treatment of punitive damages from a European perspective in 2015. Since then, we have published several contributions in this particular field in Dutch, Belgian and international legal literature.

Following a groundbreaking decision of the Italian Supreme Court in 2017, the Department of Italian and Supranational Public Law of the University of Milan organised a conference on punitive damages in May 2018. During the conference, in which we presented our research, the private international law question was addressed from the perspective of several European countries. The insights of the conference were collected in a book: S. Bariatti, L. Fumagalli & Z. Crespi Reghizzi (Eds.), *Punitive damages and private international law: State of the art and future developments*, Padova, Wolters Kluwer-Cedam, Studi e Pubblicazioni della Rivista di Diritto Internazionale Privato e Processuale Vol. 83, 2019.

As our curiosity does not stop at the European borders and the relevance of the institution of punitive damages equally extends far beyond, we decided to broaden our horizons. We found that systematic research into jurisdictions outside Europe was lacking even though there is a continuous discussion in several legal systems worldwide on the recognition and enforcement of foreign punitive damages judgments. We therefore attempted to bring researchers from different continents together to exchange understandings and foster the cross-fertilisation of ideas.

For the purpose of our project, we organised a Maastricht European Private Law Institute (M-EPLI) Roundtable in October 2021. This book is the subsequent result of that fruitful Roundtable. It intends to give an overview of the manner in which several jurisdictions across various continents deal with the enforceability of foreign judgments awarding punitive damages. The book includes an introductory chapter on the status quo of punitive damages enforcement in Europe (chapter 1) and country reports from Russia (chapter 2), China (chapter 3), South Korea (chapter 4), the Philippines and Japan (chapter 5), Commonwealth Africa (chapter 6), Argentina and Mexico (chapter 7), Brazil (chapter 8) and overarching concluding insights from the Hague Conference (chapter 9).

We wish to thank all the authors for their enriching and valuable contributions to this important global debate. Furthermore, we are very grateful to Marta Pertegás Sender for her indispensable help in realising this book. She holds the chair in private international law and transnational law at Maastricht University and we both have had the pleasure of working with her for many years now. A special thanks goes to Marielène Wertenbroek, our assistant editor. She is a student intern at M-EPLI who wrote her bachelor thesis on the insurability of punitive damages in American and Dutch law. Her careful formal review of all contributions in this book shows that she has genuine interest in the topic of punitive damages and in legal writing in general.

We hope this book may serve as a useful building block for further research into a captivating and truly transnational legal issue.

Cedric Vanleenhove and Lotte Meurkens
June 2023

Table of Contents

CONTENTS

Enforcement of Punitive Damages in Europe: An Overview

Cedric Vanleenhove[*]

1 Introduction

Punitive damages: the term itself is able to send shivers down the continental lawyer's spine. The civil remedy can be described as an additional amount of money awarded to the victim of an unlawful act on top of the normal compensatory damages. Punitive damages do not (at least primarily) aim to compensate the victim (for a harm) but instead pursue the punishment of the culprit and intend to deter him and other potential wrongdoers from repeating the harmful conduct. Other names include exemplary damages, aggravated damages[1] or multiple (usually treble) damages if they are calculated as a multiplication of the compensatory damages.

Although traces of the concept can be found as early as the 18th century BC in the Code of Hammurabi, modern-day punitive damages are predominantly present in Common Law countries. Punitive damages exist in several countries around the world. The United States, Canada, Australia, South Africa and New Zealand are the main examples of jurisdictions allowing for the remedy. Within Europe only England, Wales, Ireland, Northern Ireland and Cyprus provide for this kind of damages in their respective legal systems.

Civil Law systems are generally monistic in nature, as only compensatory damages can be awarded and punitive damages are unknown.[2] The concept of punitive damages is considered contrary to the fundamental separation of criminal and private law because punishment should not have its place within private law. Punitive damages are also held to be contrary to the principle of strict compensation and are seen as resulting in an unjust

---

* Professor of Private International Law, Ghent University and HEC Management School Liège University. I am interested to learn about the position on the enforcement of punitive damages in other European countries than the ones covered in this chapter. I can be contacted at cedric.vanleenhove@ugent.be.

1 At least in the United States. In England aggravated damages are a form of compensatory damages: A.J. Sebok & V. Wilcox, 'Aggravated Damages', in H. Koziol & V. Wilcox (Eds.), *Punitive Damages: Common Law and Civil Law Perspectives*, Vienna, Springer, 2009, p. 257.

2 A number of civil law jurisdictions are however beginning to rely on the remedy in their internal law. Examples are the gradual introduction of punitive damages in China to strengthen the protection of intellectual property rights and to deter infringers (see chapter 3 by Zhang and Zhong in this book) and the treble damages introduced in certain areas of Korean law (see chapter 4 by Suk in this book).

enrichment of the plaintiff. Punitive damages are one of the aspects of the Common Law tradition that are looked at with suspicion and scepsis in jurisdictions that do not provide for this type of remedy in their domestic laws.[3]

This difference in mentality comes to the surface and creates friction in particular when Common Law judgments containing punitive damages need to be recognised and enforced in legal systems that do not make the remedy available. The recognition and enforcement of judgments is one of the domains of private international law. This distinct field of law offers a separate perspective from which to study punitive damages. In this chapter, the situation in a number of countries in Europe will be described. It is of course impossible to discuss all relevant countries. Russia will be covered in another chapter.[4]

As the topic of the enforcement of punitive damages judgments in Europe/the EU has been discussed relatively extensively in the past, I will not reproduce in full detail what has been written already.[5] The aim of this chapter is to give a succinct overview of the existing case law (and – to a lesser extent – doctrine) regarding the enforcement of punitive damages in Europe. This will allow the reader to familiarise himself or herself quickly with the current European state of play and sets the scene for the main focus of this book, namely the enforcement of punitive damages in various non-European jurisdictions.

Before delving into the individual countries, it should be noted that the enforceability of awards for punitive damages generally depends on the interpretation of the international public policy exception. The notion of public policy or *ordre public* refers to the common core of principles and fundamental values that are vital for a legal system. In cross-border cases, a more restricted form of public policy, namely international public policy, operates as a safety valve.[6] Only *international* public policy can act as a barrier to the enforcement

---

3 Other aspects include (in my opinion at least) for instance: discovery, contingency fees and class actions (although that has changed dramatically over the last years, see for instance Directive (EU) 2020/1828 of the European Parliament and of the Council of 25 November 2020 on representative actions for the protection of the collective interests of consumers and repealing Directive 2009/22/EC obliging all EU countries to have a mechanism of representative action in place).

4 See chapter 2 by Chernyy in this book.

5 See for my own publications on the subject: C. Vanleenhove, *Punitive Damages in Private International Law: Lessons for the European Union*, Cambridge-Antwerp-Portland, Intersentia, 2016; C. Vanleenhove, 'The Current European Perspective on the Exequatur of U.S. Punitive Damages: Opening the Gate but Keeping a Guard', *Polish Yearbook of International Law*, Vol. 35, 2015, pp. 235-263; C. Vanleenhove, 'A normative framework for the enforcement of U.S. punitive damages in the European Union: transforming the traditional '¡No Pasarán!'', *Vermont Law Review*, Vol. 41, No. 2, 2016, pp. 377-401; C. Vanleenhove, 'The Enforcement of Foreign Decisions Concerning Punitive Damages – Punitive Damages in the Belgian Perspective', *European Review of Private Law*, Vol. 26, No. 5, 2018, pp. 674-680. I relied heavily on these publications while writing this chapter.

6 P. Mayer & V. Heuzé, *Droit international privé*, Paris, Montchrestien, 2004, p. 149, no. 205; A. Mills, *The Confluence of Public and Private International Law – Justice, Pluralism and Subsidiarity in the International Constitutional Ordering of Private Law*, Cambridge, Cambridge University Press, 2009, pp. 275-277; A. Mills, 'The Dimensions of Public Policy in Private International Law', *Journal of Private International Law*, Vol. 4, No. 2, 2008, p. 213.

of a foreign judgment. There is also (mostly older) case law that puts into question the civil nature of punitive damages, in light of the unenforceability of foreign penal decisions.

2 Overview of various European countries

2.1 Germany

In Germany the landmark case is *John Doe v. Eckhard Schmitz* before the *Bundesgerichtshof*, the Federal Court of Justice.[7] The plaintiff sought enforcement of a Californian judgment awarding compensatory and punitive damages for sexual abuse.

The Court ruled that punitive damages are contrary to international public policy and should thus be refused enforcement. The Court held that a foreign judgment awarding lump sum punitive damages of a not inconsiderable amount – in addition to the damages for material and immaterial losses – generally cannot be enforced in Germany. It noted that German private law seeks to compensate, but does not intend to enrich the victim. The main objectives of punitive damages are punishment and deterrence, which belong to the field of criminal law rather than of civil law. Punitive damages also allow a plaintiff to act as a private-public prosecutor, which interferes with the state's monopoly on penalisation. Furthermore, the defendant cannot rely on the special procedural guarantees that criminal law offers.

The *Bundesgerichtshof* further argued that enforcement in Germany would put foreign creditors in a better position than domestic creditors. The former would be able to gain access to the assets of German debtors to a considerably greater extent than the latter, even if the latter had suffered more damage. The fact that foreign creditors can obtain punitive damages leads, according to the Court, to a lack of equal treatment. It thus seems that the *Bundesgerichtshof* tried to shield the German industry from American judgments.[8]

It should be noted that the case's connection to the German territory (*Inlandsbeziehung*) was minimal. The crime was committed in the United States and both the victim and the perpetrator were living there at the time. The rejection of punitive damages despite the slight connection of the case to the forum indicates a strong German antipathy towards this type of damages.[9]

Even though the Federal Court of Justice rejected the punitive award, it continued its reasoning. It subjected the punitive damages to a proportionality check and found that

---

7 Bundesgerichtshof 4 June 1992, *NJW* 1992, p. 3096.

8 S. Baumgartner, 'Understanding the Obstacles to the Recognition and Enforcement of U.S. Judgments Abroad', *New York University Journal of International Law and Politics*, Vol. 44, 2013, p. 998.

9 C.I. Nagy, 'Recognition and enforcement of US judgments involving punitive damages in continental Europe', *Nederlands Internationaal Privaatrecht*, Vol. 30, No. 1, 2012, p. 8.

enforcement would be excessive because the punitive damages awarded are higher in amount than the sum of all the compensatory damages. This could be interpreted as laying down a maximum 1:1 ratio between compensatory and punitive damages for enforcement purposes.

The Court also carved out an exception to the enforceability of foreign punitive damages. It ruled that it would allow the enforcement of punitive damages if and to the extent that the punitive award serves a compensatory function (for instance the reimbursement of legal costs). This requires that the rendering court has explicitly identified the partly compensatory character of the punitive damages granted, which does not happen frequently in the United States and limits the impact of the exception significantly.[10] It has been suggested that punitive damages from U.S. states where compensation for legal costs is the only ground for awarding punitive damages nowadays should be deemed to fall under the scope of the exception.[11]

2.2 *Switzerland*

In Switzerland two cases have dealt with the enforcement of foreign punitive damages judgments. In a 1982 decision the court of first instance of Sargans refused the enforcement of a punitive damages award rendered in Texas. The American judgment awarded punitive damages in the amount of three times the actual damages for the defendant's misrepresentation in connection with the sale of real estate in Texas. The court held that punitive damages violate the principle that a tort victim should not be enriched by receiving compensation in excess of the damage suffered. Additionally, the court implied that the exemplary damages lacked "civil" character and should for that reason also be denied enforcement.[12]

In litigation between S.F. Inc. and T.C.S. AG the California District Court had awarded USD 50.000 in punitive damages under English law for the misappropriation of containers. Both the District Court of Basel and the Basel Court of Appeal enforced the USD 50.000

---

10 W. Wurmnest, 'Recognition and Enforcement of U.S. Money Judgments in Germany', *Berkeley Journal of International Law*, Vol. 23, 2005, p. 197; J. Zekoll, 'The Enforceability of American Money Judgments Abroad: A Landmark Decision by the German Federal Court of Justice', *Columbia Journal of Transnational Law*, Vol. 30, 1992, p. 657.

11 A. Stadler, 'Recognition of punitive damages in Germany and Switzerland', in S. Bariati, L. Fumagalli & Z. Crespi Reghizzi (Eds.), *Punitive Damages and Private International Law: State of the Art and Future Developments*, Milan, Wolters Kluwer, 2019, p. 141.

12 M. Berner & N.C. Ulmer, 'Recognition and Enforcement in Switzerland of US Judgments Containing an Award of Punitive Damages', *International Business Lawyer*, Vol. 22, 1994, p. 273. The case is reported in J. Drolshammer & H. Schärer, 'Die Verletzung des materiellen Ordre Public als Verweigerungsgrund bei der Vollstreckung eines U.S.- Amerikanischen "Punitive Damages-Urteils"' (Urteilsanmerkung)', *Schweizerische Juristen-Zeitung*, Vol. 82, No. 20, 1986, p. 309.

since its primary purpose was to restitute the unjust profit to the plaintiff, thereby avoiding the unjust enrichment of the defendant. The fact that the amount was a mere estimate of the defendant's unlawful profit was not seen as an obstacle to enforcement.[13]

2.3 *The Netherlands*

In the Netherlands there seems to be a principled antipathy towards foreign punitive damages. In a recent judgment the court of appeal of 's-Hertogenbosch (*Gerechtshof 's-Hertogenbosch*) declined to enforce the punitive damages contained in a judgment from the United States District Court for the Middle District of Tennessee. The compensatory damages and punitive damages awarded by the American court both amounted to USD 250.000. The court of appeal held the punitive damages to be against Dutch public policy because they are intended to punish and deter while Dutch liability law seeks to put the victim in the position he or she would have been in had the damaging event not taken place, and nothing more than that. Punishment and general and specific deterrence belong to the realm of criminal law. The court also noted that the amount of the punitive damages was "*fors*" (translation: hefty) in light of the compensatory damages. The court did leave the door open for punitive damages that compensate for costs incurred but in the case before the court the plaintiffs had not provided convincing evidence in that respect.[14] The incompatibility of punitive damages with the public policy of the Netherlands seems to already have been laid down in earlier case law.[15]

2.4 *Greece*

In Greece the Supreme Court (*Areopag*) has ruled on the enforceability of a Texas judgment awarding punitive damages in 1999. The *Areopag* accepted that punitive damages are not as such a violation of (international) public policy. Instead, it investigated the possible excessiveness of the punitive damages. It found that the punitive award was disproportionate to the compensatory part as the amount of the punitive damages was more than the

13 District Court Basel-Stadt 1 February 1989, upheld by the Basel-Stadt Court of Appeal 1 December 1989, *Basler Juristische Mitteilungen* 1991, pp. 31-38.

14 Gerechtshof 's-Hertogenbosch 31 August 2021, ECLI:NL:RBOBR:2019:4987, nos. 3.7.3-3.7.5 (available via rechtspraak.nl).

15 Rechtbank Amsterdam 12 December 2018, ECLI:NL:RBAMS:2018:9144, no. 4.10; Rechtbank Utrecht 8 February 2012, ECLI:NL:RBUTR:2012:BW163, no. 4.21: the latter judgment did not concern a request for enforcement but the application of Israeli law providing for punitive damages. There is, however, a lower court judgment that awarded punitive damages on the basis of the applicable California law, holding that Dutch public policy is not violated if the punitive damages are awarded to the plaintiffs: Rechtbank Amsterdam 15 June 2012, ECLI:NL:RBAMS:2012:BW9838, no. 4.14 (all judgments available via rechtspraak.nl).

damage sustained.[16] In a case of 2002 it ruled that punitive damages awarded in the amount of USD 60.000 were disproportionally high compared to the principal amount due of USD 100.000.[17]

Furthermore, there is a ruling by the court of first instance of Piraeus that granted enforcement to U.S. punitive damages in the significant amount of USD 10 million and despite the compensatory damages being USD 7.8 million.[18] This could be a sign that courts are starting to adopt a more flexible approach and are moving away from assessing the excessiveness of the punitive award by comparison to the compensatory damages towards a more holistic and pragmatic *ad hoc* assessment of the legal and factual background of the case. In any case, instead of requiring that the amount of punitive damages is considerably lower than the actual loss, it would suffice that the amount is not significantly higher than the actual loss.[19]

2.5 Spain

In the case of *Miller Import Corp. v. Alabastres Alfredo, S.L.* of 13 November 2001 the Spanish Supreme Court (*Tribunal Supremo*) dealt with a request for enforcement of a judgment of the Federal District Court for the Southern District of Texas (Houston Hall) containing treble damages for trademark infringement.[20]

The Spanish Supreme Court noted that the Texas judgment contained some damages that did not serve a compensatory objective but were punitive, sanction-like and preventive in nature. In light of the international public policy analysis, the Court noted that coercive, sanctioning mechanisms are not uncommon in (Spanish) substantive law. According to the Court the presence of such punitive mechanisms in private law to compensate for the shortcomings of criminal law is consistent with the legislature obligation to first counter

16 Greek Supreme Court, decision no. 17 of 1999, *Nomiko Bina i Miniaion Nomikon Periodikon* 2000, pp. 461-464; M. Requejo Isidro, 'Punitive Damages: How Do They Look Like When Seen From Abroad?', in L. Meurkens & E. Nordin (Eds.), *The Power of Punitive Damages – Is Europe Missing Out?*, Cambridge-Antwerp-Portland, Intersentia, 2012, p. 326.

17 Greek Supreme Court, decision no. 1260 of 2002, as reported by A. Tsirigos, P. Krystallis, & D. Skevi, 'Recognition and Enforcement of Foreign Court Decisions and Arbitral Awards in Greece: Is There a New Trend Towards a More Relaxed Application of the Public Policy Exception to Punitive Damages?', Kluwer Arbitration Blog, 10 June 2019 (available via https://arbitrationblog.kluwerarbitration.com/).

18 Piraeus First Instance Court, decision no. 722 of 2019, as reported by A. Tsirigos, P. Krystallis, & D. Skevi, 'Recognition and Enforcement of Foreign Court Decisions and Arbitral Awards in Greece: Is There a New Trend Towards a More Relaxed Application of the Public Policy Exception to Punitive Damages?', Kluwer Arbitration Blog, 10 June 2019 (available via https://arbitrationblog.kluwerarbitration.com/).

19 A. Tsirigos, P. Krystallis, & D. Skevi, 'Recognition and Enforcement of Foreign Court Decisions and Arbitral Awards in Greece: Is There a New Trend Towards a More Relaxed Application of the Public Policy Exception to Punitive Damages?', Kluwer Arbitration Blog, 10 June 2019 (available via https://arbitrationblog.kluwerarbitration.com/).

20 Spanish Supreme Court 13 November 2001, Exequatur no. 2039/1999, *AEDIPR* 2003, p. 914.

unwanted conduct by employing less invasive remedial intervention, such as civil penalties. Furthermore, it is often difficult to differentiate concepts of compensation. The Court refers in that regard to moral damages. They fulfil a compensatory role as well as a sanctioning function and it is not easy to distinguish between the two. In Spanish law a minimal overlap between civil law (compensation) and criminal law (punishment) is thus not completely unknown.[21] In making their public policy analysis, the Court finally added, courts should not lose sight of the degree of connection between the facts and the (Spanish) forum. All these reasons led the Court to the conclusion that punitive damages as a concept do not oppose public policy.[22]

The Supreme Court then moved to an analysis of the proportionality of the award. The Court considered two elements to be relevant when assessing the (potentially) excessive nature of the treble damages: (1) the predictability of the award and (2) the nature of the interests protected.

As to the former, the Court referred to the fact that the treble damages arose *ex lege*. The American provisions took the intentional character and the gravity of the defendant's behaviour into account and allowed a tripling of the amount of compensatory damages. This reliance on the statutory origin of the punitive damages begs the question whether punitive damages developed by case law would be predictable enough for the Spanish Supreme Court.[23] The absence of a written provision would presumably not automatically rule out the enforcement of the judgment.[24] One wonders what would happen to punitive awards coming from states where punitive damages legislation does not provide for caps.[25] In those states the only restraint on the amount of punitive damages comes from the courts, most notably from the US Supreme Court's due process case law. The Spanish Supreme Court confirmed that the U.S courts are prudent in policing the proportionality of damages awarded.[26] Furthermore, although legality leads to foreseeability, it does not guarantee proportionality. The legislature's intervention to fix the amount of the punitive damages (whether by establishing a maximum, a minimum or an appropriate range) does

21 S.R. Jablonski, 'Translation and comment: enforcing U.S. punitive damages awards in foreign courts – a recent case in the Supreme Court of Spain', *Journal of Law and Commerce*, Vol. 24, 2004-2005, p. 229.

22 Spanish Supreme Court 13 November 2001, Exequatur no. 2039/1999, *AEDIPR* 2003, p. 914; M. Otero Crespo, 'Punitive Damages Under Spanish Law: A Subtle Recognition?', in L. Meurkens & E. Nordin (Eds.), *The Power of Punitive Damages – Is Europe Missing Out?*, Cambridge-Antwerp-Portland, Intersentia, 2012, p. 289.

23 M. Requejo Isidro, 'Punitive Damages: How Do They Look Like When Seen From Abroad?', in L. Meurkens & E. Nordin (Eds.), *The Power of Punitive Damages – Is Europe Missing Out?*, Cambridge-Antwerp-Portland, Intersentia, 2012, p. 328.

24 M. Requejo Isidro, 'Punitive Damages – Europe Strikes Back?', presentation delivered at the British Institute of International and Comparative Law, 2 November 2011, London, text on file with the author.

25 *Ibid.*

26 Spanish Supreme Court 13 November 2001, Exequatur no. 2039/1999, *AEDIPR* 2003, p. 914.

not make the award proportional in all cases. The foreign jurisdiction's idea of proportionality may also vary from the Spanish legislature's estimation.[27]

As to the latter aspect of the proportionality test, the Court argued that in a market economy the safeguarding of intellectual property rights is important. Moreover, this interest in intellectual property protection is shared universally by countries with similar judicial, social and economic values.[28] The common desire to protect the interests at stake justified the awarding of an amount of twice the compensatory damages on top of the compensation granted.[29] The importance of the underlying *ratio legis* will thus determine the outcome of the proportionality analysis.[30]

2.6 France

In France the leading judgment is the decision of the *Cour de Cassation*, the French Supreme Court, in *Schlenzka & Langhorne v. Fountaine Pajot*.[31] The case revolved around a contractual dispute with regard to a catamaran bought by an American couple from a French manufacturer. The California Superior Court (Alameda County) awarded the plaintiffs USD 1.391.650,12 in actual damages and USD 1.460.000 in punitive damages to punish and deter the French company for hiding the vessel's structural problems. The California Superior Court also decided to permit an exception to the American rule on attorneys' fees which states that each party shall bear their own costs, even if they are victorious in the lawsuit. Schlenzka and Langhorne were awarded USD 402.084,33 in attorneys' fees.[32]

The couple's attempts to enforce the California judgment in France eventually brought the case all the way up to the Supreme Court. For the first time in its history the *Cour de Cassation* was required to take a stance on the enforcement of punitive damages. In late 2010 it ruled: ("[…] *the principle of awarding punitive damages is not, in itself, contrary to public policy; this is not the case when the amount awarded is disproportional to the loss*

27 M. Requejo Isidro, 'Punitive Damages – Europe Strikes Back?', presentation delivered at the British Institute of International and Comparative Law, 2 November 2011, London, text on file with the author.

28 Spanish Supreme Court 13 November 2001, Exequatur no. 2039/1999, *AEDIPR* 2003, p. 914.

29 S.R. Jablonski, 'Translation and comment: enforcing U.S. punitive damages awards in foreign courts – a recent case in the Supreme Court of Spain', *Journal of Law and Commerce*, Vol. 24, 2004-2005, p. 230.

30 M. Requejo Isidro, 'Punitive Damages: How Do They Look Like When Seen From Abroad?', in L. Meurkens & E. Nordin (Eds.), *The Power of Punitive Damages – Is Europe Missing Out?*, Cambridge-Antwerp-Portland, Intersentia, 2012, p. 328.

31 Cass. Civ. 1st, 1 December 2010, Schlenzka & Langhorne v. Fountaine Pajot S.A, no. 09-13303, *Recueil Dalloz* 2011, p. 423.

32 California Superior Court 26 February 2003, Schlenzka v. Pajot, case no. 837722-1.

suffered and to the contractual breach of the debtor [...]" (my own translation)).[33] The Court presumably means the seriousness of the defendant's breach of contract.[34] The French Supreme Court adapted its language because of the contractual origin of the litigation. The reference to the "contractual breach" could perhaps more broadly be read as the seriousness of the debtor's wrongful behaviour, the degree of culpability or the blameworthiness of the fault.[35] The judgment does confirm the principled enforceability of punitive damages awards in France.

However, an important caveat to this openness applies. Punitive damages do violate international public policy when their amount is disproportional to the damage suffered and the breach of the contractual obligations of the debtor. The *Cour de Cassation* did not offer further guidance on how to perform this proportionality check. The judgment can be interpreted as requiring a comparison between the amount of punitive damages and the amount of compensatory damages awarded (the injury suffered ("*préjudice subi*")). The Court's conclusion that the punitive damages largely exceeded the compensatory damages (the difference between both being USD 70.000)[36] thwarted the enforcement of the punitive damages. This can be seen as laying down a 1:1 maximum ratio between punitive and compensatory damages,[37] identical to the ceiling the German Supreme Court adopted 18 years earlier in *John Doe v. Eckhard Schmitz.*

2.7 *Italy*

Italian courts were traditionally unwilling to enforce punitive damages granted by foreign courts. The Italian Supreme Court also displayed this hostile attitude. In its seminal case *Fimez* the *Corte di Cassazione* classified the 1 million dollar judgment a mother obtained in Alabama following the death of her son in a traffic accident due to the defendant

33 Cass. Civ. 1st, 1 December 2010, Schlenzka & Langhorne v. Fountaine Pajot S.A, no. 09-13303, *Recueil Dalloz* 2011, p. 423. Original text: "[...] *le principe d'une condamnation à des dommages intérêts punitifs, n'est pas, en soi, contraire à l'ordre public, il en est autrement lorsque le montant alloué est disproportionné au regard du préjudice subi et des manquements aux obligations contractuelles du débiteur* [...]".

34 B. Janke & F.-X. Licari, 'Enforcing Punitive Damage Awards in France after Fountaine Pajot', *The American Journal of Comparative Law*, Vol. 60, No. 3, 2012, p. 776.

35 N. Meyer Fabre, 'Enforcement Of U.S. Punitive Damages Award in France: First Ruling Of The French Court Of Cassation In X. v. Fountaine Pajot December 1, 2010', *Mealey's International Arbitration Report*, Vol. 26, No. 1, 2011, p. 4.

36 It could be argued that the amount awarded for attorneys' fees (*in casu* USD 402.084,33) should be added to the compensatory damages when calculating the ratio. Legal costs are in essence also a form of loss caused by the defendant. Of course, this scenario is quite exceptional because US litigants almost always bear their own costs, even if they win the case.

37 N. Meyer Fabre, 'Enforcement Of U.S. Punitive Damages Award in France: First Ruling Of The French Court Of Cassation In X. v. Fountaine Pajot December 1, 2010', *Mealey's International Arbitration Report*, Vol. 26, No. 1, 2011, p. 4.

company's defectively produced crash helmet as punitive. Enforcement against the Italian defendant's assets in Italy was necessary and eventually led the case to the Supreme Court.

The Supreme Court disagreed with the contention that the U.S. decision did not violate public policy because the Italian liability system contains several legal institutions such as penalty clauses and moral damages, which pursue punitive objectives. According to the Italian Supreme Court, damages in private law are not connected to the idea of punishment or to the wrongdoer's misconduct. These damages are intended to restore damage suffered by the injured party by eliminating the consequences of the inflicted harm through the award of a sum of money. This is true for every type of civil damages, moral damages included, which are not influenced by the victim's conditions and the wrongdoer's wealth but require concrete and factual evidence of the loss suffered. The Supreme Court dismissed the analogy between penalty clauses and moral damages on the one hand and punitive damages on the other, as had the German Supreme Court in *John Doe v. Eckhard Schmitz*. It confirmed the Venice Court of Appeal's view that punitive damages are in violation of (international) public policy and declined to enforce the Alabama USD 1 million award.[38] The Italian Supreme Court affirmed its position in a judgment of 8 February 2012.[39]

A Copernican revolution took place in the Supreme Court judgment of *AXO v. NOSA*. Coincidentally, this case dealt yet again with liability arising out of a defective crash helmet. A motorcyclist had suffered brain injury in an accident which occurred during a motocross race in the United States. He brought suit in Florida against *inter alia* the Italian manufacturer AXO and the American reseller NOSA. The latter settled with the victim for USD 1 million. The District Court of Appeal of the State of Florida then granted NOSA's request to be indemnified by AXO for the amount paid to the victim. Subsequently, NOSA sought to enforce this decision in Italy against the assets of AXO.

For the first time, the *Corte di Cassazione* ruled that punitive damages do not violate Italy's (international) public policy. It held that punitive damages are not ontologically contrary to the Italian legal system. It pointed to various examples of provisions in Italian law, introduced in the last decades, that pursue a punitive goal. The Court now accepts that civil liability law has evolved to the point that the idea of a punitive function being attached to a damages award is no longer incompatible with it. New emerging functions such as prevention and sanctioning have led to a multifunctional dimension of liability law. In that context it would be inadequate to refuse any remedies not precisely fitting in the category of compensation.

38 Cass. Civ. 19 January 2007, no. 1183, *Rep Foro it 2007 v. Delibazione* no. 13 and *v. Danni Civili* no. 316; *Corr. Giur.*, 2007, 4, p. 497.

39 Supreme Court 8 February 2012, *Soc Ruffinatti v. Oyola-Rosado*, no. 1781/2012, *Danno resp.* 2012, p. 609.

This does not mean that foreign judgments will be given unhindered access to the Italian territory. There must be an adequate legal basis for the punitive damages awarded. Additionally, the facts subject to punishment must be precisely pre-identified guaranteeing the standardisation of cases in which punitive damages may be awarded. Furthermore, the awards must adhere to the principle of predictability, in that limits must be set as to the punitive damages that may be granted. The Italian courts faced with a foreign punitive award must, moreover, check the proportionality between the compensatory damages and punitive damages and between the punitive damages and the wrongful conduct.

2.8 England

As the birthplace of modern punitive damages it is interesting to observe how England reacts to requests for enforcement of foreign punitive damages. Under English law the scope of availability of such damages is less extensive than in, for example, American law. The House of Lords in *Rookes v. Barnard* restricted exemplary damages to three categories.[40] Perhaps surprisingly, the presence of the remedy in English law does not mean that England is completely receptive to enforcing punitive damages. Multiple damages cannot be enforced and it is currently uncertain whether other forms of punitive damages will be accepted for enforcement purposes by English courts.

2.8.1 Multiple damages

The Protection of Trading Interest Act (PTIA) is a 1980 statute which prohibits the enforcement of multiple damages in England. Sections 5.1 and 5.2 provide that a judgment of an overseas country cannot be registered and no court in the UK may entertain proceedings at common law for the recovery of any sum payable under such a judgment, if that judgment grants multiple damages. Section 6 even contains a claw-back provision allowing qualifying defendants who have paid multiple damages in a foreign suit to recover in a UK court the part of the multiple damages that exceeds the portion attributable to compensation (i.e. two thirds in case of treble damages). Although intended to apply to multiple damages (treble damages) arising out of antitrust litigation, a literal reading of the Act prohibits the enforcement of any type of multiple damages, irrespective of the underlying cause of action.[41] Section 5 of PTIA not only prevents the enforcement of the additional damages but deems the basic compensatory element of a multiple damages

---

40 Oppressive, arbitrary or unconstitutional action by government servants, calculated behaviour in order to make a profit which may exceed the compensation payable to the victim and punitive damages expressly provided for by statute: *Rookes v. Barnard* [1964] AC 1129 (HL), pp. 37-38.

41 T.J. Kahn, 'The Protection of Trading Interests Act of 1980: Britain's Response to U.S. Extraterritorial Antitrust Enforcement', *Northwestern Journal of International Law & Business*, Vol. 2, No. 2, 1980, p. 510.

award unenforceable as well.[42] Other heads of damages included in the same judgment are unaffected by PTIA.[43]

2.8.2 Other forms of punitive damages

The Protection of Trading Interests Act only applies to multiple damages and does not cover other punitive damages. As far as the latter are concerned, it is well settled in England that an English court will not lend its assistance to the enforcement of a foreign penal law.[44] An imposition of a penalty constitutes an act of sovereignty and cannot have any effect in the territory of another nation.[45] English courts will, therefore, refuse to enforce a foreign judgment when it is given in respect of a fine or penalty. However, a sum payable to a private individual is not a fine or penalty.[46]

This formalistic approach was confirmed in *S.A Consortium General Textiles v. Sun and Sand Agencies Ltd.*[47] In that case Lord Denning stated *in obiter* that a fine or other penalty only refers to sums payable to the state by way of punishment and that a sum payable to a private individual is not a fine or penalty.[48] Lord Denning's remarks seem to explicitly support the view that, despite their inherent criminal nature, for enforcement purposes in England punitive damages can avoid the penal label if they are awarded to a private person instead of to a state.[49] Lord Denning further ruled that English public policy does not oppose the enforcement of a claim for punitive damages, because they are "*still considered to be in conformity with the public policy in the United States and many of the great countries of the Commonwealth*".[50]

This judgment should not be interpreted as decisive authority on the issue and requires confirmation in further case law. The fact that English substantive law grants exemplary damages in certain situations does support the idea that foreign punitive damages are not against English public policy. The better view is perhaps that a foreign award for punitive damages that is manifestly excessive or disproportionate is against public policy and will not be enforced.[51]

---

42 L. Collins (Ed.), *Dicey & Morris on the conflict of laws*, 13th ed., London, Sweet and Maxwell, 2000, p. 566.

43 *Lewis v. Eliades* [2004] 1 WLR, p. 692.

44 *See e.g. Folliott v. Ogden* [1790] 3 Term Rep, p. 726; *Huntington v. Attrill* [1893] AC, p. 150; *Raulin v. Fisher* [1911] 2 KB, p. 93.

45 J. Fawcett & J.M. Carruthers, *Cheshire, North & Fawcett: Private International Law*, 14th ed., Oxford, Oxford University Press, 2008, p. 126.

46 M. Polonsky, 'Particular Issues Affecting the Recognition and Enforcement of U.S. Judgments', *International Law Practicum*, Vol. 19, No. 2, 2006, p. 156.

47 *S.A Consortium General Textiles v. Sun and Sand Agencies Ltd.* [1978] Q.B., p. 279.

48 *S.A Consortium General Textiles v. Sun and Sand Agencies Ltd.* [1978] Q.B., pp. 299-300.

49 L. Collins (Ed.), *Dicey & Morris on the conflict of laws*, 13th ed., London, Sweet and Maxwell, 2000, p. 476.

50 S.A *Consortium General Textiles v. Sun and Sand Agencies Ltd.*, p. 300.

51 A. Mills, 'Recognition of punitive damages in the United Kingdom', in S. Bariati, L. Fumagalli & Z. Crespi Reghizzi (Eds.), *Punitive Damages and Private International Law: State of the Art and Future Developments*,

3 Concluding overarching analysis

It could be argued that the overview of case law in the previous section reveals a certain trend within the countries that were investigated. Traditionally, punitive damages could not be enforced in the forum for a myriad of fundamental public policy reasons. This conservative stance was based on systemic arguments such as the penal character of punitive damages, the violation of the principle of strict compensation and the fact that they lead to an enrichment of the plaintiff and an unequal treatment of creditors.

Several European countries have, however, moved away from this principled distrust and have restricted the public policy test to an examination of the excessiveness or proportionality of the quantum of the punitive damages. This is the current position for Italy, Spain, France and Greece. Others, such as Germany, the Netherlands, Switzerland (although an increasing part of the literature calls for a quantitative approach there as well[52]) and apparently also Portugal,[53] seem to hold on to the conservative objections mentioned.

England is a stand-alone outlier within Europe due to its explicit acknowledgement of exemplary damages. It offers a mixed outlook on the enforcement of a punitive damages award. Multiple damages, the compensatory part included, are statutorily barred by the Protection of Trading Interests Act. Whether other forms of punitive damages can penetrate the English borders remains uncertain. Lord Denning's *obiter dictum* in *S.A. Consortium General Textiles v. Sun and Sand Agencies Ltd.* that punitive damages cannot be equated to an unenforceable fine or penalty provided they are awarded to a private party and that English public policy does not oppose them, needs further judicial confirmation.

The main justification for the perceived paradigm shift perhaps lies in the growing realisation that the law of the requested court itself contains private law instruments, which resemble punitive damages or pursue the same objectives. Examples include penalty clauses, double license fees and covert punitive damages disguised as moral damages.[54] When a legal system itself contains punitive-like remedies transcending the traditional private-public law divide, it cannot declare punitive damages unenforceable by using the

---

Milan, Wolters Kluwer, 2019, pp. 189-192.

52 A. Stadler, 'Recognition of punitive damages in Germany and Switzerland', in S. Bariati, L. Fumagalli & Z. Crespi Reghizzi (Eds.), *Punitive Damages and Private International Law: State of the Art and Future Developments*, Milan, Wolters Kluwer, 2019, p. 154.

53 As reported by L. De Lima Pinheiro, 'Portugal', in O. Meyer (Ed.), *Public Policy and Private International Law*, Cheltenham-Northampton, Edward Elgar Publishing, 2022, p. 314, no. 12-074: "*Some Portuguese judgments mention punitive damages as proscribed by the public policy clause*".

54 See for an extensive list: C. Vanleenhove, *Punitive Damages in Private International Law: Lessons for the European Union*, Cambridge-Antwerp-Portland, Intersentia, 2016, pp. 158-204.

international public policy shield.[55] This openness in the field of recognition and enforcement does not seem to be confined to those types of cases for which the internal law also awards punitive-like remedies.[56]

The courts' reliance on a check of the punitive award's size generates several new issues for consideration.[57] In my opinion the presence of punitive damages does not taint the compensatory damages. Furthermore, any portion of the punitive damages that serves a compensatory function (such as the recovery of legal fees) should be greenlighted,[58] provided that the foreign judgment identifies the rendering court's compensatory intention and the corresponding numerical value.

Determining the appropriate ceiling for punitive damages is a difficult undertaking. European courts have in that regard focused on the ratio between punitive and compensatory damages. In the United States the Supreme Court also laid down a 9:1 maximum ratio between punitive and compensatory damages (for most cases).[59] For enforcement purposes the acceptable ceiling for some European courts seems to float around a 1:1 ratio (see for instance the *Fountaine Pajot* judgment of the French Supreme Court and the *John Doe v. Eckhard Schmitz* ruling of the German Federal Court of Justice). Employing the proportionality between punitive and compensatory damages is understandable in order to bring a degree of measurable certainty into the excessiveness assessment. It has the benefit of not running afoul of the prohibition of review of the merits (*révision au fond*). However, it should not be seen as an immutable rule but can serve as a valuable starting point in a case-by-case analysis.

When the foreign award for punitive damages is considered to be excessive in light of the forum's public policy, the question arises whether this determination renders the entirety of the punitive damages unenforceable or whether the requested court can enforce

55 V. Behr, 'Punitive Damages in American and German Law – Tendencies Towards Approximation of Apparently Irreconcilable Concepts', *Chicago-Kent Law Review*, Vol. 78, No. 1, 2003, p. 153; M. Tolani, 'U.S. Punitive Damages Before German Courts: A Comparative Analysis with Respect to the Ordre Public', *Annual Survey of International & Comparative Law*, Vol. 17, No. 1, 2011, p. 207; F. Quarta, 'Foreign Punitive Damages Decisions and Class Actions in Italy', in D. Fairgrieve & E. Lein (Eds.), *Extraterritoriality and Collective Redress*, Oxford, Oxford University Press, 2012, p. 275.

56 Compare for instance with the situation in South Korea: see chapter 4 by Suk in this book.

57 For an in-depth discussion of these issues and a set of guidelines for European judges when dealing with the enforcement of punitive damages: C. Vanleenhove, *Punitive Damages in Private International Law: Lessons for the European Union*, Cambridge-Antwerp-Portland, Intersentia, 2016, pp. 210-243. In shortened form: C. Vanleenhove, 'A normative framework for the enforcement of U.S. punitive damages in the European Union: transforming the traditional '¡No Pasarán!'', *Vermont Law Review*, Vol. 41, No. 2, 2016, pp. 377-401.

58 See support for this contention (at least with regard to costs and expenses relating to the proceedings) in article 11(2) of the 2005 Hague Choice of Court Convention and article 10.2 of the 2019 Convention on the Recognition and Enforcement of Foreign Judgments in Civil or Commercial Matters. On these provisions see chapter 9 by Pertegas Sender and Zappatore in this book.

59 State Farm Mut. Auto. Ins. Co. v. Campbell, 538 U.S., p. 425 (2003): "*in practice, few awards exceeding a single-digit ratio between punitive and compensatory damages, to a significant degree, will satisfy due-process*".

the punitive damages up to the amount that it deems to be tolerable. In my opinion the requested court should be allowed to sever the acceptable amount of punitive damages from the excessive, non-tolerable part of the punitive award. The curtailing of the amount of the incoming judgment should not be equated to *révision au fond* because the requested court is not reforming the foreign court's examination of the facts or second-guessing the adjudication of the matter. An all-or-nothing approach is inherently unfair as one excess dollar, pound or rand is able to infect the rest of a substantial sum of punitive damages.[60]

The advancements in Europe should not be examined in isolation. In other parts of the world courts and scholars are also confronted with common law punitive damages seeking legal effect in the forum. In Europe we should keep an eye on those developments and draw inspiration from them. The rest of this book can be a help in doing just that.

60 G.A.L. Droz, 'Variations Pordea (À propos de l'arrêt de la Cour de cassation 1re Chambre civile du 16 mars 1999)', *Revue Critique de droit international privé*, Vol. 89, 2000, p. 194.

Recognition and Enforcement of Punitive Damages in Russia

*Vsevolod Chernyy**

1 Introduction

Since the fall of the Soviet Union, the Russian Federation has become substantially integrated into the international community and, more specifically, international trade. Naturally, such openness inevitably entails an increasing interaction with other legal systems, including, *inter alia*, in matters of recognition and enforcement of foreign court judgments and arbitral awards. As the title of this chapter suggests, the focus will be on court decisions and arbitral awards exclusively dealing with punitive damages.

Being a civil law jurisdiction, Russia has an inherent adverse perception of this legal phenomenon as being contrary to the compensatory function of civil liability. Nevertheless, despite this "birthmark", the Russian legal order does not completely reject punitive damages (both within its national legislation and when recognizing and enforcing foreign judgments and arbitral awards).[1] In this context, it seems to be of particular interest to investigate to what extent and under which conditions the Russian Federation is willing to admit punitive damages into its legal framework. That is the focus of this chapter.

The structure of this chapter is as follows: to start with, some Russia-specific preliminary remarks will be made in section 2, after which the genesis of the public policy exception in Russian law will be examined in section 3. Section 4 touches upon the recognition and enforcement of punitive damages in Russian case law and, finally, the respective results will be summed up in the conclusion.

* Senior Legal Officer at Chiron Management, Ph.D. candidate Lomonosov Moscow State University.

1 A.S. Akuzhinov, 'Overcompensation and Contradiction to Public Policy as a Ground to Refuse Enforcement of Arbitral Awards and Foreign Judgments in Russian and European Law', *Review of Economic Justice of the Russian Federation*, No. 8, 2022, pp. 139-150; S.A. Krasnova, 'Overcompensatory Protection in the Russian Civil Law: Forms and Limits', *Review of Economic Justice of the Russian Federation*, No. 1, 2020, pp. 68-110.

2 Preliminary remarks concerning the Russian legal order

The narrative starts by laying out a few preliminary remarks. If missed, it is highly likely that some aspects of the following chapter could be fairly confusing and lead to certain misunderstandings.

First, it is important to note that, setting aside the system of constitutional courts (which is of little interest for the purpose of this chapter), judicial power in the Russian Federation is distributed between two branches: courts of general jurisdiction and commercial (*arbitrazh*[2]) courts. For a long time, at the top of each of these branches were two stand-alone and mutually independent high courts: the Supreme Commercial Court of the Russian Federation and the Supreme Court of the Russian Federation. The former led the commercial courts while the latter oversaw the proper functioning of the courts of general jurisdiction. In 2014, however, in the pursuit of unifying the judicial system, the Supreme Commercial Court was taken over by the Supreme Court. That way, the Supreme Court is now the only final authority which supervises nearly all courts in the Russian Federation (excluding the Russian Constitutional Court).

Second, another noteworthy peculiarity of Russian judicial law-making lies in the powers of the referred supreme courts (now only the Supreme Court of the Russian Federation) to issue mandatory acts of interpretation of the effective law. The key element is that, in contrast to most (if not all) jurisdictions, the Russian legal order has gone much further and has empowered the Supreme Court to issue abstract acts of interpretation. This refers to the authority to guide lower courts as to how certain norms must be interpreted *in abstracto*, i.e. without reference to the facts of a particular dispute. In this paradigm, the Supreme Court *de facto* releases a binding commentary to the effective statutory provisions. This authority has brought the Russian judiciary very close to the legislative branch.[3] Throughout this chapter, some of those acts of interpretation will be explained further, including Plenums of the Supreme Commercial Court, Information Letters of the Supreme Commercial Court as well as Plenums of the Supreme Court.

Third, Russian courts have so far not been confronted with the recognition and enforcement of foreign punitive damages in the classic, common law understanding of this term. At the very least, unlike in other jurisdictions, these disputes have not resulted in a final court decision. As an example, a case from 2009 can be mentioned.[4] In this case,

---

2 This might sound similar to arbitral tribunals but, in fact, this branch of the judiciary consists solely of adjudicative bodies instituted by the state.

3 V.A. Belov, '"Twenty-Fifth" Resolution of the Plenum: Interpretation or … Legislation?', *The Review of Economic Justice of the Russian Federation*, No. 11, 2015, pp. 53-90; E.A Sukhanov, *Civil Law: Textbook*, Moscow, Statut, 2nd ed., Vol. 1, 2019, p. 66; V.M. Zhuykov, *On Case Law as a Source of Law*, Moscow, Jurist, 2000, pp. 78-85.

4 Case No. A40-24987/07-10-149.

the Russian court had to dive into the conflict of laws issue regarding the applicability of the RICO Act[5] and, accordingly, the prospective of awarding punitive damages thereunder. Unfortunately, this dispute has never reached the stage of adjudication since it ended in a settlement agreement. Even though foreign punitive damages as such have not yet been the subject of consideration by the Russian courts, the latter have quite a lot of experience in refusing to recognise (and, thereby, to enforce) judgments and arbitral awards because the amount conferred has a punitive nature and exceeds the losses incurred by the prevailing party. The chances are high that this approach would also be followed if a Russian court is faced with recognising a court judgment or arbitral award conferring punitive damages *in sensu proprio*. A discussion of these cases comprises the core of this chapter.

Fourth, Russian courts do not make a distinction between the application of public policy to arbitral awards[6] on the one hand and court judgments on the other hand. Accordingly, when recognising (and enforcing) both court judgments and arbitral awards, the same wording and, more generally, the concept of public policy will be referred to. Thus, for the purposes of the present chapter, it is logical and consistent not to limit its content to court decisions but also to look into arbitral awards dealing with the recognition and enforcement of punitive damages.

After these preliminary remarks, the next section goes into the public policy exception as interpreted over time by Russian courts.

3 GENESIS OF THE PUBLIC POLICY EXCEPTION IN RUSSIAN CASE LAW

As noted above, the Russian legal order, when faced with punitive damages (even in their mild form, for instance significant contract penalties), takes a hostile stand towards underlying court judgments and arbitral awards. In doing so, Russian courts, like their European colleagues, refer to the public policy exception.[7] Since the concept of public policy understandably plays a considerable role in this chapter, it makes sense to look more closely at its development within the Russian legal framework. This will give an opportunity to have a more holistic view on the subject matter at hand, as well as to observe what path the concept of public policy has taken over the past turbulent decades of Russian history.

---

5 The Racketeer Influenced and Corrupt Organizations (RICO) Act is a US federal law imposing severe criminal penalties as well as providing for civil remedies (including those of a punitive nature) for criminal acts committed as part of criminal organization's operations.

6 Regardless of whether those awards are rendered within the context of domestic or international arbitration proceedings.

7 C. Vanleenhove, *Punitive Damages in Private International Law: Lessons for the European Union*, Cambridge, Intersentia, 2016, pp. 87-147.

In the early 2000s, the content laid down by Russian courts into the public policy exception was, for the most part, quite unique and substantially diverging from the major tendencies in private international law at that time.[8] The reasons for this stemmed from the processes starting in 1990s, including, *inter alia*, the following:

One of the first reasons lied in the isolation of the Russian Federation from much of the Western world as well as in the ideological confrontation between then existing world regimes. In such circumstances, it was scarcely conceivable that Russian scholars of private international law could make extensive reference to or actively promote the Western understanding of public policy. This would obviously be regarded as a hostile action against the state ideology as well as being generally at odds with then prevailing moral values. Moreover, in the situation in which contact with foreign countries is something exceptional and extraordinary, a basic incentive for developing private international law is absent. Against this background, it should come as no surprise that this area of law was fairly abandoned in Russia at the time (i.e. prior to the 1990s). As a consequence, for decades, many issues of private international law (including the public policy exception) have not been treated by both theory and practice. With this in mind, the subsequent expeditious development of the public policy concept made perfect sense considering the opening of the Russian market for foreign capital in the 1990s and early 2000s. The then effective foreign investment-friendly policy attracted a huge number of outside investors which led to a sharp increase in disputes involving foreign legal and natural persons.[9] Finally, it is important to understand that the Russian concept of public policy has not been elaborated within the framework of national legislation or international treaties. In fact, fleshing out this notion was (and still is) the task of courts, which throughout modern Russian history have often changed their position thereon.[10]

In view of these reasons, in the early 2000s, the content of the public policy exception expectedly differed from the widely accepted international standards. As a starting point for this comparison, the notion of public policy set out in the Recommendation 1(d) of the International Law Association on the Application of Public Policy as a Ground for

8 E. Kurzinski-Singer & D.L. Davydenko, 'Substantive Ordre Public in Russian Case Law on the Recognition and Enforcement or Annulment of International Commercial Arbitration Awards', *Zakon*, No. 9, 2009, pp. 197-210.

9 S. Sutyrin & O. Trofimenko, 'Do Formal Institutions Really Matter for Foreign Direct Investments to the Russian Federation? The Case of FDI Flows from the European Union to Russia', in K. Liuhto, S. Sutyrin, J.-M. & F. Blanchard (Ed.), *The Russian Economy and Foreign Direct Investment*, New York, Routledge, 2017, p. 75; D. Zheriborov & V. Pirogov, 'Foreign Direct Investment in Russia (Late 1980s – Late 2010s)', *Academic Dialogue*, No. 7, 2020, pp. 346-359; A. Muranov, 'The Competence of General Jurisdiction Courts to Consider Business Disputes Involving Foreign Persons in the Light of the New Russian Commercial Procedure Code', *Moscow Journal of International Law*, No. 3, 2002, pp. 127-150.

10 B.R. Karabelnikov, 'The Supreme Commercial Court of the Russian Federation Explains the Public Policy', *Review of International Commercial Arbitration*, No. 1, 2013, pp. 199-203.

Refusing Recognition and Enforcement of International Arbitral Awards can be mentioned:[11]

> *"The international public policy of any State includes: (i) fundamental principles, pertaining to justice or morality, that the State wishes to protect even when it is not directly concerned; (ii) rules designed to serve the essential political, social or economic interests of the State, these being known as "lois de police" or "public policy rules"; and (iii) the duty of the State to respect its obligations towards other States or international organisations."*

This definition can be considered as an internationally accepted approach to public policy. For the Russian stand on the corresponding issue paragraph 29 of Information Letter of the Supreme Commercial Court No. 96 is of paramount importance.[12] It provided as follows:

> *"... contradicts the public policy of the Russian Federation, which presupposes good faith and equality of the parties entering into private relations as well as proportionality of civil liability to the faulty committed offence."*

One need not have great expertise in private international law to note how broadly the Supreme Commercial Court interpreted the public policy concept. From my point of view, indeed, by its wording the Supreme Commercial Court has placed public policy, principally established for private international law purposes, on an equal footing with internal public policy or, more precisely, with the violation of some of its principles. Particularly, the above aspects of public policy have already been applied to invalidate transactions as contrary to the foundations of Russian legal order or morality.[13] In Russian doctrine, the nullification of these transactions is regarded as an expression of internal public policy.[14]

That said, it is not entirely clear why only those principles were chosen as being worthy to constitute the concept of public policy. If, as it follows from the cited text, the Supreme

11 'Resolution of the ILA on Public Policy as a Bar to Enforcement of International Arbitral Awards', *Arbitration International*, Vol. 19, No. 2, 2003, pp. 213–215.

12 Information Letter of the Supreme Commercial Court of the Russian Federation 'Review of the Case Law of Commercial Courts regarding the Recognition and Enforcement of Foreign Court Judgments, Challenges to Arbitral Awards and the Issuance of Writs of Execution for the Enforcement of Arbitral Awards' No. 96, dated 22 December 2005.

13 Article 169 of the Russian Civil Code.

14 A.V. Egorov, 'Transactions Contrary to the Legal Order and Morality: in Russia and Abroad', in A.I. Muranov & V.V. Plekhanov (Eds.), *Cross-Border Commerce and Law*, Moscow, Infotropic Media, 2013, pp. 41-67.

Commercial Court referred to the principles of civil law, then why did it not mention other principles provided in article 1(1) of the Russian Civil Code (for instance, such principles as the non-interference in private affairs, the free exercise of civil rights and their judicial protection)? Without a doubt, such a sweeping interpretation could hardly be considered acceptable, including, *inter alia*, in terms of stability of transnational transactions. Such interpretation of public policy, in fact, significantly increased the number of reasons to refuse recognition and enforcement of foreign judgments and arbitral awards, which, considering the admittedly poor statistics thereof, drastically reduced the claimant's chances for obtaining contractual relief.[15]

Nevertheless, later on, instead of narrowing the formulation, the Supreme Commercial Court even further expanded the given wording. To be more specific, in a number of court decisions,[16] the Supreme Commercial Court stated that an arbitral award may be refused recognition and enforcement on public policy grounds provided its recognition would result in (i) actions either directly prohibited by law, or (ii) damaging the sovereignty or security of the state, affecting the interests of large social groups, being incompatible with the principles of economic, political, legal systems of states, affecting the constitutional rights and freedoms of citizens, as well as (iii) actions being contrary to the basic principles of civil law, such as the equality of participants in private relationships, the inviolability of property, and freedom of contract. Nearly all of these aspects forming the public policy concept have serious shortcomings that will be explained further.

First of all, it seems rather problematic to determine which actions are directly prohibited by law. How should this prohibition be formulated? Did the legislator mean those actions prohibited by ordinary mandatory provisions of national law? Does this approach encompass actions which, although not directly prohibited by law, are still forbidden based on the very essence of the legal rule (for instance concerning fraud)? And, finally, do "actions ... directly prohibited by law" include those which are not explicitly qualified as null and void *ab initio* (for instance, voidable contracts)? The third aspect forming the public policy concept continues to be subject to the critique outlined above. The Supreme Commercial Court mentioned only the principles belonging to civil law, while this list of principles remained to be arbitrary and non-consistent. In fact, only the second aspect appears to be the least questionable. In my view, this aspect was supposed to be the backbone of the public policy concept.

In light of the comments raised, it should come as no surprise that the approach adopted by the Supreme Commercial Court resulted in abusive practices on the part of

15 B.R. Karabelnikov & D. Pellew, 'Enforcement of International Arbitral Awards in Russia – Still a Mixed Picture', *ICC Court Bulletin*, Vol. 19, No. 1, 2008, pp. 65-85.

16 See for instance, the Rulings of the Supreme Commercial Court No. SCC-5156/12 in case No. A40-71402/11-50-586, dated 28 April 2012 and No. SCC-14119/11 in case No. A40-8646/2011-25-52, dated 12 December 2011.

bad faith parties. They steadily referred to the public policy exception to oppose the recognition and enforcement of perfectly legal and enforceable court judgments and arbitral awards, only because they were disadvantageous to them. It is evident that such a flawed solution was not sustainable. Having considered both the views of lower courts and the position of scholars, the Supreme Commercial Court took a radical step forward in the understanding of public policy.[17] The modifications were thoroughly discussed and have been drawn primarily from foreign as well as international experience.

An act that forged this breakthrough was Information Letter No. 156.[18] Paragraph 1 of this Letter provides as follows:

> "... *the public policy is understood as the fundamental legal principles, which are of paramount mandatory nature, are universal, are of distinctive social and public importance and form the basis of the economic, political and legal system of the state. In particular, this includes committing actions expressly prohibited by overriding mandatory provisions set out in the Russian legislation (Art. 1192 of the Civil Code) if these actions are detrimental to the sovereignty or security of the state, affect the interests of large social groups, violate the constitutional rights and freedoms of private persons.*"

At first glance, it can be noted that the new definition has been significantly narrowed compared to the previous one. It excludes elements that effectively equated international public policy with the internal one, while also expanding the criteria for classification as part of the public policy. Therefore, an essential achievement of this Letter is that for the first time a demarcation line has been drawn separating public policy in private international law from other legal concepts. Furthermore, the Letter has clearly pointed out when violations of public policy take place. According to the given example, in order to establish that a court judgment or arbitral award goes against the Russian public policy, one has to prove that: (i) the actions in question are expressly prohibited by the Russian overriding mandatory provisions, and (ii) such actions are undermining the sovereignty or security of the state, affect the interests of large social groups or violate private persons' constitutional rights and freedoms. Certainly, this is only an example but its value lies in

17 A.V. Asoskov & A.N. Kycher, 'The Presidium of the Supreme Commercial Court has Determined the Approaches to the Concept of Public Policy: A Brief Commentary to the Information Letter No. 156, dated 26 February 2013', *Review of International Commercial Arbitration*, No. 1, 2013, pp. 190-198; B.R. Karabelnikov, 'The Supreme Commercial Court of the Russian Federation Explains the Public Policy', *Review of International Commercial Arbitration*, No. 1, 2013, pp. 199-213; B.R. Karabelnikov, *International Commercial Arbitration: Textbook*, Moscow, Infotropic Media, 2012, pp. 352-401.

18 Information Letter of the Supreme Commercial Court of the Russian Federation 'Review of the Case Law of Commercial Courts regarding the Application of the Public Policy Exception as a Ground for Refusal to Recognise and Enforce Foreign Court Judgments and Arbitral Awards' No. 156, dated 26 February 2013.

setting the right context for determining whether a specific legal provision violates the public policy.

Following the general message of the Letter, paragraph 4 substantially limits the scope of public policy by stating that the public policy exception should be applied only in exceptional cases, without substituting the special grounds of refusal for recognition and enforcement provided for by international treaties and the rules of the Russian Commercial Procedure Code.[19] Pursuing the same objective, paragraph 5 expressly indicates that the recognition and enforcement of a foreign judgment or arbitral award cannot violate the public policy of the Russian Federation solely because Russian law lacks legal provisions comparable to those of the applied foreign law. As regards the recognition and enforcement of punitive damages, of greatest interest is, undoubtedly, paragraph 6 of the Letter, which enshrines a prohibition on the recognition of court judgments and arbitral awards providing for punitive remedies. This paragraph will be discussed in greater detail in the next section of this chapter.

Concluding the section on the genesis of public policy in Russian law, the stance taken by the Supreme Court after the dissolution of the Supreme Commercial Court cannot be left out. Indeed, the Supreme Court has chosen not to reinvent the notion of public policy and has just mostly restated the position formulated earlier in Letter No. 156. Accordingly, paragraph 51(2) of the Plenum No. 53 stipulates the following:[20]

> "*Public policy … means the fundamental legal principles, which are of paramount mandatory nature, are universal, are of distinctive social and public importance and form the basis of the economic, political and legal system of the state.*"

While following the Supreme Commercial Court in other aspects, there are also some noteworthy differences. An intriguing detail is the transformation of what could constitute the violation of public policy, set forth in paragraph 1 of Letter No. 156, into the effective constituent elements thereof. The Supreme Court phrases the rule as follows:

> "*In order to set aside or refuse to enforce an arbitral award on the grounds of violation of public policy, the court must establish the cumulative presence of two elements: first, the violation of fundamental principles of the economic, political*

19 Like those provided by article 244 of the Russian Commercial Procedure Code: the party against which the decision was made was not timely and properly notified of the time and place of the hearing or for other reasons could not present his arguments before the court, there is an effective court decision in the Russian Federation on a dispute between the same persons, on the same subject and on the same grounds, the court judgment under the law of the state in whose territory it was adopted has not entered into legal force, etc.

20 Resolution of the Plenum of the Supreme Court 'On the Exercise by the Courts of the Russian Federation of Facilitation and Control Functions in respect of Arbitral Proceedings, International Commercial Arbitration' No. 53, dated 10 December 2019.

and legal system of the Russian Federation, which, second, may have consequences such as undermining the sovereignty or security of the state, affecting the interests of large social groups or violating the constitutional rights and freedoms of natural or legal persons."

It can be noted that the first element has been slightly expanded compared to Letter No. 156. Now, rather than referring to overriding mandatory provisions, the Supreme Court points to a more general "violation of fundamental principles of the economic, political and legal system of the Russian Federation". However, it seems unlikely that such a change would have any significant impact on the effective case law.

The Plenum No. 24 has also reinforced the approach towards the public policy as elaborated by the Supreme Commercial Court.[21] Thus, in paragraph 12 of this Plenum, it has been confirmed that (i) Russian courts adhere to the concept of international public policy, (ii) the public policy exception can be applied only when the consequences of the recognition and enforcement of a foreign court judgment or arbitral award are clearly contrary to the public policy of the Russian Federation, and (iii) the lack of legal provisions in Russian law similar to those of the applicable foreign law does not in itself constitute a ground for invoking the public policy exception.

This was a short review of the genesis of the public policy exception in Russian law. Now the case law dealing with the recognition and enforcement of punitive damages is examined.

4 PUNITIVE DAMAGES IN RUSSIAN CASE LAW

4.1 *Ruling of the Presidium of the Supreme Commercial Court No. 5243/06 on the case No. A40-64205/05-30-394, dated 19 September 2006*

The first case relevant for the enforcement of punitive damages within the Russian legal order seems to be a Ruling of the Presidium of the Supreme Commercial Court from 2006.[22] The facts were as follows: Joy-Lad Distributors International Inc. JSC and Moscow Oil-Processing Factory JSC entered into a contract for the sale of diesel and fuel oil. In case of a dispute the contract stipulated that if the parties failed to reach an agreement, the

21 Resolution of the Plenum of the Supreme Court 'On the Application of the Rules of Private International Law by the Courts of the Russian Federation' No. 24, dated 9 July 2019.

22 Russian cases, as opposed to the US or UK ones, are not published in reports or other collections. Moreover, there are no uniform citing standards. With this in mind, I refer to the standard which is most widely used within Russian legal literature.

matter shall be referred to the Arbitration Institute of the Stockholm Chamber of Commerce. The contract was governed by Swedish law. Moscow Oil-Processing Factory failed to perform its obligations. Joy-Lad Distributors International Inc. resorted to arbitration. The arbitral tribunal satisfied Joy-Lad's claims in part and subjected Moscow Oil-Processing Factory to, *inter alia*, a contract penalty in the amount of 28.041.975 USD.[23]

The court of first instance and the cassation court refused the recognition and enforcement of the arbitral award as contrary to the public policy of the Russian Federation.[24,25] The Presidium of the Supreme Commercial Court reversed the challenged decisions and enforced the arbitral award by stating the following:

> "*The calculation of the penalty was carried out by the arbitral tribunal on the basis of the Swedish law applicable to the above contract and the supplementary agreement No. 28 dated 28 August 1997, the terms of which correspond to usual business practice in the Russian Federation and provided for in the legislation of the Russian Federation.*"

The Supreme Commercial Court also noted that:

> "*... [Russian] civil legislation proceeds from the principle of equality of rights and obligations of Russian and foreign legal entities and individuals as well as provides a punitive penalty as a possible type of liability for non-performance or undue performance of contract obligations. Thus, it [a penalty] is a part of the Russian legal system, and its collection cannot be contrary to the public policy of the Russian Federation.*
> *The defendant has not proven and from the case materials does not follow the disproportionality of the civil liability put by the arbitral tribunal to the consequences of the contract's violation ...*"

As can be seen, the Supreme Commercial Court generally allowed the recognition and enforcement of arbitral awards containing punitive remedies, provided that those are not disproportionate to the losses incurred. This approach drew strong criticism.[26] Among

23 Award of the Ad Hoc Arbitration, dated 14 June 2005.

24 Decision of the Moscow Commercial Court on the case No. A40-64205/05-30-394, dated 15 December 2005; Resolution of the Commercial Court of the Moscow District on the case No. A40-64205/05-30-394, dated 21 March 2006.

25 There are four levels of courts in the Russia Federation: first instance courts, appeal courts, cassation courts and the Supreme Court. Cases dealing with the recognition and enforcement of court decisions or arbitral awards go for a review directly to cassation courts (thereby bypassing appeal courts).

26 B.R. Karabelnikov, *Enforcement and Challenging the Arbitral Awards of International Commercial Arbitrations. Commentary to the 1958 New York Convention and Chapters 30 and 31 of the Russian*

other things, it was pointed out that in this case the Supreme Commercial Court indeed applied the concept of internal public policy (having a much more far-reaching scope compared to international public policy), thereby jeopardising a huge number of court judgments and arbitral awards. Moreover, probably inadvertently, the Court implicitly confirmed that it would not recognise and enforce an arbitral award to the extent that Russian law fails to provide for rules similar to the applicable ones in the case at hand. As a result, for example, a good many of M&A contracts governed by English law and, accordingly, embodying legal instruments unknown to Russian law (representations and warranties, indemnity, etc.) came under threat.

4.2 *Para. 6 of Information Letter No. 156*

The Supreme Commercial Court in paragraph 6 of the mentioned Information Letter No. 156 sets out a different approach:

> "*A commercial court shall recognize and enforce a foreign court judgment or arbitral award as not violating the public policy of the Russian Federation unless the evidence presented by the debtor shows that liquidated damages or penalties, which were adjudicated on the basis of a civil law contract, are of punitive nature.*"

To exemplify this rule, the Court referred to the following case:[27] a foreign company applied to a commercial court for the recognition and enforcement of a foreign *ad hoc* arbitral award. The award obliged the defendant, a Russian company, to pay the principal debt, liquidated damages, and the costs of arbitration proceedings.

The defendant opposed the application and argued that the enforcement of this award would be contrary to the public policy of the Russian Federation since it was rendered in violation of the proportionality principle of civil liability, which is a fundamental principle of Russian law. Justifying the punitive nature of the awarded liquidated damages, the defendant drew attention to the fact that the amount of liquidated damages was more than twice as high as the size of the initial debt and the losses which, in the defendant's opinion, the claimant could have incurred in connection with the alleged breach.

The court of first instance refused the recognition and enforcement of the arbitral award as contrary to public policy. The court reasoned that the recovery of liquidated

Commercial Procedure Code of 2002, Moscow, Statut, 3rd ed., 2008, pp. 410-422.

27 According to the standards used in drafting Information Letters, the Supreme Commercial Court sets out a case in abstract terms (i.e. without specifics in respect of parties, claim size, courts involved, etc.). Sometimes, such a case might be fictitious.

damages without establishing the claimant's actual losses and lost profits could lead to unjust enrichment of the claimant and punishment of the defendant. Thus, according to the court, the deviation from the compensatory nature of contractual liability tolerated by the arbitral tribunal is in itself evidence of a violation of the public policy of the Russian Federation.

In its cassation petition, the claimant argued, *inter alia*, that in determining the amount of damages to be recovered, the arbitral tribunal had, in fact, already reduced the size of damages in comparison to the sum initially agreed upon by the parties when entering into the contract.

Evaluating the arguments of the parties and the conclusions of the first instance court, the cassation court ruled that the mere fact of exceeding actual damages and lost profits cannot imply the punitive nature of the amount awarded and, consequently, lead to a violation of public policy. At the same time the court did impose one, rather vague limitation: the sum to be paid by a defendant must be reasonable. Furthermore, the cassation court noted that a number of legal concepts enshrined in the Russian civil legislation suggest a departure from the strict understanding of the exclusively compensatory nature of civil liability (for instance, amounts recoverable for intellectual property infringements). It was stressed that to implement the principle of proportionality, the requested court must, when assessing the consequences of enforcement, take into account whether the punitive nature of a debtor's liability is significant. Further, the cassation court listed some presumptions to be followed by a court in establishing the punitive nature of awarded amounts. More specifically, liquidated damages are presumed to be punitive when, in particular, (i) the size is so abnormally high that it many times exceeds the sum which the parties could reasonably foresee when concluding the contract, or (ii) there are obvious signs indicating the abuse of freedom of contract (by exploitation of a debtor's weak bargaining power, violation of public interests and interests of third parties, etc.). Finally, the court mentioned that the arbitral tribunal found that the amount of liquidated damages was voluntarily agreed upon by the parties as equal subjects in civil relations. Moreover, the sum awarded was determined by taking into account the proportionality of the recovered losses to the consequences of the defendant's breach, the severity of the breach, and the duration of the defendant's non-performance. With this in mind, the cassation court overruled the decision of the first instance court and enforced the arbitral award.

As this exemplary decision provided in paragraph 6 of the Letter is of paramount importance in terms of the overall attitude of Russian courts towards punitive damages (and is constantly referred to by lower courts), a small pause will be made here in order to list its key takeaways:

i) The mere fact that the amount of liquidated damages (or penalties) exceeds actual losses cannot per se result in the violation of Russian public policy.

ii) Russian courts have broad discretion in determining whether the punitive element in awarded sums is so significant as to be inconsistent with the Russian public policy.
iii) The Supreme Commercial Court set forth the non-exhaustive list of criteria to consider when establishing the punitive nature of certain amounts in question: (i) the size of awarded liquidated damages (or penalties) and (ii) the abuse of freedom of contract.

Nevertheless, the Supreme Commercial Court has left certain questions unanswered, including:[28]
i) Does the Court's approach apply to other contract instruments (for instance indemnity)?
ii) Would the solution be the same in the case of tort damages?
iii) Which specific evidence should be presented by a debtor to prove that the awarded amount is punitive?

After examining the background and general legal framework of the recognition and enforcement of punitive damages, several recent cases where the described approach was applied are now examined. It should be noted that, in order to avoid unnecessary repetition, the relevant provisions from paragraph 6 of Information Letter No. 156 (which each of the following decisions contain) referred to above will not be repeated here.

4.3 *Resolution of the Commercial Court of the Povolzhskiy District on the case No. A72-15958/2013, dated 23 December 2014*

The Privatization Agency of the Republic of Serbia (the claimant) applied to the commercial court for the recognition and enforcement of an arbitral award made under the auspices of the Foreign Trade Arbitration of the Serbian Chamber of Commerce.[29] The award charged Avtodetal-Servis JSC (the defendant) with a contractual penalty in the amount of 2.900.000 EUR and the costs of arbitration proceedings in the amount of 5.612.673 dinars (approximately 55.411 EUR).

The court of first instance denied the application on the ground that the imposition of such a penalty violated the public policy of the Russian Federation.[30] The cassation court reversed the decision and reasoned as follows:

---

28 As of today, there are still no responses to these questions.

29 Award of the Foreign Trade Arbitration of the Serbian Chamber of Commerce on the case No. T-9/10, dated 10 October 2011.

30 Decision of the Commercial Court of the Ulyanovsk Region on the case No. A72-15958/2013, dated 6 October 2014.

> "*A public policy exception is possible only in cases where the application of foreign law could produce a result that is intolerable from the Russian legal conscience perspective.*
> *Meanwhile, concluding that as a result of the arbitral award enforcement there would be actions directly prohibited by law, the court of first instance did not indicate which law of the Russian Federation prohibited liability in the form of contractual penalty and allocation of legal costs.*
> *As the Presidium of the Supreme Commercial Court has repeatedly pointed out when hearing similar cases on the recognition and enforcement of foreign arbitral awards, a penalty is provided for by the civil legislation and is a part of the legal system of the Russian Federation. Therefore, as such the application of this type of liability as well as charging and collecting interest on the amount of penalty cannot be contrary to the public policy of the Russian Federation.*
> ...
> *In this regard, the recognition and enforcement of foreign arbitral awards on the recovery of liquated damages is contrary to the public policy of the Russian Federation under the following conditions: if the amount of such damages is so abnormally high that many times exceeds the amount that the parties could reasonably foresee when entering into the contract; if, when agreeing on the amount of such damages, there were obvious signs of abuse of freedom of contract (by exploitation of the debtor's weak bargaining power, violation of public interests and the interests of third parties, etc.).*
> *The obligation to prove the entirety of the aforementioned conditions is borne by the debtor. In the present case, however, the debtor has not done so. Nor did the court of first instance establish the conditions necessary for the penalty to be considered punitive and the arbitral award, for its collection, to be contrary to the public policy of the Russian Federation.*
> ...
> *On the other hand, the Foreign Trade Arbitration of the Serbian Chamber of Commerce found that the debtor had freely decided to conclude the contract and had the time and opportunity to become acquainted with the contents of the rights and obligations assumed thereunder [...].*
> *The debtor's free will is also confirmed by the manner of entering into the contract for the sale of shares from the stock portfolio of Icarbus JSC dated 11 August 2008, and its content, which shows that the offer to buy the shares was made by Avtodetal-Servis JSC.*
> *In accordance with Art. 243(4) of the Commercial Procedure Code, when hearing a case, a commercial court is not entitled to review a foreign court decision on the merits.*

> *However, this is exactly what the court of first instance has done. In this case, the failure to enforce the arbitral award denies the very possibility of application in the territory of the Russian Federation the law of a foreign state, a contractual penalty for failure to perform an obligation, which is contrary to the principles of Russian law enshrined in Art. 1(1) of the Russian Civil Code.*
> *In addition, there is no rule in Russian law that allows a debtor to be completely released from liability for the breach of obligation provided that there are grounds for the imposition of the appropriate liability."*

The key observations from this passage are as follows:

i) In refusing to enforce an arbitral award the court must indicate specific laws prohibiting the result produced by the arbitral award; this prohibition cannot be derived from a legal concept that already exists in Russian law.
ii) The debtor bears the burden of proving the punitive nature of the awarded amount.
iii) The court is required to set criteria for finding the amount to be punitive.
iv) The debtor's free will in entering the underlying contract evidences the non-punitive nature of the amount at stake.
v) An arbitration award is unlikely to be annulled where its setting aside would completely release the debtor from liability.

4.4 *Resolution of the Commercial Court of the Northwest District on the case No. A13-2798/2014, dated 20 January 2015*

Novo-Angren Thermal Power Plant JSC (the claimant) applied to the commercial court for the recognition and enforcement of a judgment issued by the Tashkent Region Commercial Court of the Republic of Uzbekistan.[31] The decision obliged NPO Aconit JSC (the defendant) to pay a penalty for late delivery in the amount of 34.993,09 USD, a penalty for start-up and commissioning works in the amount of 750 USD, a penalty for failure to use the letter of credit in the amount of 12.483,90 USD as well as legal costs in the amount of 2,50 USD.

The court of first instance granted the enforcement.[32] As one of the arguments in support of the cassation petition, NPO Aconit JSC advanced that the recognition and enforcement of the judgment is contrary to the public policy of the Russian Federation

31 Decision of the Tashkent Region Commercial Court of the Republic of Uzbekistan on the case No. 11-1227/16770, dated 16 January 2013.

32 Decision of the Commercial Court of the Vologda Region on the case No. A13-2798/2014, dated 26 October 2014.

because the awarded penalties have a punitive nature. The cassation court upheld the decision of the first instance court by stating the following:

> *"Russian law is based on the principle of equality of rights and obligations of Russian and foreign legal entities and individuals, and provides for the imposition of a penalty as a possible type of liability for non-performance or undue performance of contractual obligations.*
> *In the present case, the Tashkent Region Commercial Court heard the dispute and found that NPO Aconit JSC violated its obligations, and the amount of penalty was agreed by the parties in Contract No. 320/24, in connection with which the court determined the contested amount of the penalty in light of the proportionality of the recovered losses to the consequences of the breach of obligations, the severity of their violation by the defendant, and the duration of its non-performance.*
> *When invoking Art. 244(1)(7) of the Commercial Procedure Code, it should be taken into account that the public policy exception is applicable only in those exceptional cases where the application of a foreign law could cause a result which would be intolerable from the perspective of the Russian legal conscience.*
> *In the present case, there is no reason to believe that the enforcement in the territory of the Russian Federation of the above decision on the payment of penalties by the Russian company in favour of the foreign entity under Contract No. 320/24 could produce such a result."*

The key takeaways from this case are the following:

i) Russian law proceeds from the equality of Russian and foreign persons, therefore the legality of penalties in Russian law makes it possible to apply the latter to foreign persons.
ii) The Russian court is unlikely to refuse recognition of a foreign judgment if the debtor has indeed breached the contract and the consequences of such a breach correspond to the amount awarded, the severity of the breach as well as the duration of the debtor's non-performance.
iii) The payment of a penalty to a foreign entity cannot by itself produce a result which would be intolerable from the perspective of the Russian legal conscience and, accordingly, violate the Russian public policy.

4.5 *Resolution of the Commercial Court of the Moscow District on the case No. A41-78523/2015, dated 17 February 2016*

Arsenal Group LLC (the claimant) applied to the commercial court for recognition and enforcement of a decision of the Dnepropetrovsk Region Commercial Court.[33] The court judgment charged ART LLC (the defendant) with a principal debt in the amount of 746.260 EUR, penalties in the amount of EUR 249.670,52 as well as legal costs in the amount of approximately 3.011 EUR.

The court of first instance granted the application.[34] Before the cassation court ART LLC argued that the recognition and enforcement of the decision is contrary to the public policy of the Russian Federation since the penalties awarded are of a punitive nature. The cassation court upheld the decision of the first instance court and noted as follows:

> "*In this case, while hearing the dispute, the Dnepropetrovsk Region Commercial Court established that ART LLC violated its obligations, and, according to the terms of Contract No. 15042104 dated 15 April 2014, the parties set out penalties for the non-performance of obligations, what is not contrary to the public policy of the Russian Federation, since the awarded sums in accordance with Art. 330 of the Civil Code are penalties, and the contract terms providing for the collection of several penalties at the same time do not violate the effective law.*"

This excerpt manifests the following:

i) The debtor's breach is an essential prerequisite for the enforcement of a penalty.
ii) Collection of a penalty (including a few at once), subject to its conformity to the Russian concept of a penalty, does not violate the Russian public policy.

4.6 *Resolution of the Commercial Court of Moscow District on the case No. A40-84581/19, dated 24 July 2019*

Uzbekiston Khavo Yullari JSC (the defendant) applied to the commercial court for the annulment of the award issued by the International Commercial Arbitration Court at the Chamber of Commerce and Industry of the Russian Federation.[35] The award obliged Uzbekiston Khavo Yullari to pay a penalty in the amount of 2.910.239,44 USD, interests in

33 Decision of the Commercial Court of the Dnepropetrovsk Region on the case No. 904/9328/14, dated 14 July 2015.

34 Decision of the Commercial Court of the Moscow Region on the case No. A41-78523/2015, dated 17 November 2015.

35 Award of the International Commercial Arbitration Court at the Chamber of Commerce and Industry of the Russian Federation on the case No. M-59/2018, dated 5 February 2019.

the amount of 5.854,63 USD, arbitration fees in the amount of 52.441,48 USD as well as other arbitration costs in the amount of 26.259,74 USD.

The court of first instance granted the application and annulled the award.[36] Before the cassation court BB Energy (GULF) DMCC (the claimant) asserted that the first instance court made erroneous conclusions about the alleged excessively high penalties awarded by the arbitral tribunal and their purported contradiction to the Russian public policy. The cassation court upheld the decision of the first instance court and indicated the following:

> *"The court of the first instance established that the dispute, which resulted in the challenged award, arose between the parties to the contract D345.519 dated 30 October 2014, in connection with the delayed payment for supplied oil products (aviation kerosene) by the buyer, Uzbekiston Khavo Yullari JSC.*
> *In accordance with Section 6.5 of the contract, the arbitral tribunal imposed a penalty at the rate of 0,05% for the first 15 calendar days of delay (per each day of delay) and in the amount of 0,4% for the following period on the outstanding amount (for each day of delay), which made up 2.910.239,44 USD. The arbitral tribunal declined to lower the penalty in view of its obvious disproportion to the consequences of the breach (Art. 333 of the Civil Code of the Russian Federation).*
> *The court of first instance, having examined and evaluated the presented evidence pursuant to Art. 71 of the Commercial Procedure Code, found that there are grounds for annulling the arbitral award as violating the fundamental principles of Russian law, being contrary to the public policy of the Russian Federation since the collected penalty (0.4 percent per each day of delay) is excessively high and many times exceeds the amount of reasonable penalties, including the key rate of the Central Bank of the Russian Federation.*
> ...
> *The court of first instance, having determined that the penalty applied by the arbitral tribunal bore signs of apparent disproportionality to the consequences of the breach on account of the excessively high rate, came to the right conclusion that it had grounds for annulling the award.*
> *The arguments of the cassation petition to the contrary, i.e., on the proportionality of the penalty ordered by the arbitral tribunal to the consequences of the breach, are aimed at the reassessment of the circumstances established by the court of first instance, which is not within the competence of the cassation court."*

36 Decision of the Moscow Commercial Court on the case No. A40-84581/19, dated 8 May 2019.

The conclusions drawn from this case are as follows:

i) The penalty in the amount of 0.4 percent per day is deemed by Russian courts as excessively high and thereby violating the Russian public policy.
ii) When determining a reasonable penalty (as a benchmark for evaluating the awarded amount), Russian courts take into account the key rate of the Russian Central Bank.

4.7 *Resolution of the Commercial Court of the Far Eastern District on the case No. F03-2922/2021, dated 24 June 2021*

The Harbin Scientific and Technical Company (the claimant) applied to the commercial court for the issuance of a writ of execution for the enforcement of the award issued by the International Commercial Arbitration Court at the Chamber of Commerce and Industry of the Russian Federation.[37] The award ordered AgroTechInvest LLC (the defendant) to pay the principal debt in the amount of 185.296 USD, a penalty in the amount of 49.585,21 USD as well as registration and arbitration fees in the amount of 17.248,76 USD.

The court of first instance rejected the application on the ground that recovery of the awarded sum violated the Russian public policy.[38] The cassation court partially reversed the decision of the first instance court and justified it as follows:

> "*As determined by the court of first instance, the amount of the penalty imposed by the arbitral tribunal was calculated at a rate which in USD exceeded more than twice the rate in rubles established by the Bank of Russia, and therefore it was not directed towards compensating the consequences of the breach but was clearly punitive in nature.*
>
> *Also noteworthy are the defendant's allegations of abuse on the part of the Harbin Scientific and Technical Company in determining the size of the penalty, which were not considered within the arbitral proceedings, while the above written position was brought to the attention of the arbitral tribunal and the claimant in a timely manner: the existence of mutual relationships between the Harbin Scientific and Technical Company as well as the further delivery of goods to an affiliate of the claimant, who for a significant period of time did not make payment to AgroTechInvest LLC.*
>
> *The arguments of the cassation petition concerning the fallacy of the first instance court's findings on the disproportionality of the penalties sought to the*

37 Award of the International Commercial Arbitration Court at the Chamber of Commerce and Industry of the Russian Federation on the case No. M-166/2019, dated 14 September 2019.

38 Decision of the Commercial Court of the Amur Region on the case No. A41-77728/2020, dated 15 April 2021.

consequences of the breach cannot be accepted by the cassation court as the specified is a matter of fact, rather than the application of law, [the first instance court's findings] were done within the competence of the first instance court, respectively, [the arguments of the cassation petition] may not serve as a ground for reversing (amending) the court decision.
Hence, having assessed the conformity of the award rendered by the arbitral tribunal in respect of the levied penalty with the public policy of the Russian Federation and its adherence to the fundamental principles of law, the commercial court, under its authority, ruled that the award did not comply with the principles of justice and proportionality of liability to the breach of obligations."

The crucial points to deduce from this excerpt are the following:
i) To determine the punitive nature of the penalty, Russian courts refer to the key rate of the Russian Central Bank.
ii) Upon refusal to enforce the arbitral award, of significance are the debtor's bad faith actions as well as the arbitral tribunal's failure to address those within the arbitral proceedings.

4.8 *Resolution of the Commercial Court of the Moscow District on the case No. A41-77728/2020, dated 28 January 2022*

The Agency for Dispute Resolution in Privatization Procedures of the Republic of Serbia (the claimant) applied to the commercial court for recognition and enforcement of a Belgrade Commercial Court decision.[39] The judgment obliged Metallorukav LLC (the defendant) to pay penalties in the amount of 414.341.436,2 dinars (approximately 3.527.064 EUR) and 616.730,82 EUR[40] as well as legal costs in the amount of 1.593.090 dinars (approximately 13.561 EUR).

The court of first instance denied the enforcement for the reason that, *inter alia*, the collection of the penalties violated the public policy of the Russian Federation.[41] The cassation court upheld the decision of the first instance court and briefly reasoned it as follows:

39 Decision of the Belgrade Commercial Court on the case No. 45П-4128/2010, dated 13 May 2014.

40 As mentioned in the decision of the first instance court, the penalties awarded to the Agency for Dispute Resolution in Privatization Procedures of the Republic of Serbia exceeded almost six times the price of the contract of sale entered into with Metallorukav LLC.

41 Decision of the Commercial Court of the Moscow Region on the case No. A41-77728/2020, dated 29 October 2021.

> *"Furthermore, the first instance court ... in refusing to enforce the judgment of a foreign court, proceeded on the assumption that the decision of Belgrade Commercial Court violated such a fundamental principle of Russian law as the principle of proportionality of civil liability, which, by default, cannot be used to enrich the creditor, but is intended to compensate this creditor for possible damages and to remedy one's infringed rights.*
>
> ...
>
> *The findings of the court are based on a full, comprehensive, and objective examination of the factual circumstances and the evidence at hand, are not contrary to them and are not subject to review by the cassation court by virtue of Art. 286 of the Commercial Procedural Code of the Russian Federation."*

The basic findings from this case are as follows:

i) The Russian public policy is based on the principle of proportionality.

ii) The proportionality principle implies that civil liability cannot result in the creditor's enrichment since such liability is purely compensatory in nature.

Summing up this section, one could note that, unfortunately, the Russian case law relevant for punitive damages is fairly inconsistent and lacks common lines of reasoning. The only commonalities are the reference to the debtor's breach and the use of the key rate of the Russian Central Bank as a benchmark in assessing the punitive nature of the awarded penalty.

5 Conclusions

The present chapter was devoted to the recognition and enforcement of punitive damages in the Russian Federation. The key question sought to be addressed was whether and under which conditions Russian courts would recognise and enforce court judgments or arbitral awards conferring punitive damages. To answer this question, the relevant case law was analysed and, consequently, the following conclusions were drawn:

First, over the past seventeen years the public policy exception transformed from a very broad concept to a more modern and internationally accepted understanding thereof. The Russian courts apply the same concept of public policy both to court judgments and arbitral awards (whether rendered within domestic or international arbitration proceedings).

Second, while Russian courts have not been faced with punitive damages in the classic understanding of this term, inspiration could be drawn from the cases dealing with punitive liquidated damages or punitive contractual penalties as the closest surrogate thereof. According to the current case law, Russian courts do not recognise and enforce foreign court decisions and arbitral awards ordering the payment of such "fake" punitive damages, as they are considered contrary to public policy.

Third, notwithstanding the above, a deviation from the compensatory nature of civil liability does not by itself imply a violation of the Russian public policy. The question whether there is a sufficient punitive element is considered on a case-by-case basis, with a court being given broad discretion within this analysis.

Fourth, the case law on the recovery of punitive damages is scarce and inconsistent. Unfortunately, it appears to be challenging to identify any benchmarks against which a given amount would be recognised as having a punitive nature, and, consequently, be refused recognition and enforcement.

I would hope that the Russian Supreme Court will in the near future issue detailed and comprehensive guidelines on the recognition and enforcement of punitive damages, on which Russian courts can rely to adjudicate relevant disputes by applying predefined and transparent criteria. Absent such guidelines, each case is effectively within the absolute discretion of the court, which obviously cannot be regarded as satisfactory (at least, in terms of legal certainty).

Punitive damages in China: codification, developments and global cooperation

Wenliang Zhang[*] *and Yingqi Zhong*[**]

1 Introduction

China passed its Code of Civil Law in 2021, which marks a significant progress in the development of Chinese civil law. Since China is of a civil law tradition, the basic tenet for remedies is to compensate, that is to say, parties may only claim for compensatory damages rather than punitive damages. The reality is indeed that over the past decades there were hardly any Chinese laws that allowed for punitive damages. Under this newly introduced Code, however, punitive damages are unified by several important provisions. Bearing in mind the several pieces of the Chinese special laws that were enacted before the Code and also address punitive damages in relation to specific civil and commercial issues,[1] the arrival of the Code marks a further significant development of punitive damages under Chinese law. The introduction of punitive damages in the Code is quite striking in the sense that punitive damages are now regulated at the level of general civil law, with the Code being the most important civil law. As of today, although punitive damages have crept into the Code of Civil Law, the remedy only plays a marginal role in China's legal and judicial practice.

When we talk about punitive damages in China, it will be natural for us to consider how China treats foreign punitive damages when these foreign awards seek recognition and enforcement. This is another side of China's attitude towards punitive damages. Fairly speaking, the more receptive Chinese law is to the concept of punitive, the easier it is for Chinese courts to recognise foreign punitive damages. In this respect, it becomes necessary to conduct an investigation into China's recognition landscape for foreign punitive damages judgments. No Chinese laws have ever explicitly provided for the recognisability or non-recognisability of foreign punitive damages. In China's judicial practice, however, there were sporadic cases in which foreign punitive damages sought recognition and enforcement in China. Although no single Chinese court has ever recognised or enforced foreign punitive damages, the changing landscape of China's punitive damages law shows

* Associate Professor, Renmin University of China Law School.

** PhD candidate, Renmin University of China Law School.

1 See *infra* 2.2 Punitive damages in special laws.

that China is likely to treat foreign punitive damages in a positive light. In this chapter, the basic regime of the gradually evolving punitive damages, the development and future direction of punitive damages, as well as the attitudes towards recognition and enforcement of foreign punitive damages in China will be explored.

2 The role of punitive damages in Chinese law

In the past two decades, the legislation of punitive damages in China has been continuously promoted and recent years saw a dramatic surge of the legislation or regulation on punitive damages.[2] China's legislature, judiciary and the government all started to introduce a series of laws or rules regulating the application of punitive damages. Especially in 2020, as shown in Figure 1, there was a salient surge in the relevant rules about punitive damages, ranging from the laws passed by China's legislature such as the Code of Civil Law to the Supreme People's Court (hereafter "SPC")'s judicial interpretations.[3] Remarkably, besides the general laws on punitive damages there is also a large number of judicial interpretations and rules delimiting the scope and extent of punitive damages.[4]

2 See *infra* Figure 1. The statistics in Figure 1 were collected on Wolters Kluwer Law Online, available at https://law.wkinfo.com.cn/ (last visited 15 October 2021). The authors searched for the rules and regulations relating to punitive damages and classified them according to the enacting authorities.

3 See Figure 1.

4 These judicial interpretations and the like are set to help apply the punitive damages established under the laws passed by China's legislature.

Figure 1 Number of laws regulating punitive damages in China

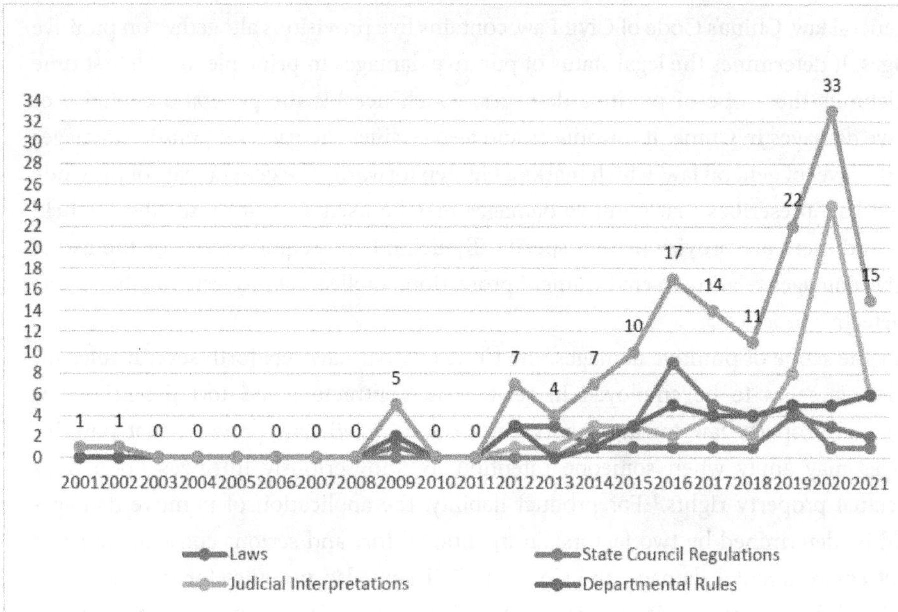

Figure 1 clearly shows the rising trend of enacted laws on punitive damages in China, which signals an increasing acceptance of punitive damages in Chinese law. Before 2012, punitive damages were hardly known in Chinese law, except in some specific laws such as the Consumers Protection Law which includes just one article to grant consumers a right to claim punitive damages in case of injury from defective goods.[5] After 2012, there was a sharp rise of punitive damages law, and in 2020, there was a dramatic surge in terms of the SPC's judicial interpretations on punitive damages. These moves were coordinated with China's desire to promote its business environment, both domestically and internationallly. Chinese courts are aiming to regulate the use of punitive damages on a wide scale. As regards the laws passed by the Chinese legislature, the National People's Congress and its Standing Committee, we also see a rise of such laws in the past decade, but that is not in proportion to the judicial interpretations of the SPC. In addition, China's central government and its departments also joined in promoting the regulation of punitive damages and the relevant laws and policy documents also increased in those years.[6]

5 Consumers Protection Law *(Revised in 2013)*, article 55.

6 China's central government and its departments referred to punitive damages on many occasions. On the one hand, regulations were passed to regulate the use of punitive damages, such as the 2019 Regulations on Optimizing the Business Environment, which calls for the establishment of a punitive compensation system for intellectual property infringement. On the other hand, there are a lot of policy documents to

2.1 *Punitive damages in the Code of Civil Law*

The general law, China's Code of Civil Law, contains five provisions altogether on punitive damages. It determines the legal status of punitive damages in principle for the first time and delimits the scope of punitive damages, which heralds the general acceptance of punitive damages in China. It introduces and also codifies the rules on punitive damages from the level of general law, which marks a big step forward. The general part of the Code of Civil Law prescribes that punitive damages may be used against those who are held liable, and there are provisions that specifically delimit the requirements for the use of punitive damages relating to environment protection, intellectual property infringements and defective products.[7]

For the scope of punitive damages, the Code of Civil Law sets forth several rules for punitive damages to be employed in relation to contractual and tort liabilities. For intellectual property law infringements, the Code of Civil Law provides that punitive damages may apply when someone intentionally and seriously infringes upon one's intellectual property rights.[8] For product liability, the application of punitive damages should be determined by two factors: an intentional tort and serious consequences.[9] In case of environmental damage, the Code of Civil Law also provides for two elements: intentional damage and serious consequences.[10] The example of environmental damage will be explained further below. Firstly, intentional damage refers to the intention to allow the result to occur, knowing that the illegal disposal and dumping of pollutants will cause environmental pollution or ecological damage. Secondly, the consequence of violating regulations shall lead to punitive liabilities. If the conduct turned out to be "no violation on state regulations", there would be no need to punish and it is enough to bear compensatory responsibility rather than punitive damages. Some scholars believe that punitive damages should only be applicable to illegal behavior.[11] For environmental damage, the judicial interpretations of the SPC affirm that punitive damages should only be applied in case of "serious consequences". If the environment is damaged and the ecosystem is destroyed, causing death, serious damage to health, major property loss,

---

promote the use of punitive damages in the field of protection of intellectual property, food security, fake commodities, protection of environment and so on.

7 Article 179 of the Code of Civil Law sets forth that "*Where the law provides for punitive damages, such provisions shall prevail*".

8 Code of Civil Law, article 1185.

9 Code of Civil Law, article 1207.

10 Code of Civil Law, article 1232.

11 See H. Xie, 'The Constructive Interpretation and Analysis of the Punitive Liability Clause for Environmental Infringement – Centered on Article 1232 of the Civil Code' (环境侵权惩罚性赔偿责任条款的构造性解释及其分析–以《民法典》第1232条规定为中心), *Journal of Law Application (法律适用)*, Vol. 464, No. 23, 2020, pp. 134-140.

serious damage to the ecological environment or major adverse social impact, this should be seen as causing serious consequences for which punitive damages can be imposed.[12]

2.2 Punitive damages in special laws

Besides the rules under the general Code of Civil Law, there are Chinese special laws in several fields regulating the application of punitive damages and prescribing the requirements that should be satisfied in order to impose punitive damages. These special areas *inter alia* include intellectual property, consumer protection and food safety.

With regard to intellectual property rights, the Trademark Law introduced punitive damages in this field when the law was amended in 2013. Now the punitive damages rules have spread over the Copyright Law, the Patent Law and the Anti-unfair Competition law.[13] These laws lay down the general requirements for application of punitive damages in the field of intellectual property, while the relevant judicial interpretations regarding intellectual property further define the specific circumstances for punitive damages.[14] For example, the Trademark Law sets forth two elements: subjective malice and objective serious circumstances. The identification of these two elements overlaps, which still remains controversial. Some scholars believe that the assessment of "subjective malice" focuses on factors such as the infringer's knowledge of the law and the legal nature of the infringed right, meaning that the infringer's behavior in the judicial procedures is particularly important.[15] The "objective serious circumstances" should focus on the conduct itself, and also be analysed in combination with the damage caused by the infringement.[16]

The Consumers Protection Law provides for the application of punitive damages in cases concerning fraud and product liability, and lays down specific provisions regarding medical products, food and other special products related to daily life. It prescribes that if producers and operators commit fraud when providing goods and services, consumers

12 Interpretation of the Supreme People's Court on the Application of Punitive Damages in the Trial of Ecological Environment Infringement Disputes, article 8.

13 Copyright Law (Revised in 2020), article 54; Patent Law (Revised in 2020), article 71; Trademark Law (Revised in 2019), article 63; Law Against Unfair Competition (Revised in 2019), article 17.

14 Several Provisions (II) of the Supreme People's Court on Issues Concerning the Application of Law in the Hearing of Cases Involving Disputes over Infringement upon the Rights of New Plant Varieties (II), article 17, paragraph 1.

15 See J. Xu, M. Ye, 'Research on the Typology of the Applicable Elements of Trademark Punitive Compensation Law' (商标惩罚性赔偿法律适用要件的类型化研究), *Intellectual Property (知识产权)*, Vol. 242, No. 4, 2021, pp. 79-96.

16 See X. Li, 'Jurisprudential Analysis and Application Approach of Punitive Damages for Intellectual Property Rights' (知识产权惩罚性赔偿的法理剖析与适用进路), *Academic Exchange (学术交流)*, Vol.333, No. 12, 2021, pp. 40-51.

may claim punitive damages.[17] In case of product liability, punitive damages may also be applied when, subjectively, producers and operators "know clearly" that there are defects in goods and, objectively, this results in death or serious damage to health.[18] The draft Vaccine Administration Law contained one provision on punitive damages, which laid down that if the vaccine was sold and inoculated with knowledge of the product's quality problems, resulting in death or serious damage to the health of the vaccinated person, punitive damages might be claimed in addition to compensation for the loss. The draft continued to use the identification of subjective and objective elements in medical products.[19] However, when the draft was approved, this provision on punitive damages was deleted.

As for food liability, as stricter requirements for liability are imposed on producers and business operators, the upper limit of punitive damages that is allowed by China's Food Safety Law has been raised. The Food Safety Law prescribes that consumers who have suffered any losses from food failing to meet the food safety standards may claim compensatory damages against the trader or producer. In addition to claiming compensatory damages, a consumer may require a producer failing to meet the food safety standards, or a trader knowingly dealing in such food, to pay an indemnity of ten times the price paid or three times the loss.[20] In order for liability to be imposed, the Food Safety Law requires producers and sellers to "know clearly" that food does not meet food safety standards, without the requirement of causing death or serious health damage. As for subjective intention, some Chinese scholars suggested approaches to identify what constitutes "know clearly". For example, if the producer or seller tampered with or forges the production date, qualification mark or other essential information, it would satisfy the fraud rules. If a producer or seller failed to take reasonable measures to fully detect whether the product has defects after clearly having been informed of the defects of the product to eliminate the possible risks of the product, it can be regarded as "knowing clearly".[21]

---

17 Consumers Protection Law (Revised in 2013), article 55, paragraph 1.

18 Consumers Protection Law (Revised in 2013), article 55, paragraph 2.

19 Vaccine Administration Law (second review draft), article 95, paragraph 3; Interpretation of the Supreme People's Court on Several Issues Concerning the Application of Law in the Trial of Medical Injury Liability Disputes (Revised in 2020), article 23.

20 Food Safety Law, article 148.

21 See Z. Wang & J. Gong, 'The Punitive Compensation Liability for Detective Products in China – Centered on the Article 1207 of Tort Liability in *Civil Code*' (我国缺陷产品惩罚性赔偿责任研究–以《民法典•侵权责任编》第1207条为中心), *Journal of Shandong University (Philosophy and Social Sciences) [山东大学学报(哲学社会科学版)]*, Vol. 244, No. 1, 2021, pp. 119-130.

2.3 *The increasing values of punitive damages in Chinese law*

Generally speaking, the theoretical basis of punitive damages lies in punishing and stopping illegal actions, especially intentional or malicious conduct. It was pointed out that punitive damages are usually used to achieve at least one of the following four functions: revenge, social justice, compensation, and punishment and deterrence.[22] In civil law jurisdictions, the basic function of damages is mostly to compensate, which aims to bring the victim to the position he would have been in had the damage not occured. China is considered to have a civil law tradition and it insists on the concept of compensation as the basic principle of civil law. For a long time, the scope of punitive damages permitted in China was limited to some specific areas based on strict requirements. Punitive damages mainly play the role of punishment or deterrence as a supplement to compensatory damages, while compensation is not the main function of punitive damages in China. Chinese scholars hold different views on the function of punishment and deterrence in specific fields. As for food liability, the Food Safety Law stipulates that punitive damages amount to ten times the commodity price.[23] Some scholars believe that such a punitive damages award is still rather meagre because of the low food price in China, meaning that the effect of punishment cannot really be achieved. In addition, the application of punitive damages in food liability has strict constraints. Ten-fold compensation is mostly seen in cases concerning buying fake products on purpose, and is said to have the function of law enforcement. Some say that only high administrative fines may achieve real punishment under the Food Safety Law, while the ten-fold compensation is only a kind of multiple compensation which cannot be considered as punitive.[24] In the field of intellectual property, punitive damages of three times the actual loss will be awarded to punish and deter malicious infringement. This is considered to have punitive effect because of the relatively large amount of damages in practice. Compared to other fields, it is more difficult for the law enforcement authorities to discover the infringement of intellectual property. Another interesting example concerns labor contracts under Chinese law. If the employer fails to conclude a written labor contract with the employee in time, a double salary may be ordered as a form of punitive damages by some Chinese courts, which has the function of punishment rather than remuneration for labour.[25]

22 R. Fowler, 'Why Punitive Damages Should be a Jury's Decision in Kansas: A Historical Perspective', *University of Kansas Law Review*, Vol. 52, No. 3, 2004, p. 631.

23 Food Safety Law, article 148, paragraph 2.

24 See Y. Li, 'Research on the Chinese Model of Punitive Compensation System' (惩罚性赔偿制度的中国模式研究), *Law and Social Development (法制与社会发展)*, Vol. 21, No. 6, 2015, pp. 109-126.

25 Labor Contract Law, article 82. The Beijing High People's Court once held that the double salary was punitive in nature. See Minutes of the Symposium of the Beijing Higher People's Court and the Beijing Labor Dispute Arbitration Commission on the Application of Law in Labor Dispute Cases (II)(北京市高级人民法院、北京市劳动争议仲裁委员会关于劳动争议案件法律适用问题研讨会会议纪要(二)).

2.3.1 First-instance cases concerning punitive damages

Following the surge of the rules on punitive damages, there is also a sharp rise of the use of punitive damages in China's judicial practice. The number of cases which applied punitive damages may be analysed according to domestic law, and such cases may be divided into different categories according to the types of disputes involved.[26] As can be seen in Figure 2.1, in the entire period from 2001 to 2016 less than 9000 first-instance cases involving punitive damage were decided, while there were more than 9000 punitive damages-related cases in 2017 alone, more than the total number of cases in the preceding 15 years. Since 2017, the number of cases involving punitive damages basically remains at the same level. Thus, we can see a clear trend that the use of punitive damages is increasing in China's judicial practice.

Figure 2.1 Number of first-instance punitive damages cases

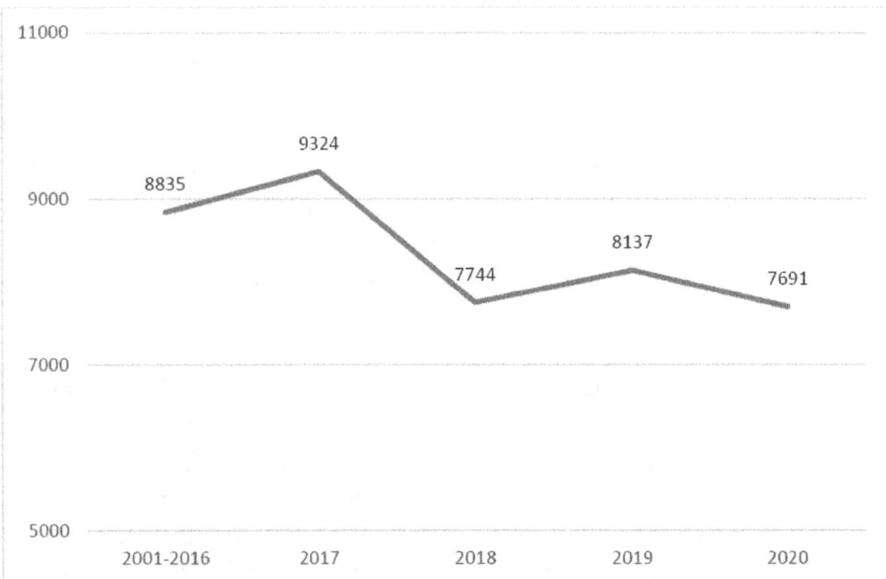

The full text can be found at https://mp.weixin.qq.com/s/InL79wVXlrbFYdZFJyn-fw, last visited 31 January 2023. For more, see Minutes of the Symposium of the Higher People's Court of Shandong Province and the Human Resources and Social Security Department of Shandong Province on Several Issues concerning the Trial of Labor and Personnel Disputes(山东省高级人民法院、山东省人力资源社会保障厅关于审理劳动人事争议案件若干问题研讨会会议纪要). The full text can be found at http://www.sdcourt.gov.cn/lypyfy/404120/404053/8497525/index.html, last visited 16 January 2023.

26 For more, see Figure 2.2.

Figure 2.2 Number of first-instance punitive damages cases in different disputes

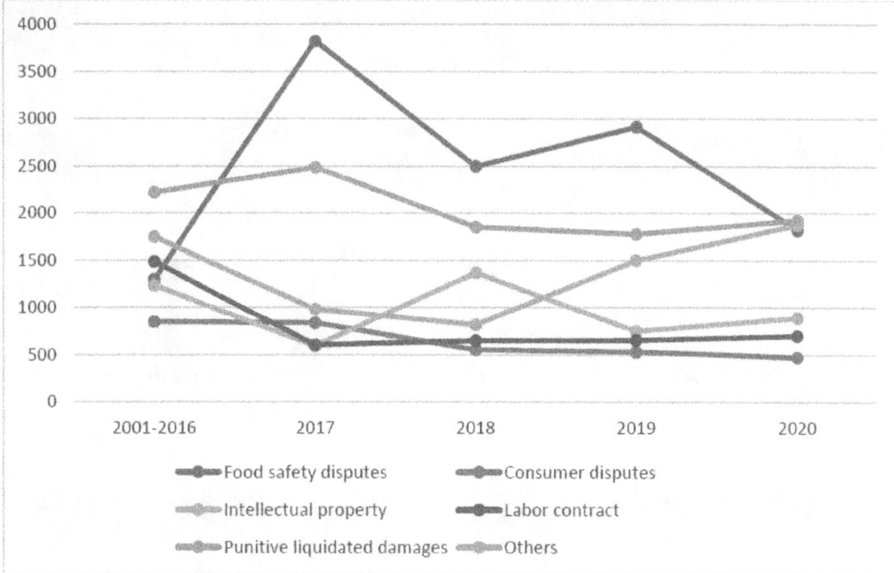

As can be seen in Figure 2.2, the number of cases differs according to the category of dispute. From this Figure, it can be drawn that in Chinese judicial practice the greatest number of cases related to food safety disputes. The sharp rise of the judicial practice on punitive damages may be explained in several ways. Firstly, there is a clear rise of rules regulating punitive damages as explained above. Secondly, the general tenet for remedies is changing and the courts tend to accept and apply punitive damages, especially in the broad context of China's deepening open-door policy and borrowing of foreign legal experience.

2.3.2 The upper limits of punitive damages

The increasing acceptance of punitive damages is also reflected in the upper limits of punitive damages in China's existing laws. Figure 2.3 below clearly shows the limits of punitive damages in different fields of China's civil law.

Figure 2.3 Upper limits of punitive damages (expressed in times of actual loss)

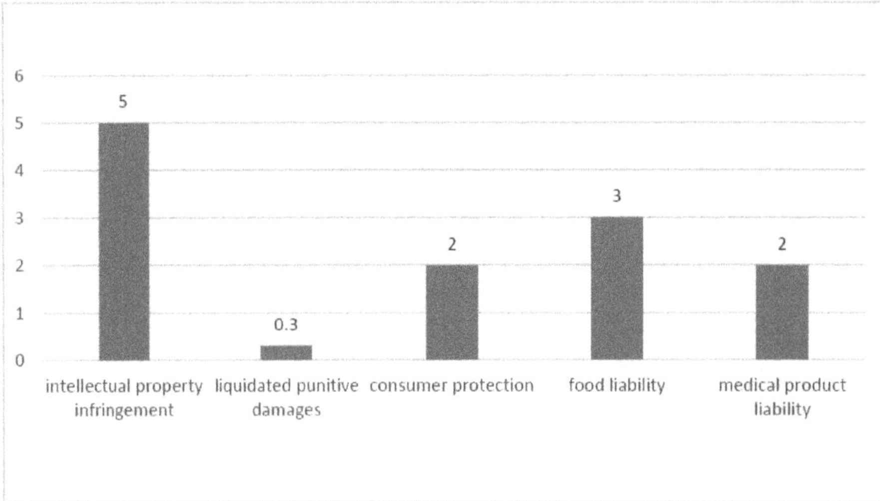

For malicious intellectual property infringements the upper limit of punitive damages that courts may apply is five times the actual loss. The law raised the upper limit from three to five times in 2019, significantly enhancing the punishment for IP infringement. However, some scholars pointed out that the calculation base of actual loss is not feasible in practice, because it is difficult to prove the actual loss suffered in the context of IP. Therefore, some suggested that if the court can find out the actual profit that was made by the infringer, this should be taken as the calculation base. If the parties cannot ascertain the actual amount of profit but the existence of profit can be determined, the court should calculate the amount of profit according to the evidence provided and take it as the calculation base for punitive damages.[27]

For product liability, the court should apply twice the actual loss in consumer disputes and medical product, and three times in food disputes.[28] For food liability, the victim has a choice to claim either three times the actual loss or ten times the product's price. It may be argued that the calculation method of ten times the product's price is not quite reasonable. The sum of damages is negligible in comparison with the huge profit gained

27 See X. Li, 'Jurisprudential Analysis and Application Approach of Punitive Damages for Intellectual Property Rights' (知识产权惩罚性赔偿的法理剖析与适用进路), *Academic Exchange (学术交流)*, Vol. 333, No. 12, 2021, pp. 40-51.

28 Minutes of the symposium on exploring the establishment of the punitive compensation system in civil public welfare litigation for food safety, which set forth that *"First, the subjective fault of the infringer is serious; Second, the number of illegal acts is large and the duration is long; Third, the amount of illegal sales is large, the amount of profits is large, and the coverage of victims is wide; Fourth, causing serious consequences of infringement or adverse social impact; Fifth, there are other serious violations of social and public interests"*.

from the tort, therefore hardly achieving the effect of punishment.[29] Considering this situation, the rules allow for a choice of remedies between the Consumer Protection Law and the Food Safety Law in order to seek higher damages.

For commercial contracts, the Interpretation of the Supreme People's Court on Several Issues concerning the application of the contract law of the People's Republic of China (II) limits the amount of punitive damages, which may be agreed on by the parties, to 30 percent of the actual loss. This rule equally applies to foreign-related contracts.[30] For contract fraud, the Interpretation of the Supreme People's Court on Several Issues Concerning the Application of Law in the Trial of Disputes over Commercial Housing Sales Contracts imposes punitive damages on the seller. If the seller concealed the fact that it had not obtained the pre-sale license of commercial housing or provided fake certificates, it will have to bear punitive liability of not more than twice the purchase price in addition to the return of the money paid.[31]

For environmental damages, in practice, the amount of punitive damages shall range from one to three times the actual loss with reference to the Consumer Protection Law, the Food Safety Law and other regulations. As the public environment is akin to the protection of rights and interests of consumers, food safety and product liability, which all relate to public interests, the one-to-three times environmental punitive damages exhibit a certain rationality.[32]

2.4 *Interim conclusion*

Punitive damages have been firmly anchored in Chinese substantive rules regarding civil and commercial damages. According to the above analysis, we can conclude that China's adoption of punitive damages is wide but scattered in certain areas of civil law. Generally speaking though, the introduction of punitive damages in China is still in its nascence. This field of law is developing quite fast. Above all, the arrival of China's Code of Civil Law is unprecedented although it merely brings in very general rules for punitive damages. Besides this Code of Civil Law, we also see the emergence of punitive damages in some

29 See S. Li & X. Mo, 'Research on the 10 times punitive compensation mechanism in China's Food Safety Law' (我国《食品安全法》中的10倍惩罚性赔偿机制探究), *Science and Technology of Food Industry (食品工业科技)*, Vol. 37, No. 13, 2016, pp. 30-32.

30 Contract Law, article 114 paragraph 2; Interpretation of the Supreme People's Court on Issues Concerning the Application of the Contract Law of the People's Republic of China (II), article 29, paragraph 2. The laws mentioned here may be found on the website of National Laws Database established by National People's Congress of China, https://flk.npc.gov.cn/index.html, visited on 25 April 2023.

31 Interpretation of the Supreme People's Court on Several Issues Concerning the Application of Law in the Hearing of Cases Involving Disputes over Contracts of Purchase and Sale of Commercial Housing (amended in 2020), article 9. *Id.*

32 (2020) Gan 0222 Min Chu No. 796.

other areas, though still limited. The salient feature of China's existing punitive damages regime is the cap placed upon the amount of punitive damages. The various forms of limitation on punitive damages also reflect that the basic tenet for civil remedies is still mainly to compensate rather than to punish or deter. The modest amount of punitive damages in different areas of law reflects China's conservative attitude towards punitive damages.

However, from a historical perspective, we see the dramatically changing landscape for punitive damages in China. In recent years, there has been a sharp rise of the rules in this field, which is a key step in accepting punitive damages at the general level. For the time being, we may say that China is using punitive damages more than ever. In China's judicial practice, more and more cases grant punitive damages, which confirms the increasing acceptance of punitive damages. China's legislation and practice affirm the application of punitive damages in both domestic and non-domestic contexts, and the consideration of punitive damages is equally applicable in both contexts. For example, the relevant practice affirmed the application of liquidated damages in foreign related and non-foreign related breach of contract, and adopts a unified standard to determine the amount of liquidated punitive damages, namely the punitive damages agreed upon by the parties.

3 FOREIGN PUNITIVE DAMAGES AWARDS BEFORE CHINESE COURTS

3.1 A glance at foreign judgments recognition in China

The reception of foreign punitive damages awards and China's development of punitive damages regime are two closely related issues, with the latter deeply influencing the former while the former strongly strengthens the latter. In reality, the landscape for the recognition and enforcement of global judgments is changing dramatically over the recent years. States work together under the auspices of the Hague Conference on Private International Law (HCCH) and significant progress has been made with the arrival of the Convention of 30 June 2005 on Choice of Court Agreements (HCCH 2005 Choice of Court Convention)[33] and the Convention of 2 July 2019 on the Recognition and Enforcement of Foreign Judgments in Civil or Commercial Matters (Hague 2019 Judgments Convention).[34] Regionally, the EU has been taking the leading role in promoting the recognition of regional judgments by reference to the Brussels I Regulation Recast in particular. With the

33 The full text of the Convention can be found at https://www.hcch.net/en/instruments/conventions/full-text/?cid=98, visited on 14 January 2023.

34 The full text of the Convention can be found at https://www.hcch.net/en/instruments/conventions/full-text/?cid=137, visited on 14 January 2023.

deepening of international communications, more foreign judgments are expected to circulate at the global stage. For China, the efforts in this field are also intensifying.

Punitive damages awards are but one category of civil and commercial judgments. Currently, there are no special rules for the recognition and enforcement of foreign punitive damages in China. Thus, the general rules for recognition and enforcement of foreign judgments apply to the recognition and enforcement of foreign punitive damages in China. Roughly speaking, recognition and enforcement of foreign judgments in China may follow an international treaty path or a domestic law path based on the principle of reciprocity. As of today, China has concluded 39 bilateral treaties on judicial assistance in civil and commercial matters, 35 of which provide for the recognition of judgments.[35] These bilateral treaties contain relatively detailed rules on the recognition of judgments, although their provisions have evolved since China concluded its first bilateral treaty with France in 1987.[36] Such bilateral treaties do not contain specific rules for the recognition and enforcement of punitive damages. The biggest contribution of such bilateral treaties is that these treaties ensure reciprocity in the recognition and enforcement of foreign judgments. In fact, the first successful recognition cases in China were brought under such treaties, although these cases did not concern punitive damages awards.[37] However, the role of such treaties should not be exaggerated. Only a limited number of countries have signed bilateral judicial assistance treaties with China. No such treaties exist between China and its biggest trading partners, including the United States, Japan, South Korea, Germany, the United Kingdom, and Australia.[38] There appears to be little hope for such treaties between China and these countries, at least in the short term. That is to say, the punitive damages awards from these countries cannot enjoy the assistance of bilateral treaties.

Multilateral conventions provide a potentially more promising path. In recent years, China has been actively participating in the Hague Conference on Private International

35 For a detailed analysis, see W.S. Dodge & W. Zhang, 'Reciprocity in China-US judgments recognition', *Vanderbilt Journal of Transnational Law*, Vol. 53, 2020, pp. 1541-1583.

36 For a detailed analysis, see W. Zhang, 'Recognition and Enforcement of Foreign Judgments in China: Rules, Practice and Strategies', Doctoral dissertation, Ghent University, 2014, pp. 206–227; K. F. Tsang, 'Chinese Bilateral Judgment Enforcement Treaties', *Loyola of Los Angeles International and Comparative Law Review*, Vol. 40, No. 1, 2017, pp. 1-49.

37 The earliest recognition of foreign judgments in China occurred in the early 2000s under bilateral treaties. For example, a Foshan court recognized an Italian judgment in 2000, and a Guangzhou court recognised a French judgment in 2005, both under bilateral treaties. In contrast, recognition was denied to all the foreign judgments coming from other countries without a bilateral treaty with China. See W. Zhang, 'Recognition and Enforcement of Foreign Judgments in China: A Call for Special Attention Paid to Both the "Due Service Requirement" and the "Principle of Reciprocity"', *Chinese Journal of International Law*, Vol. 12, 2013, pp. 143–174.

38 See B. Sun, 'The Future of Cross-Border Litigation in China: Enforcement of Foreign Commercial Judgments Based on Reciprocity', *New York University Journal of International Law and Politics*, Vol. 50, 2018, pp. 1135–1136.

Law (HCCH). China signed the 2005 Hague Convention on Choice of Court Agreements in 2017,[39] and it is likely that China will also ratify the Convention. The 2005 Convention prescribes that

> "*Recognition or enforcement of a judgment may be refused if, and to the extent that, the judgment awards damages, including exemplary or punitive damages, that do not compensate a party for actual loss or harm suffered.*"[40]

Thus, the 2005 Convention does not impose an obligation to recognise and enforce punitive damages awards from a Contracting State. Non-recognition of punitive damages in any case does not affect the recognition and enforcement of the other parts of the judgment. As the Explanatory Report by Hartley and Dogauchi states, if an award of punitive damages is not enforced by reason of article 11, the remainder of the award must be enforced if it satisfies the requirements of article 8.[41] It is also true that such treaties do not exclude the recognition and enforcement of the punitive damages awards either.

In the absence of any international convention or bilateral treaty, recognition and enforcement of foreign judgments, including punitive damages awards, in China must be based on Chinese domestic law under the principle of reciprocity. This domestic law approach applies to the recognition and enforcement of foreign judgments from most countries, and practice shows that it is more uncertain than the recognition under a treaty. For reciprocity-based recognition of foreign judgments in China, the overarching rules come from the Civil Procedure Law (hereafter "CPL").[42] These rules are subject to further interpretations by the SPC in practice. To be specific, China's recognition of foreign judgments, including punitive damages, starts with article 289 CPL.[43] To summarise, the

39 China signed the Convention on 12 September 2017, but has not yet ratified it. See Convention of 30 June 2005 on Choice of Court Agreements. The full text can be found at: https://www.hcch.net/en/instruments/conventions/status-table/?cid=98 (last updated 17 January 2023).

40 Convention of 30 June 2005 on Choice of Court Agreements, article 11.

41 T. Hartley and M. Dogauchi, Explanatory Report on the 2005 Hague Choice of Court Convention, paragraph 217.

42 See Civil Procedure Law (revised in 2021), article 289. In the areas of bankruptcy and maritime matters, there are additional laws governing the recognition of foreign judgments passed by the Nation People's Congress Standing Committee, which have the same authority as laws passed by the Nation People's Congress itself and complement the Civil Procedure Law; Enterprise Bankruptcy Law (effective on 1 June 2007), article 5 (the full text can be found at http://www.npc.gov.cn/npc/c198/200608/82c5645b09b24b5ebefe76e365db72c9.shtml, last visited 17 January 2023); Special Maritime Procedure Law (promulgated 25 December 1999), article 11 (the full text can be found at https://whhsfy.hbfy.gov.cn/DocManage/ViewDoc?docId=6b9a4118-d9fb-450c-8c88-ac4a7d07a0ff), last visited 17 January 2023.

43 Article 289 of CPL prescribes that *"After a People's Court of the PRC reviews an application or request for the recognition and enforcement of a legally effective judgment or ruling delivered by a foreign court according to the international treaties concluded or acceded to by the PRC or based on the principle of reciprocity, if [the People's Court] considers that such a judgment or ruling neither contradicts the basic principles of the laws [of the PRC] nor violates the national sovereignty, security, and social and public interests of the PRC, [the People's*

following requirements are set forth under the CPL: the foreign judgment is legally effective, the recognition is supported by an international treaty or the principle of reciprocity, and the judgment does not violate Chinese public policy. For recognition and enforcement of foreign punitive damages awards, these requirements under the CPL apply on the same footing.

Under China's Belt and Road Initiative, the SPC takes measures to provide a sound legal environment, which include efforts to promote the recognition of foreign judgments.[44] Such efforts may also improve the environment for the recognition and enforcement of foreign punitive damages awards. In 2015, the SPC issued Several Opinions of the SPC on the Provision of Judicial Services and Safeguards to the Establishment of One Belt and One Road, which provide that People's Courts "*shall promote the mutual recognition and enforcement of judgments rendered by countries along the 'Belt and Road'*".[45] A softened approach to address the reciprocity requirement under the CPL is expected following these moves. The SPC has also sought to update China's rules on the recognition of foreign judgments by signing recognition memorandums with its counterparts in other jurisdictions. In 2018, the SPC and the Singapore Supreme Court signed a Judgments Recognition Memorandum, which determines how Chinese judgments may be recognised in Singapore and vice versa.[46] Although the memorandum is expressly stated to have "no binding legal effect,"[47] it clearly reflects the current positive attitude of the SPC towards foreign judgments.

3.2 *Foreign punitive damages receiving a special treatment*

Punitive damages awards are getting more and more accepted in domestic laws around the globe, especially in common law jurisdictions such as the United States which have a long tradition of employing punitive damages to promote important judicial policies. In Chinese law, as shown above, punitive damages are also increasingly accepted. In this

---

Court] shall make a ruling to recognise its effects. Where the enforcement is of necessity, [the People's Court] shall issue an order to enforce the foreign judgment according to the relevant provisions of the present law. If a legally effective judgment or ruling delivered by a foreign court contradicts the basic principles of the law [of the PRC] or the national sovereignty, security, social and public interests of the PRC, the People's Courts shall refuse to grant the recognition and enforcement."

44 The salient efforts in this area include Several Opinions of the SPC on the Provision of Judicial Services and Safeguards to the Establishment of One Belt and One Road], Fa Fa No. 9 (2015). The full text can be found at: https://www.court.gov.cn/zixun-xiangqing-14900.html, last visited 7 February 2023.

45 *Ibid.*

46 See Memorandum of Guidance Between the Supreme People's Court of the People's Republic of China and the Supreme Court of Singapore on Recognition and Enforcement of Money Judgments in Commercial Cases. The full text can be found at https://www.pkulaw.com/en_treaties/20cd7dbf296b7ca7f9f7e98a20133061bdfb.html, last visited 31 January 2023.

47 *Id.*, article 2.

context, cross-border recognition of punitive damages becomes necessary to expand the usefulness and effects of such awards.

The recognition and enforcement of punitive damages has long been a controversial issue in national legislation, judicial practice and legal theory. As for the punitive damages rendered by foreign courts, especially those from the United States, although some countries display an open attitude, a lot more countries still adhere to the traditional cautious approach. Generally speaking, recognition of punitive damages shares the same basic legal and judicial structure as foreign judgments recognition. All barriers to the general foreign judgment recognition equally apply in the context of recognition of punitive damages. Recognition of punitive damages may however encounter more obstacles, among which public policy is of a big concern. All of these factors create a special picture for the recognition of punitive damages. The international community actively co-operated in the hope of reaching an effective convention on the recognition and enforcement of foreign judgments, and within the framework of the HCCH the 2019 Hague Judgments Convention was adopted. However, it will take time for this new global instrument to attract a large membership. As an alternative, States have also attempted to co-operate bilaterally or regionally. Indeed, bilateral co-operation is an option, but it is far from ideal. As regards regional instruments in this respect, some but not many successful examples have been witnessed. To put it another way, recognition and enforcement of punitive damages is still a matter that is predominantly handled by individual countries relying on their own disparate laws, which exacerbates the inconsistencies among the laws of countries and the ensuing conflicts that inevitably surface. It seems more meaningful and necessary to investigate individual countries' laws and practice on the requirements imposed on punitive damages, since the domestic law of individual countries still predominates in the handling of recognition and enforcement of punitive damages for the time being and the status quo will probably last for a considerable period of time.[48]

In the past, there were hardly any cases where Chinese courts were requested to recognise and enforce foreign judgments containing punitive damages. This situation changed in 2022 when the Guangzhou Intermediate People's Court was requested to recognise and enforce three U.S. EB-5 visa fraud judgments containing both compensatory and punitive damages.[49] In these three connected cases, the defendants Fang Zeng and CIIF Corporation defrauded eight Chinese nationals who wanted to go abroad, by lying that they could get the opportunity of investment immigration by the EB-5 real estate

48 W. Zhang, 'Recognition and enforcement of foreign judgments in China: A call for special attention to both the "due service requirement" and the "principle of reciprocity"', *Chinese Journal of International Law*, Vol. 12, No. 1, 2013, pp. 143-174.

49 These three cases are Anqin WANG v. Fang ZENG etc., (2019) Yue 01 Xie Wai Ren No. 3; Hui JIANG, Jun HUANG v. Fang ZENG etc.,(2019) Yue Xie Wai Ren No. 58; Yeqing XIA v. Fang ZENG etc., (2019) Yue 01 Xie Wai Ren No. 22.

project. The project, however, turned out to be fabricated and the investment funds were stolen by Fang Zeng and the CIIF Corporation. Two of these three U.S. judgments dealt with the lawsuit the victims had brought against Fang Zeng, CIIF and other defendants before the United States District Court for the Central District of California. The court held that the defendants were jointly and severally liable. To be more specific, in the first case, Anqin Wang, applied for recognition and enforcement of the judgment of the United States District Court for the Central District of California for \$1.800.000, comprised of \$560.000 as compensatory damages and \$1.240.000 as punitive damages.[50] In the second case, six people including Hui Jiang jointly applied for \$2.140.000 for each person.[51] In the third case, Yeqing Xia applied for recognition and enforcement of the judgment of the Superior Court of California County of Los Angeles for \$2.060.173,75, comprising of \$1.060.000 as compensatory damages and \$1.000.000 as punitive damages, with the interest in the amount of \$173,75.[52]

The defendants however did not voluntarily carry out their obligations under the judgments. Since defendant Fang Zeng lived in Guangzhou and owned property there, the plaintiffs applied for recognition and enforcement of the judgments in Guangzhou. The Guangzhou Intermediate People's Court held that, according to article 289 CPL,[53] the US judgments did not violate the basic principles of Chinese law, and also did not infringe China's sovereignty, national security, and social public interests. Therefore, the US judgments could be recognised and enforced in accordance with the reciprocity between China and the US. However, the punitive damages that obviously exceeded the actual losses were not recognised and enforced. The Guangzhou Intermediate People's Court only recognised the compensatory damages in the three judgments. As regards why the punitive damages under the three judgments could not be recognised or enforced, the Guangzhou Intermediate People's Court did not furnish any reasoning. The Court could have referred to the public policy defense to refuse the punitive damages, but not elaborating on the ground for refusal of the punitive part is not an advisable approach to address such cases.

The Chinese courts' handling of recognition and enforcement of foreign punitive damages is just at the beginning. A Chinese court's refusal of foreign punitive damages is not unique, considering foreign courts' practice in relation to recognition of foreign punitive damages. As has long been established, especially in civil law jurisdictions, it is rare to recognise punitive damages exceeding actual losses.[54]

---

50 Anqin WANG v. Fang ZENG etc., (2019) Yue 01 Xie Wai Ren No. 3.

51 Hui JIANG, Jun HUANG v. Fang ZENG etc., (2019) Yue Xie Wai Ren No. 58.

52 Yeqing XIA v. Fang ZENG etc., (2019) Yue 01 Xie Wai Ren No. 22.

53 Civil Procedure Law (Revised in 2021), article 289.

54 See for instance chapter 1 on Europe by Vanleenhove in this book.

For the treatment of foreign punitive damages in China, it is also necessary to briefly consider Chinese courts' recognition and enforcement of foreign arbitral awards containing punitive damages. In the 2014 case of *ECOM Company v. Shenzhen Guotai Hua Investment Company*, the award was made in accordance with the bylaws of the International Cotton Association. The seat of arbitration was England and the governing law was English law. The award ordered Guotaihua to pay approximately $450.000 to ECOM, including damages for delayed performance amounting to more than $110.000. Guotaihua claimed that the damages for delayed performance were punitive in nature, and that such amount violated the basic principle of fairness in Chinese civil law, which constituted a violation of China's public policy. In response to this argument, the Shenzhen Intermediate People's Court opined that, according to the SPC's standpoint, deviation from mandatory rules of Chinese law does not necessarily violate China's public policy. Irrespective of whether Guotaihua has the qualification for cotton state-owned trade or has obtained import and export quotas when signing the contract, the arbitral award will not violate public policy. Further, the Shenzhen Court said that even if the award did violate the basic principles of equality, fairness or good faith in Chinese civil law, it did not violate China's public policy. Based on these reasons, the court dismissed the challenge of recognition based on public policy. In this case, the Shenzhen Court narrowed the scope of the use of the public policy defense against foreign arbitral awards containing punitive damages.

At present, as the functions of punishment and deterrence of punitive damages may conflict with basic legal principles, resulting in the infringement of the public policy of a country, there are few cases in which foreign punitive damages judgments were recognised and enforced in civil law jurisdictions.[55]

Compared with foreign practice invoking the public policy defense, China's attitude towards the nature of punitive damages can be deemed to be tolerant. Chinese courts confined the application of public policy in the recognition and enforcement of arbitral awards. In other cases of foreign judgements involving punitive damages, Chinese courts did not respond whether the claimed punitive damages violate basic legal principles of compensation or public policy in China, and rejected the recognition and enforcement of the whole judgment on procedural grounds such as the unfinished domestic parallel proceedings,[56] and the absence of reciprocal relations between the two countries.[57] At least we can infer that China's courts will probably not refuse foreign punitive damages for the simple reason that the nature and function of punitive damages violate public policy.

55 For an overview see for instance chapter 1 by Vanleenhove in this book.

56 AMC v. Jason Charles Dean, Juan CHEN, (2018) Yue 03 Min Chu No. 420.

57 (2017) Su 02 Xie Wai Ren No. 1 Zhi Er.

3.3 *Interim Conclusion*

With China's deepening reform and opening up, the country has become increasingly active in international judicial cooperation. Efforts have intensified over the years to promote Sino-foreign circulation of judgments, which paves the way for recognising more foreign punitive damages awards. As regards recognition of foreign punitive damages in China, the newest practice shows the standpoint of Chinese courts in treating foreign punitive damages. On the one hand, Chinese courts only recognise foreign compensatory damages but refuse to recognise the punitive part exceeding the actual loss suffered. On the other hand, the courts narrowed the application of the public policy defense in the context of foreign punitive damages and interpreted this defense in a restrictive way, which indicates that Chinese courts will not simply refuse foreign punitive damages because of their function and nature and also shows Chinese courts' increasingly tolerant attitude towards foreign punitive damages. It is thus predicted that the future may see Chinese courts recognising and enforcing foreign punitive damages awards.

4 FURTHER PATHS TO RECOGNISE FOREIGN PUNITIVE DAMAGES AWARDS IN CHINA

4.1 *The common denominator for punitive damages*

Recent practice seems to suggest that civil law and common law jurisdictions are to some extent starting to converge on their understanding of the nature of punitive damages. In Italy, a civil law jurisdiction, in the 2017 case of *AXO Sport SpA v. NOSA Inc.* the Supreme Court, when ruling on a request for enforcement of foreign punitive damages, acknowledged the function of punishment as part of civil liability, together with the function of compensation.[58] Equally, in the French case of *Schlenzka & Langhorne v. Fountaine Pajot S. A.*, the court noted that punitive damages do not conflict with public policy, and the Court did not consider the punitive damages as criminal.[59] The shift in the attitudes towards the nature of punitive damages in civil law jurisdictions is illustrative of their tolerance or acceptance of punitive damages, which creates more room for recognition and enforcement of foreign punitive damages.

58 See A. Venchiarutti, 'The Recognition of Punitive Damages in Italy: A Commentary on Cass Sez Un 5 July 2017, 16601, *AXO Sport, SpA v. NOSA Inc*', *Journal of European Tort Law*, Vol. 9, No. 1, 2018, pp. 104-122.

59 See B. Janke & F. Licari, 'Enforcing Punitive Damage Awards in France after Fountaine Pajot', *American Journal of Comparative Law*, Vol. 60, 2012, pp. 775-804.

In common law jurisdictions, when it comes to the nature and function of punitive damages, the courts tend to address the concerns in specific situations. On the one hand, the function of punishment and deterrence can be achieved through civil liability in the form of punitive damages as long as the conduct involved has not been punished by the authorities. For example, in *Borders (UK) Ltd v. the Commissioner of Police of the Metropolis & Another*, the appellate court upheld the punitive damages of £100.000 and explained that the prohibition against double jeopardy is not violated by awarding punitive damages alongside criminal punishment, because the conduct actionable in civil litigation exceeds far beyond the stealing which had been punished in criminal proceedings.[60] On the other hand, the punitive damages were paid to the victims rather than to the authorities, which also supports the characterisation of punitive damages as civil in nature. The idea about qualification according to the recipient of punitive damages was approved by Lord Denning in the *SA Consortium* case in 1978. It was held that the sum paid to individuals or private sectors cannot be classified as a fine or punishment, which means that punitive damages cannot be classified as criminal.[61]

In order to keep a balance between the principle of compensation of domestic law and the recognition and enforcement of foreign punitive damages, both civil law and common law jurisdictions have put forward the method of partial recognition. The following two approaches can avoid using the public policy defense to reject the recognition and enforcement of foreign punitive damages as a whole.

On the one hand, some countries, especially those from a civil law tradition, divide the civil damages into a punitive and a compensatory part. In a Japanese case, *Bryant v. Mansei Kogyo Co*, the court partially recognised and enforced the US judgment. The Japanese Supreme Court ruled that the aim of Japanese tort law is to compensate for the loss suffered by the victims and to return them to the state they would have been in had the tort not taken place. The punishment and deterrence pursued by punitive damages does not belong to the basic principles of tort law.[62] The court therefore recognises and enforces the compensatory part, while rejecting the punitive part. If the punitive damages also fulfill a compensatory function they can be recognised to that extent.[63] Punitive damages can indeed sometimes be awarded as compensation for damages that are difficult to prove, or as a means of depriving the defendant of the proceeds obtained through illegal behavior.[64]

---

60 Borders (UK) Ltd v. the Commissioner of Police of the Metropolis & Another, [2005] EWCA Civ 197.

61 See C. Vanleenhove, *Punitive Damages in Private International Law: Lessons for the European Union*, Cambridge-Antwerp-Portland, Intersentia, 2016, p. 145.

62 J. Y. Gotanda, 'Damages in Private International Law', *Collected Courses of the Hague Academy of International Law*, Vol. 326, 2007, p. 388.

63 See for instance the German case of *John Doe v. Eckhard Schmitz*, discussed in chapter 1 by Vanleenhove in this book.

64 See E. C. Stiefel, R. Stürner, & A. Stadler, 'The enforceability of excessive US punitive damage awards in Germany', *American Journal of Comparative Law*, Vol. 39, No. 4, 1991, pp. 779-802.

In the English case of *Lewis v. Eliades*, Nelson J agreed to enforce the basic compensatory part without multiplication, and did not recognise and enforce the multiple damages. Jacob LJ pointed out that it would be unreasonable to deprive a party of the purely compensatory damages. The judgment of the Court of Appeal supports the idea that compensatory damages can be separated from multiple damages. It seems reasonable to assume that the compensatory part of the award would have been enforceable if the plaintiff had not sought to enforce the multiple damages.[65]

Globally, some multilateral arrangements also adopted a restrictive interpretation of public policy and partial recognition of foreign judgments to the extent of compensatory damages was adopted in article 11 of the 2005 Hague Choice of Court Convention, as a salient example.[66] The Explanatory Report on the 2005 Hague Choice of Court Convention makes it clear that recognition and enforcement may only be refused to the extent that the judgment goes beyond the actual loss or harm suffered. This avoids a possible "all or nothing approach" which some legal systems apply to the public policy exception[67] and thus furnishes an approach to address the issue of recognition of foreign punitive damages.

4.2 *China's punitive damages following the global trend*

China's judicial practice has seemingly followed the international trend of partial recognition of foreign judgments containing a punitive part and divides foreign judgments into compensatory and punitive damages. Article 45 of the 2021 *Minutes of the Symposium on Foreign-related Commercial Maritime Trials of National Courts* states that if the damages in a foreign judgment clearly exceed the actual loss, the courts should reject the recognition and enforcement of the excessive part.[68] It represents the stance of Chinese judicial practice concerning the recognisability of foreign punitive damages, although this document, as a piece of the SPC's judicial policy, is not legally binding. China thus still adheres to the principle of compensation, with the compensatory part being the sole part of foreign judgments that is recognisable and enforceable. In the 2022 cases decided by the Guangdong Intermediate People's Court mentioned above, the court stated that the punitive damages within the US judgments, which clearly exceeded the actual loss, would

65 See *Lewis v. Eliades and others*, [2004] 1 All ER 1196, [2003] EWCA Civ 1758. For further analysis see E. Kellman, 'Enforcement of Judgments and Blocking Statutes: *Lewis v. Eliades*', *International & Comparative Law Quarterly*, Vol. 53, No. 4, 2004, pp. 1027-1030.

66 Convention of 30 June 2005 on Choice of Court Agreements, article 11.

67 Explanatory Report on the 2005 Hague Choice of Court Convention, paragraph 205(g).

68 Minutes of the Symposium on Foreign-related Commercial Maritime Trials of National Courts (全国法院涉外商事海事审判工作座谈会会议纪要). The full text of the document can be found at https://cicc.court.gov.cn/html/1/218/62/409/2172.html (last visited 17 January 2023).

not be recognised and enforced.[69] These decisions echoed the SPC's stance in the 2021 *Minutes of the Symposium on Foreign-related Commercial Maritime Trials of National Courts*, which recognised compensatory damages and regarded punitive damages as excessive, using actual loss as the standard of division.

China has gradually explored bilateral judicial assistance mechanisms and actively participated in the construction of international multilateral judicial assistance mechanisms. The Arrangement on Mutual Recognition and Enforcement of Judgments in Civil and Commercial Cases between the Courts of the Mainland and the Hong Kong Special Administrative Region issued in 2019 opens the door to the recognition and enforcement of punitive damages for intellectual property infringement, unfair competition disputes, counterfeit disputes and trade secrets disputes.[70] It reflects the favorable practice of differentiating between recognition of compensatory and of punitive damages, which is called "partial recognition". This flexible practice reflects the legal reality of China, which still takes "covering the loss" as the core principle of civil law.[71] This approach also follows the global trend of gradual relaxation of the traditional harsh restrictions on the recognition of foreign judgments. In any case, China's recognition rules are still cautious about the recognition and enforcement of foreign punitive damages, but partial recognition of punitive damages has been made possible in the field of intellectual property between Mainland and Hong Kong, which is a good attempt to promote the recognition and enforcement of foreign punitive damages. As for multilateral arrangements, China has signed the 2005 Convention on Choice of Court Agreements and it may consider to sign the 2019 Convention on the Recognition and Enforcement of Foreign Judgments in Civil and Commercial Matters. Considering that both conventions allow for domestic courts to refuse the recognition of a foreign punitive damages award if it does not compensate a party for actual loss or harm suffered, the Conventions thus leave open the problem of recognising and enforcing punitive damages judgments. It is clear that it is hard for the international community to reach a uniform arrangement on the issue.[72]

69 Hui JIANG, Jun HUANG v. Fang ZENG etc., (2019) Yue 01 Xie Wai Ren No. 58.

70 The Arrangement on Mutual Recognition and Enforcement of Judgments in Civil and Commercial Cases between the Courts of the Mainland and the Hong Kong Special Administrative Region, article 17.

71 See L. Song & X. Chen, 'Practical differences and coordination of recognition and enforcement of foreign punitive damages judgments' (外国惩罚性赔偿判决承认与执行的实践分歧与协调), *Jianghuai Tribune (江淮论坛)*, No. 3, 2021, pp. 111-119.

72 The Arrangement on Mutual Recognition and Enforcement of Judgments in Civil and Commercial Cases between the Courts of the Mainland and the Hong Kong Special Administrative Region, article 16 paragraph 2; Convention of 30 June 2005 on Choice of Court Agreements, article 11; Convention of 2 July 2019 on the Recognition and Enforcement of Foreign Judgments in Civil or Commercial Matters, article 10.

4.3 *The possible introduction of special recognition rules for foreign punitive damages*

As things stand today, there are no rules under the existing Chinese laws that specifically regulate the recognition and enforcement of foreign punitive damages. However, there has already been sporadic judicial practice applying the public policy defense in the recognition and enforcement of foreign judgments to deny recognition and enforcement of the punitive part of the damages. As more and more Chinese domestic laws were passed to bring in punitive damages, with the promulgation of the Code of Civil Law in particular, this type of damages has gained wider and wider recognition in China's legislation. This in theory provides an argument for recognising foreign punitive damages in China, but it does not necessarily mean Chinese domestic law has allowed for the recognition and enforcement of punitive damages.

It is worth considering if there is a need to introduce special rules for the recognition and enforcement of foreign punitive damages in the future. Some common law jurisdictions have chosen to pass laws that oblige courts to refuse the recognition of excessive foreign punitive damages. For instance, the Protection of Trading Interests Act 1980 enacted by the UK prohibits domestic courts from recognising and enforcing foreign multiple damages.[73] The Federal Parliament of Canada also passed a blocking statute to refuse to recognise or enforce a foreign judgment of treble damages in antitrust cases if it (1) adversely affects significant Canadian interests in relation to international trade or commerce, or (2) either infringes or is likely to infringe Canadian sovereignty.[74] The refusal of foreign punitive damages was not limited to antitrust cases when the recognition and enforcement would adversely affect or be likely to adversely affect the significant interests of Canada.[75] In the case of a judgment for a specified amount of money, for the purposes of recognition and enforcement of foreign judgments in Canada, the amount of the judgments shall be deemed to be reduced to such an amount as is specified in the order.[76] The UK explicitly refused multiple damages which are awarded by doubling, trebling or otherwise multiplying a sum assessed as compensation for the loss or damage sustained by the person, but did not mention whether the court could recognise or enforce the sum within the sustained loss.

For China, the recognition and enforcement of foreign judgments is predominantly regulated by the Civil Procedure Law, without any clauses specifically designed for recognition of foreign punitive damages. Despite the shortage of laws passed by China's legislature to address foreign punitive damages, the judicial interpretations released by the

73 The Protection of Trading Interests Act (1980), article 5(2)(a) and article 5(3).
74 Foreign Extraterritorial Measures Act, ch. 49, § 8 (1984), article 8(1).
75 Foreign Extraterritorial Measures Act, ch. 49, § 8 (1984), article 8(1.1).
76 Foreign Extraterritorial Measures Act, ch. 49, § 8 (1984), article 8(1).

SPC might be an answer to the problem. The future SPC stance may shift towards more acceptance of foreign punitive damages, to further echo the practical needs of the market.[77]

Considering the relevant international practice, foreign punitive damages should not be denied recognition simply due to their nature and function of punishment and deterrence. Punitive damages have generally been accepted in China's domestic legislation. As for the limitation on the recognition of foreign punitive damages, Canada would recognise foreign punitive damages in the amount that its domestic law would award in similar situations. The Uniform Law Conference of Canada drafted a Uniform Enforcement of Foreign Judgments Act which, although not legally binding, permits Canadian courts to enforce only the amount of punitive damages that could have been awarded in similar circumstances had the action been filed in Canada, thus absorbing the viewpoint of the Foreign Extraterritorial Measures Act.[78] The mainstream of Chinese judicial practice is that the recognition and enforcement of foreign judgments should be determined on the basis of actual loss. It is in line with the basic principle of compensation, as punitive damages that punish the infringer exist as an exception to compensatory damages. It also adheres to the current situation of China's civil compensation rules that take actual loss as the basis for determining punitive damages.

To take intellectual property infringement as an example, article 54 of China's Copyright Law, article 71 of the Patent Law and article 63 of the Trademark Law all adopt the same theory of compensating for the actual loss. If the circumstances of intentional infringement are serious, the damages shall be no less than one time but no more than five times the actual loss.[79] In order to appropriately recognise and enforce foreign punitive damages, the amount of the actual loss or compensatory damages can be used as a reference to quantify the severity of the infringement in order to evaluate whether the awarded punitive damages meet the requirements of proportionality. This method can control foreign punitive damages within a reasonable and acceptable range. The Canadian approach to treat foreign punitive damages may also be copied in the sense of only recognising foreign punitive damages that are recoverable under the local laws.

77 In particular, the Arrangement on Mutual Recognition and Enforcement of Judgments in Civil and Commercial Cases between the Courts of the Mainland and the Hong Kong Special Administrative Region remarkably already allows for the recognition of punitive damages.

78 Uniform Enforcement of Foreign Judgments Act, drafted by Uniform Law Conference of Canada (ULCC), article 6(2).

79 Copyright Law, article 54 paragraph 1; Patent Law, article 71 paragraph 1; Trademark Law, article 63 paragraph 1.

5 Conclusion

Punitive damages have become increasingly prominent in Chinese legislation, due to China's zealous efforts to internationalise its legal structure and judicial practice. More extensive legislative developments can be expected to occur in the area of punitive damages. Echoing the arrival of more Chinese rules on punitive damages, Chinese judicial practice also sees a sharp rise in the number of cases on punitive damages, which shows that the role of punitive damages is getting more and more significant in Chinese law and judicial practice. China's increasing adoption of punitive damages in its civil law also affects the landscape of the treatment of foreign punitive damages by Chinese courts. This may facilitate Chinese courts' recognition of foreign punitive damages in China. As punitive damages are becoming more prevalent in China's substantive law, the environment thus improves as well for the recognition and enforcement of foreign punitive damages awards in the country.

Although punitive damages per se no longer trigger alarm bells during the recognition and enforcement process around the world, punitive damages of an excessive nature are still problematic in light of the lasting international public policy concerns. There has already been some practice of foreign punitive damages seeking recognition and enforcement in China. As of today, no Chinese courts have ever recognised or enforced any foreign punitive damages. Foreign punitive damages are still regarded by Chinese courts as problematic, i.e. a violation of Chinese public policy. However, foreign punitive damages of a moderate nature, especially when Chinese laws provide for the same or similar punitive damages, are likely to be enforced in the future, in parallel with the successful recognition of a foreign arbitral award containing punitive damages. Importation of foreign punitive damages is also promising considering the improving environment for the recognition and enforcement of foreign judgments in general. Above all, the increasing acceptance of puntive damages under Chinese laws is believed to pave the way for Chinese courts to recognise foreign puntive damages to a certain extent.

Recognition and Enforcement in Korea of Judgments of Foreign Countries Awarding Punitive Damages

Kwang Hyun Suk[*]

1 Introduction

Judgments given in a court of a certain country are the result of the exercise of jurisdiction, i.e. sovereignty, and therefore only have effect in that country; such effect does not automatically extend to other countries. However, in order to stabilise international legal relations and quickly settle international civil and commercial disputes, many countries now recognise and allow enforcement of foreign judgments that satisfy certain requirements. According to articles 217 and 217-2 of the Civil Procedure Act ("CPA") of the Republic of Korea ("Korea"), a foreign judgment on the one hand has *res judicata* effect and other effects (excluding enforcement power) in Korea without a separate procedure if the requirements for recognition are satisfied. This is called the "principle of automatic recognition". On the other hand, in order to enforce a foreign judgment, an enforcement judgment (or declaration of enforceability) (so-called "exequatur") of a Korean court should be obtained according to articles 26 and 27 of the Civil Execution Act ("CEA") of Korea.

In this chapter, the recognition and enforcement in Korea of judgments of foreign courts ("foreign judgments") ordering the payment of non-compensatory damages will be discussed. Non-compensatory damages refer to damages that exceed the scope of damage that was actually suffered by the victim. These include not only punitive damages based upon common law, but also multiple damages based on statutes in United States law such as the Clayton Antitrust Act of 1914 and the Racketeer Influenced and Corrupt Organizations (RICO) Act of 1970. In this chapter the former is referred to as "punitive damages" and the latter as "multiple damages". As will be shown, multiple damages not only include treble damages, but also quintuple damages.

---

[*] Visiting Professor, School of Law, Inha University. I would like to express thanks to Mr. Issey Park for providing assistance in preparing this chapter. Unofficial English translations of Korean law including the Civil Procedure Act and Act on Private International Law are available on the website of the Ministry of Government Legislation of Korea. See https://www.law.go.kr/LSW/eng/engMain.do?eventGubun=060124.

If, as is often the case, the damages award imposed by a foreign court consists of compensatory damages, punitive damages or multiple damages, and litigation costs, the recognition and enforcement needs to be judged separately for each head of damages. Firstly, the ordinary compensatory damages can be recognised and enforced when the requirements for recognition and enforcement are satisfied. Secondly, there is controversy regarding the recognition and enforcement of foreign judgments ordering the payment of punitive damages, multiple damages, or grossly excessive compensatory damages. Thirdly, when costs and expenses relating to the proceedings including lawyer's fees ("litigation costs") are excessive according to Korean standards, there is controversy over the recognition and enforcement of the foreign judgment.

To start with, articles 217 and 217-2 of the CPA which constitute the legal basis for the recognition of foreign judgments under Korean law will be reviewed (section 2). Then the recognition and enforcement of foreign judgments ordering punitive damages, multiple damages, and grossly excessive compensatory damages will be reviewed (sections 3, 4 and 5 respectively). Finally, a proposal for amendment of article 217-2 of the CPA will be discussed (section 6), followed by a conclusion (section 7).

2 Analysis of articles 217 and 217-2 of the CPA

2.1 Overview of recognition and enforcement of foreign judgments under Korean law[1]

Korea has not entered into any bilateral or multilateral treaties regarding the recognition and enforcement of foreign judgments. More specifically, Korea is not a party to the Hague Convention on Choice of Court Agreements ("Choice of Court Convention"). Accordingly, the relevant provisions of the CPA and the CEA regulate the issue of recognition and enforcement of foreign judgments. In order to give finality to a dispute settlement achieved by foreign judgments and prevent conflicting legal relationships between the same parties, articles 217 and 217-2 of the CPA and articles 26 and 27 of the CEA provide for the recognition and enforcement of foreign judgments, respectively.

In order to obtain an enforcement judgment from a Korean court, the following requirements for recognition under article 217 of the CPA must be satisfied: (i) the foreign judgment must be final, conclusive and no longer subject to ordinary review; (ii) the foreign court must have had international jurisdiction to adjudicate the case in question;

1 For more detailed information on the recognition and enforcement of foreign judgments under Korean law, see K. H. Suk, 'Recognition and Enforcement of Judgments Between China, Japan and South Korea in the New Era: South Korean Law Perspective', *Frontiers of Law in China*, Vol. 13 No. 2, 2018, p. 171 ff.

(iii) the defendant who lost the case must have been served with the complaint and the summons or any orders in a lawful manner in advance so that he or she had sufficient time to prepare for his or her defense; (iv) the recognition of the foreign judgment must not be contrary to the public policy of Korea; and (v) there must be a guarantee of reciprocity between Korea and the country to which the foreign court belongs.

The court hearing a lawsuit in which enforcement is sought can only examine whether the requirements for recognition are met, and cannot examine whether the judgment is right or wrong. In other words, Korean courts are prohibited from reviewing the merits of the foreign judgment in deciding whether or not to recognise and enforce it. This is also known as the principle of prohibition of *révision au fond* (review of the merits). Korean courts may only review the merits of the case to the extent necessary to determine whether the conditions for recognition and enforcement are satisfied.[2] In particular, Korean courts may review the merits of the case in deciding whether a U.S. judgment awarding punitive damages is consistent with the public policy of Korea. Since recognition and enforcement of foreign judgments ordering the payment of punitive damages and multiple damages are discussed here, the most important provisions on the requirements of recognition are article 217(1)(iii) of the CPA setting forth the public policy requirement ("Public Policy Clause") and article 217-2. Therefore, the focus of the discussion in this chapter is on these two articles.

Article 217 of the CPA regarding the recognition of foreign judgments was amended and article 217-2 of the CPA about the recognition of foreign judgments imposing damages was newly added in May 2014. This is the result of legislative efforts made under the leadership of the National Assembly as a measure to protect Korean companies from unfair foreign judgments. The direct impetus for the new legislation is known to be the case of *E.I. Du Pont de Nemours and Co. v. Kolon Industries Inc. et al.* of 2011,[3] which ordered Kolon Industries (a Korean company) to pay punitive damages and to stop infringement of the trade secrets of DuPont. It is reported that the Korean Supreme Court has rendered until recently three judgments on the new article 217-2. The reasons for the amendment of the Public Policy Clause, and the introduction of article 217-2 as stated in the report of the National Assembly are as follows:

---

2 Supreme Court judgment of 9 February 1988, Docket No. 84Daka1003 concerning the recognition of a foreign arbitral award.

3 The background of the case is as follows: DuPont, a U.S. chemical company, filed a lawsuit against Kolon Industries, a Korean company, for damages due to the alleged trade secret infringement in 2009, in the Federal District Court in the Eastern District of Virginia. In September 2011, the Federal District Court ordered Kolon Industries to pay nearly $920 million in compensation to DuPont for infringing on the trade secrets of aramid technology. However, Kolon Industries was able to avoid the crisis since on 3 April 2014 the 4th Circuit Federal Court of Appeals of the United States accepted the appeal of Kolon Industries and reversed the lower court judgment. Reportedly, Kolon Industries has since agreed to pay $275 million to DuPont.

> *"It is expected that litigation in foreign countries will increase along with the increase in economic activities of Korean companies abroad due to the entry into force of the Korea-US FTA and other factors. Since foreign litigation is likely to proceed unfavorably for Korean companies, it is necessary to protect Korean companies from unfair judgments of foreign courts by having a domestic court investigate ex officio whether a Korean company has been subjected to an unfair trial in a procedural aspect in a foreign court or whether the judgment of a foreign court violates the legal order or good morals of Korea, where a foreign party seeks recognition and enforcement of foreign judgments in Korea."*[4]

2.2 *Article 217 of the CPA as amended and the Public Policy Clause*

The Public Policy Clause provides, as one of the requirements for recognition of a foreign judgment, that "the recognition of such final, and conclusive judgment or any other decision acknowledged to have the same force ("final judgment, etc.") does not violate good morals or other social order of Korea in light of the contents thereof and judicial procedures." The Public Policy Clause clearly stipulates that public policy consists of substantive public policy and procedural public policy. The Korean Supreme Court has already ruled to that effect.[5]

The Public Policy Clause functions as an emergency brake or measure to protect Korea's basic moral beliefs and social order in the context of the recognition of foreign judgments. In connection with the recognition of a foreign arbitral award, the Supreme Court held in its judgment of 1990[6] that in determining whether or not to recognise a foreign arbitral award, the Korean court should take into account the need for stability of international transactions, as well as the domestic situation. This statement is considered to be relevant to the recognition of foreign judgments as well. Accordingly, it is generally accepted that Korean courts will interpret the public policy test to refer to "international public policy", rather than "domestic public policy" as mentioned in article 103 of the Civil Act. In determining the question of public policy, the court may examine the reasons of the foreign judgment, although Korean courts should adhere to the principle that they should not re-examine the merits of the case (CEA, article 27(1)).

---

4 Refer to Legislative Judiciary Committee of the National Assembly, Review Report on the Bill of the Amendment to the Civil Procedure Act, April 2014, p. 2.

5 Supreme Court judgment of 28 October 2004, Docket No. 2002Da74213. This is a case dealing with the question whether fraud in obtaining a foreign judgment falls under the grounds for refusal of recognition and enforcement of foreign judgments.

6 Supreme Court judgment of 10 April 1990, Docket No. 89Daka20252.

2.3 *Article 217-2 of the CPA: Recognition of a foreign judgment ordering compensation of damage*

Article 217-2 of the CPA that was newly introduced in May 2014 reads as follows:

> *"Article 217-2 (Recognition of Final Judgment, etc. on Compensation of Damage)*
> *(1) Where final judgment, etc. on compensation of damage give rise to a result being significantly against the basic order of the law of Korea or international treaties entered into by Korea, a court shall not recognise the whole or part of the relevant final judgment, etc.*
> *(2) Where a court examines the requirements under paragraph , it shall consider whether the scope of damages awarded by a foreign court comprises litigation costs and expenses, including lawyer's fees, and the scope thereof."*

Article 217-2(2) was influenced by article 11 of the Choice of Court Convention, which was adopted in 2015 under the auspices of the Hague Conference on Private International Law, and article 33 of the preliminary draft Convention on Jurisdiction and Foreign judgments in Civil and Commercial Matters published in October 1999 ("Preliminary Draft"). On the face of it, it does not really show that article 217-2(1) was influenced by the Choice of Court Convention and the Preliminary Draft. However, considering the earlier draft of article 217-2(1) and the Supreme Court's interpretation thereof as shown in the three Supreme Court judgments of 2015, 2016 and 2022 referred to below it seems reasonable to acknowledge the influence that the (draft) Convention had in the end.

2.4 *Relationship between article 217-2 and the Public Policy Clause of the CPA*

The relationship between the Public Policy Clause and article 217-2 is unclear. Although there is not much discussion on this issue in Korea, I understand that Article 217-2 seeks to enhance legal certainty, even though the Public Policy Clause can solve the situation in the absence of article 217-2. Therefore, it is reasonable to say that the recognition of a foreign judgment ordering the payment of punitive damages or multiple damages should be resolved by article 217-2, whereas the recognition of a foreign judgment ordering grossly excessive compensatory damages should be resolved by the Public Policy Clause. In other words, in my opinion the purpose of article 217-2 was to set forth clearer criteria than those under the Public Policy Clause, rather than introducing new and stricter requirements for the recognition of foreign judgments ordering the payment of damages.

While article 11[7] of the Choice of Court Convention does not refer to the recognition of a foreign judgment ordering grossly excessive compensatory damages, article 33(2)[8] of the Preliminary Draft clearly specifies that the court of the recognising country may reduce the amount awarded by the foreign court. In this respect I believe that the stance taken by the Preliminary Draft is more persuasive. In particular, considering that article 52(4)[9] of the Act on Private International Law ("APIL") of Korea provides for a mechanism to allow Korean courts not to apply the foreign law awarding grossly excessive damages where the litigation is pending in Korea, it is reasonable to interpret it as explained above even at the stage of recognition of a foreign judgment.

3 Recognition and enforcement of foreign judgments ordering the payment of punitive damages

3.1 *Recognition of a foreign judgment ordering the payment of punitive damages*

Article 217-2(1) does not use the term "punitive damages" or "non-compensatory damages", but its purpose is understood to limit the scope of recognition of non-compensatory damages awarded by a foreign judgment to an appropriate level. The Supreme Court judgments of 2015[10] and 2016,[11] which will be explained below, are

7 Article 11 of the Choice of Court Convention reads as follows:
"*Article 11 Damages*
1. Recognition or enforcement of a judgment may be refused if, and to the extent that, the judgment awards damages, including exemplary or punitive damages, that do not compensate a party for actual loss or harm suffered.
2. The court addressed shall take into account whether and to what extent the damages awarded by the court of origin serve to cover costs and expenses relating to the proceedings."
Article 10 of the Convention on the Recognition and Enforcement of Foreign Judgments in Civil or Commercial Matters concluded in 2019 provides the same.

8 Article 33(2) of the Preliminary Draft reads as follows:
"*a) Where the debtor, after proceedings in which the creditor has the opportunity to be heard, satisfies the court addressed that in the circumstances, including those existing in the State of origin, grossly excessive damages have been awarded, recognition may be limited to a lesser amount.*
b) In no event shall the court addressed recognise the judgment in an amount less than that which could have been awarded in the State addressed in the same circumstances, including those existing in the State of origin."

9 Article 52(4) of the APIL reads as follows:
"*In cases where a tort is governed by foreign law under the provisions of paragraphs 1 to 3, damages arising from the tort shall not be awarded if the nature of the damages is clearly not appropriate to merit compensation to the injured party or if the extent of the damages substantially exceeds appropriate compensation to the injured party.*"

10 Supreme Court judgment of 28 January 2016, Docket No. 2015Da207747.

11 Supreme Court judgment of 15 October 2015, Docket No. 2015Da1284.

understood to the same effect. In addition, the most recent Supreme Court judgment of 2022 held as follows:[12]

> *"Article 217-2 of the CPA, in relation to article 217(1)(iii) of the CPA, was prepared to limit the recognition of foreign judgments to an appropriate extent where the contents of foreign judgments that ordered payment of damages exceeding the scope of compensatory damages reaches an unacceptable level in light of the fundamental principles, ideology and the damage compensation system recognised in the laws of Korea or international treaties concluded by Korea."*

As mentioned, the term "damages exceeding the scope of compensatory damages" referred to in this Supreme Court judgment is understood to include multiple damages as well as punitive damages.

Before article 217-2 was introduced in 2014, the key issue in dealing with the recognition and enforcement of U.S. judgments ordering punitive damages was whether they are against substantive public policy under the Public Policy Clause. A prevailing view in the past had been that the recognition and enforcement of a U.S. judgment ordering the payment of punitive damages which a U.S. judge or jury imposes for the purpose of sanctioning the perpetrator and general prevention, irrespective of the degree of damage suffered by the victim, was not permitted as contrary to Korean public policy.[13] However, this does not mean that recognition and enforcement of a foreign judgment ordering punitive damages should be rejected in its entirety. It rather means that a foreign judgment ordering punitive damages can be recognised and enforced partially if part of it performs a compensatory function.

By concluding that the recognition and enforcement of foreign judgments ordering punitive damages is against Korean public policy, parties can predict in advance the final outcome in the recognising country (i.e. Korea) and thereby increase legal certainty. From a Korean point of view, it has the effect of discouraging victims from filing lawsuits in a foreign country against Korean individuals or companies with a view to enforcing the judgment later in Korea.

Prior to the introduction of article 217-2, on 24 April 2009 the Suwon District Court Pyeongtaek Branch rendered a judgment on the recognition of a foreign judgment

12 Supreme Court judgment of 11 March 2022, Docket No. 2018Da231550. An introduction and brief commentary on the above judgment in English is available at http://arbitrationblog.kluwerarbitration.com/2022/10/22/korean-supreme-courts-recent-recognition-of-treble-damages-implications-for-the-enforcement-of-arbitral-awards/.

13 B. H. Yang, "On Public Policy Requirements and Punitive Damages Judgments", *Ilgam Law Review*, Vol. 4 , 1999, p. 52 (in Korean).

ordering the payment of punitive damages.[14] Although this judgment is significant for our discussion, it deals with treble damages for breach of the compensation payment agreement signed by the parties, and is thus not a typical case of punitive damages based on tort. Since a system of awarding punitive damages other than multiple damages was not yet introduced in Korea at that time, an act which constituted the cause for damage of the foreign judgment cannot be a cause for punitive damages within the area of individual laws of Korea. However, since treble damages for product liability have been introduced in Korea, as will be shown in section 4, if the foreign court orders the payment of punitive damages in addition to compensatory damages, the compensatory damages portion can of course be recognised and enforced if the other requirements for recognition are satisfied. In addition, one may argue that recognition and enforcement should be allowed up to an amount equalling three times the compensatory damages based on the reasoning of the Supreme Court judgment of 2022 on treble damages that will be explained below in section 4.3.

3.2 *Recognition and enforcement of litigation costs and compensatory damages in foreign judgments ordering punitive damages*

Article 217-2(2) requires a Korean court to consider whether the scope of damages awarded by a foreign court comprises litigation costs and the extent thereof when examining the requirements of article 217-2(1). This reflects the view that, in principle, recognition of a judgment ordering the payment of punitive damages is against public policy of Korea, but that punitive damages are not rejected in their entirety. In particular, if a portion of them performs a compensatory function, that part can be recognised. As mentioned above, article 217-2(2) was modelled after article 33(3) of the Preliminary Draft[15] and article 11(2) of the Choice of Court Convention[16] and shows an attitude favourable to recognition and enforcement. This is justifiable because even though it is included in punitive damages, that part actually serves a compensatory function. This is particularly meaningful in the case of U.S. judgments that include litigation costs in calculating the amount of damages to be paid by the defendant.

---

14 Suwon District Court Pyeongtaek Branch judgment of 24 April 2009, Docket No. 2007Gahap1076.

15 Article 33(3) of the Preliminary Draft reads as follows:
"In applying paragraph 1 or 2, the court addressed shall take into account whether and to what extent the damages awarded by the court of origin serve to cover costs and expenses relating to the proceedings."

16 Article 10(2) of the Convention on the Recognition and Enforcement of Foreign Judgments in Civil or Commercial Matters concluded in 2019 provides the same.

4 RECOGNITION AND ENFORCEMENT OF FOREIGN JUDGMENTS ORDERING THE PAYMENT OF MULTIPLE DAMAGES

The main stream of recent individual laws of Korea setting forth multiple damages still provides for treble damages, but there are also laws that allow quintuple damages. Therefore "multiple damages" and "treble damages" are used interchangeably below unless the context requires otherwise.

4.1 Recognition of foreign judgments ordering multiple damages

There is a question of whether a U.S. judgment ordering the payment of treble damages (or other multiple damages) could be recognised in Korea under the CPA. In the past, when the Korean legal system did not know multiple damages in its substantive law, there was consensus in Korea that foreign judgments ordering the payment of multiple damages could not be recognised or enforced in Korea on the grounds that the fundamental ideology underlying multiple damages was different from that of the damage compensation system of Korea, which aims to compensate for actual damages.[17] However, in 2011, for the first time, namely in the Fair Transactions in Subcontracting Act ("Subcontracting Act"), compensation of damages exceeding the scope of compensatory damages was introduced, allowing the court to order the payment of damages up to three times the actual damage (article 35 with respect to compensation for damages caused by the principal contractor's unfair conduct). Subsequently, in the Monopoly Regulation and Fair Trade Act ("Fair Trade Act") and through amendments to individual laws in the fields of personal information and labour relations, etc., rules were introduced to allow compensation of damage exceeding the scope of compensatory damages up to three to five times the actual damage for certain types of conduct. In other words, Korea is gradually introducing the multiple damages system through individual laws and the scope of such laws is steadily expanding. Therefore, we can no longer definitely say that the recognition of a foreign judgment ordering the payment of multiple damages would be either contrary to Korean public policy or trigger a result significantly contrary to the basic order of Korean law or treaties to which Korea is a party. In the case of a foreign judgment ordering the payment of treble damages, opinions may differ as to whether the part exceeding the actual damage (i.e. 200%) could be recognised and enforced.[18]

---

17 B. H. Yang, "On Public Policy Requirements and Punitive Damages Judgments", Ilgam Law Review, Vol. 4 , 1999, p. 52 (in Korean).

18 In the case of a foreign judgment ordering the payment of treble damages, the issue is whether the part exceeding the compensatory damages (i.e. 200%) can be recognised and enforced since the compensatory damages portion can be recognised and enforced without any doubt.

The first opinion is that it is no longer possible to refuse the recognition and enforcement of a foreign judgment ordering treble damages. Since Korea has introduced treble damages in various individual laws, the recognition is not against the basic order of Korean law, and even if it is against the basic order, it is not a significant or manifest violation.

The second opinion considers that recognition and enforcement can be refused outside of the specific areas, i.e. individual laws in which Korea has introduced the treble damages system. Recognition of a foreign judgment ordering the payment of treble damages in areas where Korea has not yet introduced treble damages would be significantly contrary to the basic order of Korean law, since the fact that the treble damages were not introduced in a specific area is the result of the policy judgment of the Korean legislator according to Korea's ideology and justice in light of the Korean damage compensation system as well as the meaning and purposes of individual laws.

In my opinion, the second theory should be maintained for the time being, but the first theory will eventually prevail at some stage if the multiple damages continue to spread under Korean substantive law in the future.

4.2 *Recognition and enforcement of litigation costs and compensatory damages in foreign judgments ordering the payment of multiple damages*

As mentioned, article 217-2(2) requires a Korean court to consider whether the scope of damages awarded by a foreign court comprises the litigation costs, and the extent thereof when examining the requirements of article 217-2(1). The explanation given above (see section 3.2) with respect to the recognition and enforcement of litigation costs and compensatory damages in foreign judgments ordering punitive damages is also valid for the recognition and enforcement of a foreign judgment ordering the payment of multiple damages.

4.3 *The Supreme Court judgment of 2022 and evaluation thereof*

On 11 March 2022 the Supreme Court rendered a judgment directly dealing with the recognition and enforcement of a foreign judgment ordering the payment of treble damages.[19]

In this case, the plaintiffs received from the court of the U.S. State of Hawaii a favourable judgment ordering the defendant to pay treble damages for the harm suffered by the plaintiffs, on the ground that the defendant violated Section 480-2(a) of the Hawaii

19 Supreme Court judgment of 11 March 2022, Docket No. 2018Da231550.

Revised Statutes (HRS) by unfair competition methods and unfair deception through the interference with the exclusive import and sales contracts of foodstuffs. Then the plaintiffs filed a suit in Korea seeking for an enforcement judgment. In its judgment the Seoul High Court (the appellate court) dismissed the part of the judgment awarding treble damages.[20] The reason was that the effect of the recognition of the part ordering the payment of treble damages would be against the public policy of Korea because there is no individual Korean law allowing treble damages for the type of illegal act which constituted the cause of damage of the foreign judgment. It is clear that this judgment followed the second opinion that was explained in section 4.1.

However, in its judgment of 11 March 2022 the Supreme Court reversed the judgment of the Seoul High Court by holding that recognising the judgment of the State of Hawaii ordering the payment of treble damages is not unacceptable in light of the principles, ideology, and system of the Korean damage compensation system.[21]

As a result, recognition and enforcement of foreign judgments ordering the payment of treble damages is now possible in Korea if the foreign law on which the treble damages were based falls within the area of individual laws of Korea setting forth treble damages. The Supreme Court, in my opinion, also followed the second opinion explained in section 4.1. The reason why the Supreme Court reached a different conclusion from the one of the Seoul High Court was because their view on whether the law of the State of Hawaii underlying the Hawaii State judgment fell within the area of individual Korean laws was different. It is noteworthy that the Supreme Court presented the basis for such a conclusion and the criteria for determination in individual cases. Although it is rather long, the rationale of the Supreme Court judgment is introduced below since it is important to understand the position of Korean law:[22]

> *"1) The fundamental ideology of the Korean compensation of damage system was to restore to the state before the damage occurred by compensating the actual damage suffered by the victim. Then, in 2011, for the first time in the Subcontracting Act, with respect to compensation for damage caused by the principal contractor's unfair conduct, damages exceeding the scope of compensatory damages were introduced with a limit of 3 times the actual damage (article 35). Subsequently, in the Fair Trade Act and through amendments to individual laws in the fields of personal information, labour relations, intellectual property rights, consumer protection, etc., rules were introduced to allow compensation of damage exceeding the scope of compensatory damages up to 3*

20 Seoul High Court judgment of 23 March 2018, Docket No. 2017Na2057753.

21 Supreme Court judgment of 11 March 2022, Docket No. 2018Da231550.

22 Supreme Court judgment of 11 March 2022, Docket No. 2018Da231550, section 2 na.

to 5 times the actual damage for certain types of conduct. This is to suppress the occurrence of torts through such compensation and to compensate the victims for substantial damage.

2) In view of the fact that the Korean damage compensation system allows compensation of damage that exceeds the scope of compensatory damages in accordance with special circumstances in a specific area through individual laws, while providing compensatory damages in principle, the scope of compensation of damage in the event that the act which constituted the cause of damage of the foreign judgment falls within the area of individual laws, it is difficult to say that it is unacceptable, because it does not significantly violate the basic order of the Korean laws concerning compensation of damage. In this case, even if the foreign law applied to a foreign judgment automatically sets a certain multiple of the actual amount of damages as the final amount of compensation, Korean courts cannot refuse to recognise the foreign judgment because of that fact, and should rather decide whether to recognise it or not in consideration, inter alia, of the upper limit of the amount of damages set forth in the relevant laws of Korea.

In short, Korean courts should determine in concrete cases whether or not to recognise all or part of a foreign judgment ordering the payment of damages exceeding the scope of compensatory damages by comprehensively considering, under the premises of the fundamental principles or ideology and the Korean damage compensation system, the relationship between the foreign judgment and related Korean laws, whether the act which constituted the cause of damage compensation of the foreign judgment falls within the area of individual laws that allow damages exceeding the scope of compensatory damages in Korea, and if so, considering the extent to which the damages awarded in the foreign judgment differs from the contents stipulated in the individual Korean laws (especially the upper limit of the amount of damages)."

4.4 *Evaluation of Supreme Court judgment of 2022*

The approach in the Supreme Court's judgment of 2022 is similar to the second opinion presented above, so it is in principle acceptable. But it is not without criticism.

First, the principle of prohibition of review of the merits in the process of recognition and enforcement of foreign judgments should be respected. The Supreme Court's position excessively derogates from that principle. The statement of the Supreme Court that

> "*[The Korean court should] consider whether the act which constituted the cause for compensation of damage of the foreign judgment falls within the area of*

> *individual laws that allow damages exceeding the scope of compensatory damages in Korea, and if that is the case, consider the extent to which the damages awarded in the foreign judgment differs from the contents stipulated in the individual Korean laws (especially the upper limit of the amount of damages)"*

went a little bit too far. The Supreme Court's position is not unfounded, as review of the merits is permitted within the scope necessary to determine whether it is in violation of the public policy of Korea. Considering the rapid spread of the multiple damages system in Korea in recent years, one could argue that the time for generally recognising and enforcing foreign judgments ordering multiple damages is already mature, unless the recognition of the foreign judgment is in violation of Korean public policy. It is a matter for each country to decide, on a policy basis, in which individual legal areas multiple damages can be introduced. In other words, rather than allowing a broad review of the merits as the Supreme Court has suggested, the review should be limited to determining whether the public policy of Korea is violated.[23]

Secondly, it may be difficult to determine whether an illegal act that is regulated by a foreign law falls within the area of Korea's individual laws by comparing the individual laws of the foreign country and Korea's individual laws. This was clearly shown in the Supreme Court judgment in 2022. In that case, the Hawaii State Court ordered treble damages based on the Hawaii State law stipulating that threefold compensation of damage may be ordered for the defendant's unfair method of competition and deceit. However, as to whether there is a Korean individual law that allows treble damages for such types of illegal acts, the Seoul High Court answered this question negatively, whereas the Supreme Court answered positively. This presents a tricky problem that inevitably arises when comparing the laws of two countries.

Thirdly, the Supreme Court held that the fundamental ideology of the Korean damage compensation system was to restore the victim to the state before the damage occurred by compensating for the actual damage suffered, and further that the multiple damages system intends to suppress the occurrence of torts through such compensation and to compensate the victims for substantial damage. However, the concept of "the substantial compensation of damage" and the relationship between this notion and "the compensation for actual damage" has yet to be clarified since the notion of substantial compensation of damage is not well known to the current Korean damage compensation system.

23 As mentioned above, this view is similar to the first opinion. However, this view does not exclude the possibility of a violation of public policy.

5 Recognition and Enforcement of Foreign Judgments Ordering the Payment of Grossly Excessive Compensatory Damages

5.1 Analysis of the CPA

In my view, even if the foreign judgment does not have a punitive nature, a Korean court can still refuse to recognise it when it exceeds the limits Korean law can tolerate. The legal basis for such a refusal is the Public Policy Clause rather than article 217-2.[24] It should be noted that when a Korean court limits the recognition of a foreign judgment ordering grossly excessive damages, the decision whether the damages are grossly excessive shall not be judged mechanically based on the amount that would have been awarded if a Korean court had dealt with the case. There must be room for a certain "leeway", the volume of which must be determined in consideration of various elements under the circumstances.

The issue of grossly excessive damages also arises with regard to the recognition of foreign judgments ordering the payment of excessive damages for mental suffering. This is because, according to some, the amount of damages for mental suffering awarded by Korean courts is too low in light of the sound common sense of the Korean legal community, the volume of the national economy of Korea, and precedents of foreign countries.[25] If this situation is not improved, only a small amount of damages for mental suffering will be awarded by Korean courts, whereas foreign judgments ordering the payment of grossly excessive damages for mental suffering will be fully recognised and enforced in Korea. This causes a severe imbalance between domestic and foreign litigations and therefore a disadvantage to plaintiffs suing in Korea. Therefore, it is necessary to allow Korean courts either to increase damages awards for mental suffering or to reduce the large foreign damages awards for mental suffering to an appropriate level in consideration of the circumstances of the case.

There may be objections to this view. Even if human life and health are financially valued more highly in foreign countries than in Korea, Korea should still tolerate that foreign valuation. However, in my view, the opinion mentioned above is more persuasive than the objections.

24 If it is grossly excessive, it can be considered that the punitive nature has already been reflected, so within that scope there is room for refusal of recognition on the basis of article 217-2.

25 D. J. Lee, "Judicial Policy Research on the Appropriateness of Compensation for Mental Suffering," Research Report Submitted to the Supreme Court, 2013, p. 3 and p. 115 (in Korean).

5.2 *Approach of lower courts before the introduction of Article 217-2 of the CPA*

Even before article 217-2 was introduced in 2014, scholars took the view that the recognition and enforcement of a U.S. judgment ordering the payment of grossly excessive compensatory damages on the grounds of tort was against Korean public policy.[26] In fact there were several lower court judgments that recognised and enforced only a part (for example 50%) of U.S. judgments ordering the payment of grossly excessive compensatory damages.[27]

The pioneering one was the judgment of the Eastern Branch of the Seoul District Court.[28] This is a case dealing with the recognition and enforcement of a judgment of the Minnesota State Court in the United States, which ordered the defendant to pay a damages award of US$ 500.000 (including compensation for mental anguish, physical injury, consequent medical expenses, loss of earning, etc.), plus reasonable compensation for damage arising out of the defendant's sexual assault and rape.

The Eastern Branch of the Seoul District Court found that the amount of the award was much higher than what would be acceptable under Korean law for such damages. Thus, the court reduced the amount of compensation that could be recognised and enforced in Korea to 50% of the original amount, on the ground that recognition and enforcement of the portion in excess of US$ 250.000 would be against the public policy of Korea. The conclusion of the judgment was upheld by the Supreme Court in its judgment of 1997.[29] However, the position of the Supreme Court is unclear as the issue does not appear to have been directly addressed. The rationale of the judgment is as follows:[30]

> *"In light of article 13(3)*[31] *of the then current APIL (limiting the scope of damages and serving as the guiding principles of the compensation of damage law of*

---

26 B. H. Yang, "On Public Policy Requirements and Punitive Damages Judgments", *Ilgam Law Review*, Vol. 4 , 1999, p. 52 (in Korean); K. H. Suk, *Private International Law and International Litigation*, Vol. 1, 2002, p. 402 (in Korean).

27 For example, the Eastern Branch of the Seoul District Court judgment of 10 February 1995, Docket No. 93Gahap19069 and the Southern Branch of Seoul District Court judgment of 20 October 2000, Docket No. 99Gahap14496 which are mentioned below.

28 The reason why the judgment attracted particular attention is that, in similar cases, the German Federal Supreme Court (BGH) in 1992 (BGH, 4 June 1992, *BGHZ* 118, 312) and the Tokyo District Court of 18 February 1991 (*Hanreijiho*, Vol. 1376, p. 79) also refused to recognise, on the grounds of a violation of public policy, part of the judgments of the State of California ordering the payment of damages including punitive damages and because the Korean judgment appears to have been influenced by those judgments.

29 Supreme Court judgment of 9 September 1997, Docket No.96Da47517.

30 The Eastern Branch of the Seoul District Court judgment of 10 February 1995, Docket No. 93Gahap19069. Section 2 ma (3) (ga).

31 The article read as follows:
"Even if the fact that occurred in a foreign country constitutes tort under Korean law, the victim may not

> *Korea) and the so-called "principle of proportionality" originally derived from the constitutional principle and incorporated into the civil law order, it is against the public policy to the extent that the damages significantly exceed a reasonable amount that can be awarded in Korea."*

Since then, various lower courts have followed this approach, and it is now generally accepted that Korean courts can recognise only part of a foreign judgment ordering the payment of grossly excessive damages based upon the public policy exception.

For example, there is the judgment of the Southern Branch of the Seoul District Court of 20 October 2000[32] and the judgment of the Busan High Court of 23 July 2009.[33] In the former case, the plaintiff (a U.S. company) filed a suit against the defendant (a Korean company) and received a judgment from the Southern District Court of New York ordering the defendant to pay damages on the ground that the defendant infringed the plaintiff's copyright. Based on that judgment, the plaintiff requested the Korean court to issue an enforcement judgment. In this case, the Korean court reduced the amount of damages and allowed the enforcement of only 50% of the damages awarded by the New York court.

In the latter case, the plaintiffs (the wife and children of the victim who died in an accident while working at a factory in the State of California with an injection molding machine manufactured by the defendant) filed a suit against the defendant (a Korean company) and received from the Californian court a judgment ordering the defendant to pay damages (consisting of compensation of economic and non-economic damage). Based on that judgment, the plaintiffs requested the Busan District Court to issue an enforcement judgment. The Busan District Court recognised only the amount of economic damage.[34] On the other hand, the Busan High Court recognised and allowed to enforce the amount of economic damage awarded by the Californian court, and in addition recognised and allowed to enforce part of the amount of non-economic damage by considering the adjusting function of damages for mental suffering.[35]

---

seek remedies other than compensation for damage or other dispositions recognised by Korean law."

32 Seoul District Court Southern Branch judgment of 23 July 2009, Docket No. 99Gahap14496.

33 Busan High Court judgment of 23 July 2009, Docket No. 2009Na3067.

34 The grounds of the Busan District Court judgment are as follows: recognition of the full amount of damages awarded by the court of California may have severe consequences contrary to the basic principles of the Korean damage compensation law, that is, the fair and reasonable allocation of damage and it is against the public policy of Korea.

35 The rationale of the Busan High Court judgment is as follows: Non-economic damage is equivalent to damage for mental suffering in the Korean damage compensation law system, and not awarding damages for mental suffering at all is unacceptable even in the light of the Korean damage compensation legal system.

5.3 Supreme Court judgments after the introduction of Article 217-2 of the CPA

After the introduction of article 217-2, the Korean Supreme Court rendered three reported judgments directly dealing with the application of this provision. These are the above-mentioned judgment of 2022 dealing with multiple damages, and the two judgments of 2015 and 2016 which were also mentioned above. The latter two judgments dealt with the recognition and enforcement of U.S. judgments ordering the payment of compensatory damages.

The judgment of 2015 dealt with the recognition and enforcement of a judgment of the United States District Court for the Eastern District of Texas Lufkin Division, where the court ordered damages on the ground that the defendants' bill counters sold in the United States infringed the plaintiff's patent rights.[36]

Meanwhile, the judgment of 2016 dealt with the recognition and enforcement of a judgment of the Woodford Circuit Court of Kentucky, United States, which ordered damages for breach of a sales contract regarding a stallion.[37] In its judgment of 2016, the Supreme Court laid down abstract legal principles:[38]

> *"Article 217(1)(iii) of the CPA stipulates as one of the requirements for recognition of a foreign judgment that the recognition of a final judgment, etc. by a foreign court does not violate good morals or other social order in Korea. Here, in determining whether the recognition is in violation of the good morals or other*

---

36 The specific issue in this case was how to calculate damages in case of patent infringement. The U.S. court first calculated the loss of profit on the sales volume that would have been attributed to the plaintiff if there had been no patent infringement among the volume of defendant's bill counter sales, and calculated the reasonable royalty for the sales volume that would not have been attributed to the plaintiff. When calculating the loss of profits, the U.S. court applied the entire market value rule, which is based on the total price of products that the plaintiff could sell when calculating the loss of profits. The U.S. court then added the loss of profit and the reasonable royalty fee. The damages awarded by the U.S. court were of a compensatory nature and did not include damages of a punitive nature, such as punitive damages. The Korean first-instance court, following the lower courts of the past, allowed enforcement of only 70% of the damages awarded by the U.S. court. On the other hand, the Korean court of appeal held that it is difficult to see that the amount of damages awarded by the U.S. court exceeds the scope of compensatory damages or that the method of calculating the amount of damage in the U.S. judgment is fundamentally different from the method used by Korean courts, and allowed enforcement of 100% of the damages. The Supreme Court accepted the conclusion of the court of appeal.

37 What is interesting is the judgment of the court of appeal of 4 February 2015 (Docket No. 2013Na1152). The court of appeal recognised only 50% of the total of consulting costs, legal costs before litigation and litigation costs, on the ground that the recognition of the other half is against the Public Policy. It is noteworthy that the court of appeal in particular pointed out that the costs of litigation awarded by the U.S. court in the case were excessive compared to the amount of attorney's fee which can be included in the litigation costs by applying Korea's "Rules on the Inclusion of Attorney's Fees in Litigation Costs" of the Supreme Court.

38 Supreme Court judgment of 28 January 2016, Docket No. 2015Da207747, section 1 ga.

social order of Korea, the Korean court should judge, at the time of deciding whether to recognise a final judgment, etc., the impact of the recognition of the final judgment, etc. on the basic moral beliefs and social order that Korea's domestic legal order protects in light of the degree of relevance between the case dealt with by the final judgment, etc. and Korea (Refer to the Supreme Court judgment of May 24, 2012, Docket No. 2009Da22549).

And article 217-2(1) of the CPA was prepared to limit the recognition of foreign judgments to an appropriate extent where the foreign judgments ordered the payment of damages exceeding the scope of compensatory damages such as punitive damages. Accordingly, in the case where the final judgment of a foreign court orders the payment of damages to compensate the actual damage suffered by the party, the recognition cannot be restricted on the basis of article 217-2(1) of the CPA (Refer to Supreme Court judgment of October 15, 2015, Docket No. 2015Da1284)."

After the introduction of article 217-2, the Supreme Court is now presumed to have abandoned the attitude of lower courts that used to be tolerated by the Supreme Court in the past. This means that the recognition and enforcement of foreign judgments ordering the payment of grossly excessive damages can no longer be refused on the basis of the Public Policy Clause insofar as the nature of the damages is compensatory. In my view, the main reason for this is that in the judgments of 2015 and 2016, the damages awarded by the U.S. courts were not found to be grossly excessive. If this is true, the status of Korean companies seems to be in a disadvantageous situation compared to the one before the introduction of article 217-2, as a result of the immature legislation, contrary to the intention of the National Assembly. Therefore, the Supreme Court should clarify the relationship between article 217-2 and the Public Policy Clause (i.e. article 217(1)(iii)). If the Supreme Court maintains the current position, the National Assembly needs to amend the CPA so that the Public Policy Clause can control the recognition of foreign judgments ordering the grossly excessive damages.

5.4 *Evaluation of the Supreme Court judgments after the introduction of article 217-2*

Since the Supreme Court judgment of 2022 was discussed already, the other two judgments are further explained here.

5.4.1 The Purpose of Article 217-2(1) and a foreign judgment ordering the payment of grossly excessive compensatory damages

As noted, the Supreme Court judgments of 2015 and 2016 laid down abstract legal principles as follows:[39]

> *"Article 217-2(1) of the CPA is a provision to limit to an appropriate level the recognition of foreign judgments ordering the payment of damages exceeding the scope of compensatory damages, such as punitive damages. Therefore, article 217-2(1) of the CPA does not apply to foreign judgments that order the payment of compensatory damages."*

The Supreme Court judgment of 2022 reaffirmed this point. Although such a conclusion is not naturally drawn from the text of article 217-2(1) because the current text uses only general language without referring to punitive or non-compensatory damages, the conclusion can be supported considering the background of the introduction of the provision and the earlier drafts. An important question is whether the Public Policy Clause (i.e. article 217(1)(iii)) applies to a foreign judgment that ordered grossly excessive damages. The Supreme Court's conclusion on this point is still unclear because the damages awarded by the U.S. judgments in the two judgments were not grossly excessive.[40]

5.4.2 Relationship between article 217-2 and the Public Policy Clause

In my view, the recognition of a foreign judgment ordering the payment of punitive damages should be blocked by article 217-2, and the recognition of a foreign judgment ordering the payment of grossly excessive damages should be examined by reference to article 217-2 and then by the Public Policy Clause by way of supplement. Of course, the decision that the recognition of a foreign judgment is in violation of the public policy must be made very carefully. The standard is the scope of what the Korean legal order can tolerate in consideration of the basic principle ("fair and reasonable allocation of damage") of the Korean damage compensation system. Since all three Supreme Court judgments mentioned refer to both the Public Policy Clause and article 217-2, the Supreme Court appears to have taken the view that the Public Policy Clause is also applicable to the recognition of a foreign judgment ordering excessive compensatory damages. However, it

---

39 Supreme Court judgment of 15 October 2015, Docket No. 2015Da1284, section 1 ga and Supreme Court judgment of 28 January 2016, Docket No. 2015Da207747, section 2 ga.

40 In a similar situation and regarding the draft of a Hague Judgments Convention, Fausto Pocar and Peter Nygh appear to take the view that public policy provisions in article 28(1) are not applicable since there is a special provision in article 33 on compensation for damages in the Preliminary Draft (which corresponds to article 217-2 of the CPA). See the Preliminary Document No. 11 of August 2000 for the attention of the Nineteenth Session of June 2001, p. 117.

is regrettable that the Supreme Court has not clarified the relationship between the Public Policy Clause and article 217-2.

5.4.3 Judgment of the Supreme Court regarding article 217-2(2) concerning litigation costs

In its judgment of 2016 the Supreme Court held that "*[e]ven if the U.S. judgment in this case made the defendant pay more attorneys' fees than the level accepted by Korean courts, recognising the U.S. judgment in this case is not contrary to Korea's basic moral beliefs and social order.*" However, as seen above, if we follow the logic of the Supreme Court according to which article 217-2 (1) does not apply to compensatory damages, we cannot limit the recognition and enforcement of the U.S. judgment ordering the payment of lawyer's fees even if the amount of lawyer's fees for U.S. lawyers included in the litigation costs is very high according to Korean standards. So as far as the lawyer's fees are concerned, there will be a severe imbalance between domestic and foreign litigation if the recognition and enforcement of a U.S. judgment ordering the payment of (usually U.S.) lawyer's fees is not limited, while Korean courts strictly control the amount of lawyer's fees (usually of Korean lawyers) which can be included in the litigation costs and may be recovered from the losing party. It is undesirable to leave this issue unaddressed, therefore a solution should be considered here as well.

5.5 *Interpretation of article 11 of the Choice of Court Convention*

Since article 217-2 of the CPA has been influenced by the Choice of Court Convention and the Preliminary Draft, the relevant provisions of those two instruments are briefly mentioned here.

According to the Choice of Court Convention (article 11(1)), in principle, it seems that the recognition and enforcement of a foreign judgment awarding compensatory damages cannot be refused. Hartley and Dogauchi admit that in exceptional cases, damages which are characterised as compensatory by the court of origin could also fall under article 11(1) without clarifying the meaning of exceptional cases.[41] Thus, it is not clear whether the recognition and enforcement of a foreign judgment may be restricted if the compensatory damages awarded are grossly excessive. On the other hand, article 33(2) of the Preliminary Draft clearly stipulates that even if it is a judgment awarding compensatory damages, recognition may be limited to a lesser amount if it is grossly excessive. It is interesting to

41 T. Hartley & M. Dogauchi, Explanatory Report on Convention of 30 June 2005 on Choice of Court Convention, para. 205.

find out what the correct interpretation of article 11(1) of the Choice of Court Convention is.

According to Brand and Herrup, article 11 of the Choice of Court Convention does not permit the refusal of recognition of a foreign judgment awarding damages with a compensatory purpose.[42] However, it is difficult to support this conclusion. The reason is that, as can be seen from the Explanatory Report, article 11 of the Choice of Court Convention is merely a simplification, not intended to change the intentions of the drafters reflected in the Preliminary Draft.[43] Hartley and Dogauchi state as follows:[44]

> *"To sum up: the new article 11 is shorter than the old article 15, it is more in line with the general drafting of the Convention, and it addresses the real issues without adding complex and sophisticated rules which might be understood in the wrong way. Therefore the Working Group proposes that this provision be adopted."*

It should be noted that the old article 15 is the same as article 33 of the Preliminary Draft. In short, although article 11 of the Choice of Court Convention seems to apply, on its face, only to foreign judgments awarding punitive damages, it should be interpreted in such a way that even recognition and enforcement of a foreign judgment ordering grossly excessive damages could be refused. As article 11 of the 2019 Hague Convention on the Recognition and Enforcement of Foreign Judgments in Civil or Commercial Matters ("Judgment Convention") is identical to article 11 of the Choice of Court Convention, this is also an issue under the Judgment Convention.

Even if article 11 of the Choice of Court Convention is not interpreted that way, such a conclusion can be drawn from the public policy clause (article 9(e) of the Choice of Court Convention). What I am concerned about is that, even after Korea's accession to the Choice of Court Convention (or after acceding to the Judgment Convention), there is a possibility that Korean courts apply article 11 of the two conventions only to non-compensatory damages following the reasoning of the Supreme Court judgments (2015, 2016 and 2022) mentioned above. In addition, at the international level, I am afraid that the uniform interpretation of the two conventions may not be achieved.

---

42 R. A. Brand & P. M. Herrup, *The 2005 Hague Convention on Choice of Court Agreements: Commentary and Documents*, Cambridge, Cambridge University Press, 2008, p. 126.

43 T. Hartley & M. Dogauchi, Explanatory Report on Convention of 30 June 2005 on Choice of Court Convention, para. 205.

44 For more information on the rationale of article 33 of the Preliminary Draft, see the Preliminary Document No. 11 of August 2000 for the attention of the Nineteenth Session of June 2001, p. 112 ff.

6 Proposal for amendment of article 217-2 of the CPA

Strictly speaking, article 217-2(1) is unnecessary because the rationale behind this provision is similar to the Public Policy Clause. This is because the issue of recognition and enforcement of foreign judgments ordering punitive damages and other non-compensatory damages can be resolved with the Public Policy Clause, and lower courts have actually done so in the past. However, if the meaning of article 217-2 is to be interpreted in good faith according to the will of the legislator, it should be understood as follows: the recognition of foreign judgments ordering punitive damages should be assessed under article 217-2, while foreign judgments ordering grossly excessive damages should be limited based on the Public Policy Clause to the extent acceptable by Korean law.

With the issuance of the Supreme Court's judgment of 2022, the recognition and enforcement of foreign judgments ordering the payment of multiple damages was resolved to some extent. On the other hand, if article 217-2 and the Public Policy Clause cannot prevent the recognition and enforcement of foreign judgments ordering grossly excessive damages, Korean companies will be at a more disadvantageous position compared to the past. As this is contrary to the purpose of article 217-2, the National Assembly needs to rectify the situation through legislation.

7 Conclusion

The points discussed in this chapter can be summarised as follows.

First, the recognition and enforcement of a foreign judgment ordering the payment of punitive damages may be refused in whole or in part in accordance with article 217-2 of the CPA. However, recognition and enforcement is permitted to the extent the damages awarded by the foreign court serve to cover compensatory damages and litigation costs. It should be noted that recognition and enforcement is not limited to the amount that would have been awarded if the Korean court had decided the case, but a certain amount of leeway may be allowed. The exact extent of damages which can be recognised in Korea is a matter to be determined on a case-by-case basis. In addition, since treble damages were introduced in Korea through the Product Liability Act and other series of recent legislation, a U.S. judgment ordering the payment of punitive damages for product liability could be recognised and enforced within the limit of treble damages.

Second, recognition and enforcement of a foreign judgment ordering the payment of multiple damages is permitted under article 217-2 of the CPA if the conduct that constituted the cause for compensation of damage of the foreign judgment falls within the area of individual Korean laws that provide for multiple damages in Korea. However, as for the exact scope of damages which can be recognised in Korea, the Korean courts must comprehensively consider in concrete cases, inter alia, the extent to which damages awarded in foreign courts differ from those stipulated in individual Korean laws (especially the upper limit of the amount of damages).

Third, the recognition and enforcement of a foreign judgment ordering the payment of grossly excessive damages is likely to be possible under the available Supreme Court rulings. However, there is a persuasive opinion that Korean courts can reduce, on the basis of the Public Policy Clause, the grossly excessive damages and litigation costs to an appropriate level. The opinion underlines that Korean courts should be allowed to limit the amount of compensation for mental suffering and the amount of the lawyer's fees included in the litigation costs. If the Supreme Court does not accept this opinion, legislative measures will be necessary to improve the situation.

In this chapter, I have discussed the possibility of recognition and enforcement in Korea of foreign judgments ordering the payment of damages by classifying them into three types. Determining the type under which a certain foreign judgment falls, is a matter of characterisation. However, in some cases, it may be difficult to classify the damages ordered by the foreign court. For example, there may be cases in which the nature of the damages is not clearly apparent from the reasoning of the foreign judgment. This is particularly likely in the case of a default judgment. In that case, the Korean court in charge will have no choice but to make a decision considering the totality of the circumstances.

As has been argued in this chapter, it should be borne in mind that the change of the damage compensation system of Korea in substantive law may trigger a revision of the provisions of the APIL. Although not discussed here in more detail, article 52(4) of the APIL, which limits the application of foreign tort law if the nature of the damages is clearly not appropriate to merit compensation for the victim or if the extent of the damages substantially exceeds appropriate compensation for the victim, also needs to be amended to reflect the ongoing introduction of a multiple damages system in Korean law. At the same time, it is also necessary to review the current Korean practice of calculating the amount of compensation for mental suffering and the tight control on the amount of lawyer's fees recoverable under the head of litigation costs in Korean litigation.

Recognition and Enforcement of Foreign Judgments Awarding Punitive Damages in the Philippines and Japan

*Béligh Elbalti**

1 Introduction

Describing the recognition and enforcement of punitive damages as a highly controversial issue is commonplace.[1] Interestingly, however, the discussion has somehow focused on European courts' attitudes and reactions.[2] This chapter offers a different perspective as it examines how punitive damages fare in two Asian jurisdictions,[3] notably the Philippines and Japan. The choice of these jurisdictions deserves a brief explanation.

First, unlike most of the jurisdictions in Asia, the courts in the two selected jurisdictions have had the opportunity to deal with the question examined here. The same is true for South Korea and Taiwan.[4] However, these two jurisdictions will not be addressed here

---

* Associate Professor, Graduate School of Law and Politics, Osaka University.

1 See e.g. B. Elbalti, 'Spontaneous Harmonization and the Liberalization of the Recognition and Enforcement of Foreign Judgments', *Japanese Yearbook of Private International Law*, Vol. 16, 2014, p. 274; C.I. Nagy, 'Recognition and Enforcement of US Judgments Involving Punitive Damages in Continental Europe', *Nederlands Internationaal Privaatrecht*, Vol. 30(1), 2012, p. 4. For this chapter's purpose, the terms 'recognition' and 'enforcement' will be used interchangeably unless otherwise indicated. In addition, 'punitive damages', irrespective of their designation (aggravated damages, treble damages, exemplary damages, multiple damages, etc.), are understood broadly to mean "*non-compensatory damages that seek to punish the defendant and to deter similar conduct by others.*" W.P. Statsky, *Essential of Torts*, USA, Cengage Learning, 3rd ed., 2011 p. 221.

2 See e.g. M. Requejo Isidro, 'Punitive Damages from a Private International Law Perspective', in H. Koziol and V. Wilcox (eds.), *Punitive Damages: Common Law and Civil Law Perspectives*, Vienna, Springer, 2009, pp. 237 ff. *et sp.* 245-249; S. Bariatti *et al.* (eds.), *Punitive Damages and Private International Law: State of Art and Future Developments*, Assago, Wolters Kluwer Italia, 2019 and in particular, C. Vanleenhove, 'A Helicopter Overview of the Recognition and Enforcement of Punitive Damages', pp. 235 ff.; C. I. Nagy, 'Recognition and Enforcement of US Judgments Involving Punitive Damages in Continental Europe', *Nederlands Internationaal Privaatrecht*, Vol. 30(1), 2012, pp. 4 ff. (but the author included a few lines about Japan).

3 'Asia' should be understood to denote East and South East Asian jurisdictions.

4 For South Korea, see e.g. K.H. Suk, 'Recognition and Enforcement of Judgments between China, Japan and South Korea in the New Era: South Korean Perspective', *Frontiers of Law in China*, Vol. 13(2), 2018, pp. 186-188 outlining the recognition of punitive damages in South Korea. For Taiwan, see e.g. F. Li and Y. Wu, 'Taiwan', in A. Reyes (Ed.), *Recognition and Enforcement of Judgments in Civil and Commercial Matters*,

since the situation in South Korea is examined in a different chapter in this book[5] and due to the difficulties for the author in accessing local documentation regarding Taiwan.[6]

With respect to the other Asian jurisdictions, the question has not been sufficiently addressed thus far. One reason is that the parochial legal framework in some Asian jurisdictions has prevented the courts from addressing the question of punitive damages as an independent issue. For example, in some jurisdictions, foreign judgments cannot be given effect in the first place in the absence of a treaty.[7] In other jurisdictions, the recognition and enforcement regime is yet to be fully developed.[8] This situation makes it difficult for the question of the effect of foreign judgments, let alone punitive damages awards, to be brought before the courts or sufficiently discussed in literature.[9] In some other Asian jurisdictions, especially where the rules and principles on foreign judgments recognition and enforcement are well established and developed, the issue of the

Great Britain, Hart Publishing, 2019, p. 90, citing Taiwanese court decisions dealing with American punitive damages.

5 See chapter 4 by Suk in this book.

6 For an overview, see e.g. R.-C. Chen, 'The Recent Development of Private International Law in Taiwan', in W.-Y. Wang (Ed.), *Codification in East Asia*, Switzerland, Springer International Publishing, 2014, pp. 245-247.

7 This is the example of Indonesia, Lao PDR, and Thailand. See A. Chong (Ed.), *Recognition and Enforcement of Foreign Judgments in Asia*, Singapore, Asian Business Law Institute, 2017 notably the following chapters: Y. Oppusunggu, 'The Republic of Indonesia', p. 104 (stating that "*[a]s a rule, foreign judgments are not enforceable in Indonesia*"); X. Chanthala and K. Santivong, 'Lao', p. 117 (stating that absent a bilateral or multilateral agreement, "*a Lao court will refuse to recognise or enforce a foreign judgment*"); P. Sooksripaisarnkit, 'Kingdom of Thailand', p. 210 (stating that "*[i]n the absence of law on the recognition and enforcement of foreign judgments in Thailand, a litigant with a foreign judgment needs to commence proceedings afresh*".). See also A. Reyes (Ed.), *Recognition and Enforcement of Judgments in Civil and Commercial Matters*, Great Britain, Hart Publishing, 2019 notably the following chapters: A. Kusumadara, 'Indonesia', p. 243 (stating that "*[a]s a matter of general principle, foreign judgments are not enforceable in Indonesia*"); A. Laowonsiri, 'Thailand', p. 259 (describing private international law in Thailand, and arguably the recognition and enforcement of foreign judgments as "*uncertain*" and "*unsettled*").

8 See e.g. Y. Bun, 'Cambodia', in A. Chong (Ed.), *Recognition and Enforcement of Foreign Judgments in Asia*, Singapore, Asian Business Law Institute, 2017 p. 38 (indicating that "*to date, we are unaware of any foreign judgment that has been recognised and enforced or refused to be recognised and enforced by the Cambodian Courts*"); A. Larkin & P. Yun, 'Cambodia', in A. Reyes (Ed.), *Recognition and Enforcement of Judgments in Civil and Commercial Matters*, Great Britain, Hart Publishing, 2019, p. 207 (after pointing out the shortcomings of the "*current legal framework*", the authors indicate that "*[t]o date, no foreign judgments have been enforced in Cambodia*"). Also, M. Naing Oo, 'Myanmar', in A. Chong (Ed.), *Recognition and Enforcement of Foreign Judgments in Asia*, Singapore, Asian Business Law Institute, 2017, p. 137 (describing the enforcement system in place as "*dated and archaic*" and indicating that "*there have not been many instances of foreign judgments being enforced in Myanmar in recent history*"); Z. Thura, 'Myanmar', in A. Reyes (Ed.), *Recognition and Enforcement of Judgments in Civil and Commercial Matters*, Great Britain, Hart Publishing, 2019, p. 210 (describing how rules that date back to colonial times remain in force in Myanmar).

9 See A. Chong, 'Moving Towards Harmonisation in the Recognition and Enforcement of Foreign Judgments Rules in Asia', *Journal of Private International Law*, Vol. 16(1), p. 35, pointing out that "*details on how the law applies*" in Cambodia, Laos, and Myanmar "*are scant*" and that "*[t]he number of successful instances of foreign judgments enforcement is obscure, and very likely low*".

recognition and enforcement of punitive damages has yet to be brought before local courts.[10]

Second, and most importantly, as will be shown below, courts in the Philippines and Japan have followed two different approaches when dealing with the issue of punitive damages. The courts' attitude in both jurisdictions is interesting to contrast from a comparative perspective, as this shows that there is no monolithic approach to dealing with the issue of punitive damages in the region.

This being said, this chapter will proceed as follows. Section 2 will briefly describe the recognition system in both the Philippines and Japan, as this is necessary in order to put the question of the reception of punitive damages into its broader context. Sections 3 and 4 will introduce relevant cases brought before the Philippine and Japanese courts and then provide a succinct overview of the academic debate on the issue. Section 5 will then offer analyses that highlight the differences in the courts' approaches in both jurisdictions. Finally, section 6 ends the present chapter with some concluding remarks.

2 RECOGNITION AND ENFORCEMENT IN THE PHILIPPINES AND JAPAN – GENERAL FRAMEWORK

The Philippines and Japan have long traditions of recognising and enforcing foreign judgments. However, the approaches followed in both jurisdictions differ. In this section, only a brief outline of the recognition and enforcement frameworks in both jurisdictions will be given, for this has been sufficiently done elsewhere.[11]

2.1 *The Philippines*[12]

The Philippines is a mixed jurisdiction whose legal system integrates elements of the civil law legal tradition (introduced via the Spanish colonisation) and the common law legal

10 See e.g. for China, chapter 3 by Zhang & Zhong in this book. For Singapore, T. Yeo, 'The Hague Judgments Convention – A View from Singapore', *Singapore Academy of Law Journal*, Vol. 32, 2020, p. 1163 (suggesting that Singapore courts have yet to clarify their position at common law). It should be indicated that statutory schemes, notably the Choice of Court Agreement Act of 2016 in Singapore, contain provisions dealing with the enforcement of punitive damages awards under the HCCH 2005 Choice of Court Convention. For other Asian jurisdictions, see relevant chapters in A. Chong (Ed.), *Recognition and Enforcement of Foreign Judgments in Asia*, Singapore, Asian Business Law Institute, 2017 and A. Reyes (Ed.), *Recognition and Enforcement of Judgments in Civil and Commercial Matters*, Great Britain, Hart Publishing, 2019.

11 See references cited below (*infra* footnote 12 for the Philippines and 35 for Japan).

12 This section is based on B. Elbalti, 'The Recognition and Enforcement of Foreign Judgments around the World (8), (9) and (10) – The Philippines (Parts I, II and III)', *JCA Journal*, Vol. 68(4), (6) and (7), 2021, pp. 38 ff., pp. 45 ff. and pp. 40 ff. (in Japanese). On the recognition and enforcement of foreign judgments in the Philippines, see A.A. Jo and J.P. Cruz, 'The Philippines', in A. Reyes (Ed.), *Recognition and Enforcement*

tradition (introduced via the American colonization).[13] The Philippines has not concluded any general convention dealing with the recognition and enforcement of foreign judgments.[14] The recognition and enforcement system in the Philippines dates back to the Code of Civil Procedure of 1901 (Act No. 190, hereafter: '1901 CCP'), which was adopted after the USA took control of the country.[15] The 1901 CCP included a provision dealing with the effect of foreign judgments (article 311), which was an almost verbatim copy of the old article 1915 of the California 1872 CCP.[16] The same rule has survived the different modifications and reforms of the civil procedure law, and it remains (almost) unchanged under Rule 39, Section 48, in the current Rules of Civil Procedure of 1997 as subsequently modified.[17]

The Philippine law of foreign judgments has gained the notorious reputation of allowing review of the merits of foreign judgments.[18] It is true that Rule 39, Section 49, considers judgments against persons as "*presumptive evidence*" and that it allows foreign judgments to "*be repelled by evidence of [...] clear mistake of law or fact*". In addition, in some cases, the Supreme Court of the Philippines did deny effect to foreign judgments

---

of Judgments in Civil and Commercial Matters, Great Britain, Hart Publishing, 2019, pp. 223 ff.; E. Aguiling-Pangalangan, 'Republic of the Philippines', in A. Chong (Ed.), *Recognition and Enforcement of Foreign Judgments in Asia*, Singapore, Asian Business Law Institute, 2017, pp. 146. See also J.R. Salonga, *Private International Law*, Manila, Regina Publishing Company, 2nd ed., 1961, pp. 385 ff.; C.Y.C. Ong, *Cross-Border Litigation within ASEAN*, The Netherlands, Kluwer Law International, 1997, pp. 184 ff.; R.E. Agpalo, *Conflict of laws*, Manila, Rex Bookstore, 2004, pp. 574 ff.; G.R.A. Pe Benito, *Conflict of Laws*, The Philippines, Rex Book Store, 2016, pp. 407 ff.

13 On the mixed jurisdiction nature of the Philippines legal system, see P. Agabin, 'The Philippines', in V.V. Palmer (Ed.), *Mixed Jurisdictions Worldwide – The Third Legal Family*, United Kingdom, Cambridge University Press, 2012, p. 453.

14 Some sectorial conventions dealing with specific subject matter concluded by the Philippines, such as 1992 Convention on Civil Liability for Oil Pollution (1992 CLC Convention), contain rules on the recognition and enforcement of foreign judgments.

15 As indicated in numerous decisions of the Philippine Supreme Court (see e.g. *Ingenohl v. Olsen*, No. L-22288 (15 January 1925), *Mijares et al. v. Ranada et al.*, G.R. 139325 (12 April 2005)), the 1901 CCP was copied from the California Code of Civil Procedure of 1872 (1872 CCP). The 1901 CCP abolished the then existing code of civil procedure (*Ley de Enjuiciamiento Civil de Filipinas* of 1888) introduced by the Spanish colonial government. The 1888 code of civil procedure contained rules dealing with the recognition and enforcement of foreign judgments (articles 934 *et seq.*), which were almost identical to the rules that were in force in Spain (*Ley de Enjuciamiento Civil* of 1881, articles 951 *et seq.*) but now abolished and replaced by articles 41-55 of the Law 29/2015 of 30 July 2015 on Internationl Legal Cooperation in Civil Matters.

16 Article 1915 of the 1872 CCP was later abolished in 1907. On this provision's abolition background and its context, see e.g. J.F. Coyle, 'Rethinking Judgment Reciprocity', *North Carolina Law Review*, Vol. 92, 2014, pp. 1132 ff.

17 The most recent reform of the Rules of Civil Procedure took place in the 2019. However, Rule 39 Section 48 was not modified.

18 See A. Reyes, 'Conclusion: Towards an Asia of Judgments of Judgments without Borders', in A. Reyes (Ed.), *Recognition and Enforcement of Judgments in Civil and Commercial Matters*, Great Britain, Hart Publishing, 2019, p. 319; S. Gautama, 'Recognition and Enforcement of Foreign Judgments and Arbitral Awards in the ASEAN Region', *Malay Law Review*, Vol. 32, 1990, p. 178; P.M.C. Koh, 'Foreign judgments in ASEAN – A Proposal', *International & Comparative Law Quarterly*, Vol. 45, 1996, p. 852.

after engaging a merit-based examination of the foreign judgment.[19] However, later, the Supreme Court clarified its position by pointing out the adverse effects that the review of the merits would entail.[20] Then, the Court made it clear that Philippine courts can only exercise limited control on the foreign judgment as they "*are not allowed to delve into the merits of a foreign judgment*".[21] It should be indicated, however, that despite the affirmation of the principle of prohibition of any review of the merits of the case, it remains unclear how the courts would verify whether that was a "*clear mistake of law or fact*" without examining the merits of the foreign judgment.[22] In practice, it is not uncommon that the parties raise merit-based challenges or that the lower courts go beyond an external review of the foreign judgment, thereby touching upon the legal reasoning and/or the determination of facts made by the foreign courts.[23]

The Supreme Court distinguishes between the 'recognition' and 'enforcement' of foreign judgments[24] and considers that, in either case, foreign judgments cannot produce their normative effect without prior judicial confirmation by the Philippine courts.[25] Judicial confirmation can take place when the foreign judgment is invoked before the Philippine Courts in the course of proceedings on the merits[26] or by way of a legal action by which recognition or enforcement is sought.[27]

It is established in the Philippines that foreign judgments create "*a right of action, and its non-satisfaction is the cause of action by which a suit can be brought upon for [their]*

19 *Ingenohl v. Olsen*, G.R. No. L-22288 (12 January 1925), *Nagarmull v. Binalbagan-Isabela Sugar Co.*, No. L-22470 (28 May 1970).

20 *Mijares et al. v. Ranada et al.*, G.R. No. 13932 (12 April 2004) stating that "*If every judgment of a foreign court were reviewable on the merits, the plaintiff would be forced back on his/her original cause of action, rendering immaterial the previously concluded litigation*".

21 *Fujiki v. Marinay et al.*, G.R. No. 196049 (26 June 2013). The Supreme Court reiterated its position in subsequent cases. See e.g. *Bank of the Philippines Islands Securities Corp. v. Edgardo v. Guevara*, G.R. No. 167052 (11 March 2015), *Mateo Encarnacion v. Thomas Johnson.*, G.R. No. 192285 (11 July 2018).

22 See different interpretations in literature, A.A. Jo and J.P. Cruz, 'The Philippines', in A. Reyes (Ed.), *Recognition and Enforcement of Judgments in Civil and Commercial Matters*, Great Britain, Hart Publishing, 2019, p. 235; E. Aguiling-Pangalangan, 'Republic of the Philippines', in A. Chong (Ed.), *Recognition and Enforcement of Foreign Judgments in Asia*, Singapore, Asian Business Law Institute, 2017, p. 157.

23 For illustrative examples, see *Bank of the Philippines Islands Securities Corp. v. Edgardo v. Guevara*, G.R. No. 167052 (11 March 2015); *Mercantile Insurance Co. v. Sara Yi*, G.R. No. 234501 (18 March 2019).

24 *Hang Lung Bank v. Sauloga et al.* G.R. No. 73765 (26 August 1991); *Fujiki v. Marinay et al.*, G.R. No. 196049 (26 June 2013).

25 *Fujiki v. Marinay et al.*, G.R. No. 196049 (26 June 2013); *Philsec Investment Co. et al. v. Court of Appeals and al.*, G.R. No. 103493 (19 June 1997); *Corpuz v. Tomas et al.*, G.R. No. 186571 (11 August 2010).

26 *Gorayeb v. Hashem*, G.R. No. 25577 (3 March 1927).

27 In this regard, the form of the proceedings differs depending on whether one seeks recognition or enforcement. In the case of simple recognition, 'a special proceeding', which aims to establish a status, a right or a particular fact, needs to be initiated (*Fujiki v. Marinay et al.*, G.R. No. 196049 (26 June 2013), *Corpuz v. Tomas et al.*, G.R. No. 186571 (11 August 2010)). When a party seeks to 'enforce' a foreign judgment, a 'civil action' by which a party sues another for the enforcement or protection of a right needs to be engaged (*Mijares et al. v. Ranada et al.*, G.R. No. 13932 (12 April 2004)).

enforcement".[28] The recognition and enforcement require only proof of the existence and authenticity of the foreign judgment. The party seeking recognition and enforcement bears the burden of proof, as he or she must submit the necessary evidence pursuant to the formalities prescribed by the applicable regulations (Rule 132, Sections 24 and 25 of the Rules of Evidence as recently modified in 2019). Once proven, the foreign judgment "*enjoys a disputable presumption of validity*"[29] that can be challenged by the opposing party. In this case, the party resisting recognition or enforcement bears the burden of establishing that the foreign judgment does not satisfy any of the grounds explicitly laid down in the Rule 39, Section 48.[30] These are: (1) want of jurisdiction, (2) want of notice, (3) collusion, (4) fraud, and (5) clear mistake of law or fact.[31] In addition to these requirements, the foreign judgment should be final[32] and consistent with the public policy of the Philippines.[33] On the other hand, recognition or enforcement in the Philippines does not depend on proof of reciprocity.[34]

---

28 *Bank of the Philippines Islands Securities Corp. v. Edgardo v. Guevara*, G.R. No. 167052 (11 March 2015); *Mercantile Insurance Co. v. Sara Yi*, G.R. No. 234501 (18 March 2019).

29 *Bank of the Philippines Islands Securities Corp. v. Edgardo v. Guevara*, G.R. No. 167052 (11 March 2015).

30 See e.g. *Northwest Orient Airlines v. Court of Appeals et al.*, G.R. No. 112573 (9 February 1995), *Asiavest Lmtd v. Court of Appeals et al.*, G.R. No. 128803 (25 September 1998), *Philippine Aluminum Wheels v. FASGI Enterprises*, G.R. No. 137378 (12 October 2000), *Asiavest Merchant Bankers Berhad v. Court of Appeals et al.*, G.R. No. 110263 (20 July 2001), *Mijares et al. v. Ranada et al.*, G.R. 139325 (12 April 2005), *St. Aviation Services v. Grand Int'l Airways*, G.R. No. 140288 (23 October 2006), *Mercantile Insurance Co. v. Sara Yi*, G.R. No. 234501 (18 March 2019).

31 On the interpretation and application of these requirements, see references cited *supra* footnote 12.

32 The condition of finality is referred to in Rule 32, Section 48 as well as the Supreme Court's decisions. See e.g. *St. Aviation Services v. Grand Int'l Airways*, G.R. No. 140288 (23 October 2006); *Bank of the Philippines Islands Securities Corp. v. Edgardo v. Guevara*, G.R. No. 167052 (11 March 2015).

33 See article 17(3) of the Civil Code of the Philippines which reads as follows: "*Prohibitive laws concerning persons, their acts or property, and those which have, for their object, public order, public policy and good customs shall not be rendered ineffective by laws or judgments promulgated, or by determinations or conventions agreed upon in a foreign country* (emphasis added)". See also *Mijares et al. v. Ranada et al.*, G.R. 139325 (12 April 2005).

34 Some scholarly opinions suggest that reciprocity is part of the foreign judgments regime in the Philippines. See e.g. E. Aguiling-Pangalangan, 'Republic of the Philippines', in A. Chong (Ed.), *Recognition and Enforcement of Foreign Judgments in Asia*, Singapore, Asian Business Law Institute, 2017, p. 152. However, as correctly indicated, reciprocity, as a ground for non-recognition, has never been considered by the Philippine Supreme Court. See A.A. Jo and J.P. Cruz, 'The Philippines', in A. Reyes (Ed.), *Recognition and Enforcement of Judgments in Civil and Commercial Matters*, Great Britain, Hart Publishing, 2019, p. 226.

2.2 Japan[35]

Like the Philippines, Japan has not concluded any general convention on the recognition and enforcement of foreign judgments.[36] This means that the circulation of foreign judgments in Japan mainly depends on domestic legislation. It is generally admitted in Japan that the recognition and enforcement system is modeled after the German one.[37] The system in place dates back to 1890 when the first Code of Civil Procedure (CCP) was adopted. The CCP initially lacked provisions on the 'recognition' of foreign judgments and dealt only with their 'enforcement'.[38] However, this was changed in 1926 with the inclusion of the former article 200 CCP, whereas the provisions on enforcement were maintained. Later, rules on enforcement were moved in 1979 to article 24 of the Civil Execution Act (CEA). Finally, on the occasion of the comprehensive reform of the CCP in 1996, minor but important modifications were made to former article 200, which since then became the current article 118 CCP.[39]

The current legal framework in Japan distinguishes between 'recognition' and 'enforcement' conceptually and from a procedural point of view. Where 'recognition'

35 For detailed analyses, see e.g. B. Elbalti, 'Foreign Judgments Recognition and Enforcement in Civil and Commercial Matters in Japan', *Osaka University Law Review*, Vol. 66, 2019, pp. 1 ff.; T. Kono, 'Japan', in A. Chong (Ed.), *Recognition and Enforcement of Foreign Judgments in Asia*, Singapore, Asian Business Law Institute, 2017, pp. 105 ff.; K. Nishioka & Y. Nishitani, *Japanese Private International Law*, Great Britain, Hart Publishing, 2021, pp. 204 ff.; J. Yokoyama, *Private International Law in Japan*, The Netherlands, Kluwer Law, 2nd ed., 2019, paras. 436 ff.; K. Nishioka, 'Japan', in A. Reyes (Ed.), *Recognition and Enforcement of Judgments in Civil and Commercial Matters*, Great Britain, Hart Publishing, 2019, pp. 97 ff.; Y. Okuda, 'Recognition and Enforcement of Foreign Judgments in Japan', *Yearbook of Private International Law*, Vol. 15, 2013/2014, pp. 411 ff.; T. Kono, N. Tada & M. Shin, 'Recognition and Enforcement of Foreign Judgments relating to IP Rights and Unfair Competition: The Transparency Proposal', in J. Basedow *et al.* (Eds.), *Intellectual Property in the Global Arena*, Germany, Mohr Siebeck, 2010, pp. 293 ff.; N. Tada, 'Enforcement of Foreign Judgments in Japan regarding Business Activities', *Japanese Annual of International Law*, Vol. 46, 2003, pp. 75 ff.; M. Takeshita, 'The Recognition of Foreign Judgments by the Japanese Courts', *Japanese Annual of International Law*, Vol. 39, 1996, pp. 55 ff.; M. Pryles & K. Iwasaki, *Dispute Resolution in Australia-Japan Transactions*, Sydney, The Law Book Company Limited, 1983, pp. 79 ff.

36 However, some sectorial conventions dealing with specific subject matter concluded by Japan, such as (1992 CLC Convention), include rules on the recognition and enforcement of foreign judgments. For more details, see B. Elbalti, 'Foreign Judgments Recognition and Enforcement in Civil and Commercial Matters in Japan', *Osaka University Law Review*, Vol. 66, 2019, pp. 4-5.

37 See section 6 below and the references cited therein, especially *infra* footnote 108.

38 Former articles 514 and 515 of the Old CCP of 1890.

39 It should be noted that on the occasion of the introduction of new rules on international jurisdiction in family law matters, a new provision on the 'recognition' of foreign decisions and decrees on status and family matters was introduced in Japan (article 79-2 Domestic Relation Cases Procedure Act). Article 24 CEA was also modified accordingly. For an overview, see Y. Nishitani, 'New International Civil Procedure Law of Japan in Status and Family Matters', *Japanese Yearbook of International Law*, Vol. 62, 2019, pp. 119 ff. *et sp.* 141 ff. For detailed analyses, see M. Iwamoto, 'Recognition and Enforcement of Foreign Decisions on Personal Status Litigation and Family Relation Cases', *Japanese Yearbook of International Law*, Vol. 62, 2019, pp. 226 ff.

operates *de jure* if the requirements of article 118 CCP are met, 'enforcement' can take place only if Japanese courts render a judgment to that effect through a specific procedure regulated by article 24 CEA. In either case, the courts cannot review the merits of the foreign judgment (article 24(2) CEA). In order to be recognized and enforced, a foreign judgment must satisfy all the requirements laid down in article 118 CCP. These are: (1) finality, (2) indirect jurisdiction, (3) service, (4) public policy, and (5) reciprocity.[40] As a matter of principle, it is generally admitted that the ascertainment of whether the foreign judgment fulfills the requirements of article 118 CCP needs to be made *ex officio* by the court.[41] However, in practice, it is not unusual for the courts to rely on the evidence submitted by the parties.[42]

3 Recognition and enforcement of punitive damages in the Philippines

This section will introduce two relevant Supreme Court decisions (3.1) before briefly outlining the academic debate on the issue (3.2).

3.1 Case law

3.1.1 The Mijares v. Ranada case[43]

This case concerned an action to enforce an award of over 2.25 billion USD, including 1.2 billion USD as exemplary damages, ordered by the U.S. District Court of the State of Hawaii and confirmed by the U.S. Court of Appeal of the Ninth Circuit.[44] The award was obtained in a class action litigation initiated by a number of Filipino citizens against the Estate of former Philippine President Ferdinand E. Marcos. In this case, the American court assumed jurisdiction based on the Alien Tort Statute (ATS) and examined allegations of human rights abuses such as arbitrary detention, torture, and rape during the Marcos

40 For details about these requirements and the related court decisions, see B. Elbalti, 'Foreign Judgments Recognition and Enforcement in Civil and Commercial Matters in Japan', *Osaka University Law Review*, Vol. 66, 2019, pp. 13 ff.

41 See, e.g. J. Yokoyama, *Private International Law in Japan*, The Netherlands, Kluwer Law, 2nd ed., 2019, p. 166; Y. Nishitani, 'Coordination of Legal Systems by the Recognition of Foreign Judgments – Rethinking Reciprocity in Sino-Japanese Relationship', *Frontiers of Law in China*, Vol. 14(2), p. 198. However, there are divergent views as to whether the *ex officio* determination concerns all the requirements or only some of them. It can be argued that the assessment of the requirements that primarily aim to protect the rights of the parties (the defendant) – such as service – would depend on arguments raised by those parties.

42 M. Pryles & K. Iwasaki, *Dispute Resolution in Australia-Japan Transactions*, Sydney, The Law Book Company Limited, 1983, p. 112.

43 G.R. No. 139325 (12 April 2005).

44 *In re Estate of Ferdinand Marcos*, 94 F.3d 539 (9th Cir. 1996).

regime. Later, the plaintiffs sought the enforcement of the American judgment in the Philippines.

Before the Trial Court,[45] the defendant raised the question of the non-payment of the correct docket and filing fees since the plaintiffs paid only the minimal fees payable only when the subject matter of the claim was not capable of calculation (410 PHP = about 14 USD). The Trial Court agreed, considering that the subject matter of the complaint (the enforcement of a foreign judgment ordering the payment of a definite sum of money) was capable of pecuniary estimation. Therefore, since the plaintiffs eventually did not pay the proper filing fees (estimated to be approximately 472 million PHP = about 16 million USD), the plaintiffs' complaint was dismissed without prejudice.

Before the Supreme Court, the central question was to determine whether the action to recognise and enforce a foreign judgment is one capable (or not) of pecuniary estimation and, therefore, whether the minimum filing fees would apply or not. Although the case did not examine the question of enforceability of the American judgment as such, the Supreme Court nonetheless seised the opportunity to clarify in a detailed landmark decision the principles underlying the recognition regime in the Philippines, including the relevance of public policy.[46] Finally, the Court overruled the appealed decision, suggesting that the foreign judgment would have been entitled to recognition and enforcement in the Philippines had the conditions for its enforceability been examined and had the defendant been allowed to challenge it.[47]

Interestingly, the question of consistency (or not) of punitive damages with the Philippine public policy did not seem to have triggered any discussion before the courts despite the fact that a considerable amount was awarded by the American court.

3.1.2 The Mercantile Insurance Co. v. Sara Yi case[48]

This case concerned the enforcement of a California default judgment ordered against a Philippine insurance company (hereafter 'Y'). The underlying facts of the case are as follows. The case initially originated as a personal injury action brought by the plaintiff (hereafter 'X') against a California business establishment (hereafter 'A1') and its owners (hereafter 'A2' and 'A3'). In this case, X sought compensation for damages resulting from an injury she suffered on A1's premises. The damages were secured by an insurance policy issued by Y through its California broker. Y first acknowledged that there was a valid policy in favor of A1 and, through its counsel, defended A1 in the action brought by X. However, later, Y withdrew its representation. As a result, a judgment was rendered in

45 Cited in *Mijares et al. v. Ranada et al.*, G.R. No. 13932 (12 April 2004).

46 *Ibid.*

47 *Ibid.*

48 G.R No 234501 (18 March 2019).

favor of X ordering A1, A2, and A3 to pay 350.000 USD. Later, X, A2, and A3 brought an action in California against Y for, *inter alia*, breach of the insurance contract. As Y did not file any pleading, a default judgment was rendered against it, ordering the payment of the following: (i) compensatory damages in favor of X in addition to 66.547 USD as interests arising out of the period between the two California judgments; (ii) 100.000 USD to A2 and (iii) 100.000 USD to A3 as general damages for emotional distress; (iv) 150.000 USD as punitive damages to the plaintiffs; (v) 8.000 USD as attorney's fees, and (vi) 2.000 USD as premiums.[49] X filed an action to enforce the California judgment in the Philippines.

The Trial Court[50] first refused to enforce the California judgment, *inter alia*, on the ground that X did not prove with sufficient evidence that she was entitled to her claim.[51] The Court of Appeals[52] reversed the trial court judgment and ordered Y to pay the amount adjudged in the California judgment. Y appealed to the Supreme Court.

The central question the Court had to answer was whether the California judgment, as a default judgment, satisfied the jurisdictional and proper notice requirements. In this respect, the Court's answer was affirmative and considered that the California judgment fulfilled the conditions prescribed under Philippine law for its enforcement.

Again, the public policy issue was not raised at all by the parties or the courts. This suggests that there was no problem enforcing the foreign judgment awarding punitive damages in the Philippines.

3.1.3 Mitich et. al. v. Mercantile Insurance Company[53]

This case also concerned the enforcement of a California default judgment ordered against a Philippine insurance company (hereafter 'Y', the same company as in the previous case). The underlying facts of the case show that it originated as a wrongful death action filed in California against X (plaintiff in the Philippine proceedings) by the heirs of a gunfight victim. At the time of the action, X had a comprehensive general liability insurance policy issued by Y.[54] Based on the insurance policy, Y hired a US attorney to represent X. Because Y failed to pay the attorney's legal fees, X proceeded with the trial without Y's assistance and eventually was held liable to pay compensation. Later, X and the victim's heir filed a complaint against Y for insurance bad faith. As Y did not appear, the court ruled in favor

49 Later, upon application of X, the California court issued a Notice of Renewal of Judgment in which the adjusted amount inclusive of interests amounted to 1.552,664 USD.

50 Cited in *Mercantile Insurance Co. v. Sara Yi*, G.R. No. 234501 (18 March 2019).

51 Notably, the court considered that the existence of the insurance policy was not established.

52 Cited in *Mercantile Insurance Co. v. Sara Yi*, G.R. No. 234501 (18 March 2019).

53 The case consists of two appeals *Bankruptcy Estate of Charles B. Mitich et al. v. Mercantile Insurance Company*, G.R. No. 238041 and *Mercantile Insurance Company v. Bankruptcy Estate of Charles B. Mitich et al.*, G.R. No. 238041 (15 February 2022).

54 It is worth mentioning that the insurance policy contained a choice of court agreement by which Y agreed to submit to the jurisdiction of "*any court of the United States*".

of the plaintiffs and ordered Y the payment of 1.135.929,14 USD with interests divided as follows: 635.929,14 USD as compensatory damages (including the amount X was ordered to pay in the wrongful death litigation (285.500 USD), emotional distress (250.000 USD) as well as pre-judgment interests and attorney's fees) in addition to punitive damages (500.000 USD). The judgment became final as Y did not file an appeal. X subsequently sought the recognition and enforcement of the California judgment in the Philippines.

Before the trial court, Y challenged the recognition and enforcement of the California judgment, *inter alia*, on the ground that service was invalid. However, the trial court admitted the petition and rendered a judgment ordering the enforcement of the California judgment (the total amount of the judgment) in addition to post-judgment interests according to California law as well as attorney's fees and litigation costs based on Philippine law. Unhappy with the result, Y appealed to the Court of Appeals, arguing, *inter alia*, that the foreign court lacked jurisdiction. However, the Court of Appeals upheld the trial court judgment with regard to the enforcement of compensatory and punitive damages but rejected the part relating to the payment of post-judgment interests since their rate was not included in the foreign judgments.[55] Both X and Y appealed to the Supreme Court. The main issues the Supreme Court had to address were whether the foreign default judgment was entitled to be recognised and enforced and whether the payment of X was entitled to post-judgment interests whose computation was not included in the judgment.[56] With respect to the first issue, Y challenged the recognition of the foreign judgment based, *inter alia*, on the fact that the foreign court lacked jurisdiction and that service was not properly effectuated. However, the Supreme Court rejected Y's argument and upheld the Court of Appeals' ruling as to the recognition and enforcement of California default judgment.

In this case again, the issue of the enforceability of punitive damages and their consistency with the public policy of the Philippines was not raised at any level of the proceedings. Interestingly, the Supreme Court referred to the punitive damages part of the

55 The Court of Appeals also rejected the payment of the attorney's fees. However, the Supreme Court disagreed with the Court of Appeals on this point. This issue will be not be addressed here.

56 With respect to the second question, the Supreme Court ruled that X was not entitled to the post-judgment interests whose computation was not included in the judgment as it considered that the determination of the interest rate and the method of computation would require delving into the merits of the foreign judgments and lead Philippine courts to substitute their judgment on how the case was decided. This aspect of the judgment was criticised in a dissenting opinion issued by one of the Supreme Court justices. The position of the Supreme Court on the enforcement of interests not included in the foreign judgment can be contrasted with that of Supreme Court of Japan which allows the payment of such interests. See e.g., Supreme Court Ruling of 28 April 1998, *Minshū*, Vol. 52(3), 1998, p. 853. An English translation is available at https://www.courts.go.jp/app/hanrei_en/detail?id=392. See also *Japanese Annual of International Law*, No. 42, 1999, p. 155. For comments on this case in English, see T. Kono, 'Case No. 68', in M. Bälz *et al.* (Eds.), *Business Law in Japan - Cases and Comments*, The Netherlands, Kluwer Law International, 2012, p. 745 ff.

California judgment and pointed out that the total amount of punitive damages (500.000 USD) and moral damages for emotional distress (250.000 USD) ordered by the foreign courts was by itself "*almost triple*" the amount X was entitled to under the insurance policy (285.000 USD). Yet, the Court did not appear to be concerned with punitive damages. The Court, however, expressed serious concern about the amount of the post-judgment interests. For the Court, such an amount ordered by the trial court – which was the accumulation of 27 years' worth of interests – was *"certainly shocking to the senses and would drive [Y] to bankruptcy"*. The Court then added that *"[p]ost-judgment interests were never meant to drive a litigant to the ground, especially when the right to litigate and its exercise are allowed by law and rules"*.

3.2 Academic debate

The issue of the recognition and enforcement of punitive damages in the Philippines has not triggered much discussion in legal literature. However, since Philippine law is heavily influenced by American law and scholarship,[57] one can assume that similar analyses would also be followed in the Philippines.

In the United States, it is admitted that foreign monetary judgments are entitled to recognition and enforcement unless the judgment has a penal character.[58] A judgment would be considered as "penal" when its "*purpose is to punish an offence against the public justice of the State rather than to afford a private remedy to a person injured by the wrongful act*".[59] However, for the purpose of recognition and enforcement, judgments awarding multiple or punitive damages are not considered penal.[60] The law of other common law jurisdictions echoes the American proposition since English common law distinguishes punitive damages that are enforceable from penal damages that are not. A judgment would be considered as 'penal' when the sum ordered by the court is payable to the

---

57 The Supreme Court of the Philippines has not only cited American courts case law, but also American legal writings and restatements of laws. See e.g. in *Mijares et al. v. Ranada et al.*, G.R. 139325 (12 April 2005), the Court citing "*the leading American case of Hilton v. Guyot*" (159 U.S. 113 (1895)) and Section 98 of the *Restatement, Second, Conflicts of Laws* (1971) dealing with the recognition of foreign nation judgments. The Court also frequently referred to American scholarly writings such as E. Scoles and P. Hay, *Conflict of Laws* (2nd ed., 1982) or H. Steiner & D. Vagts, *Transnational Legal Problems: Materials and Text* (2nd ed., 1976) (references cited here as they are mentioned in the Supreme Court's decision).

58 See e.g. in the context of international arbitration, the decision of the US District Court for the Northern District of Georgia of 18 February 1980 in *Laminoirs etc.* v. *Southwire Co.*, 484 F. Supp. 1063 (1980).

59 Restatement (Fourth) of Foreign Relations Law Section 489, comment (b), quoting *Huntington v. Attrill*, 146 U.S. 657, 674-674 (1892).

60 Restatement (Fourth) of Foreign Relations Law Section 489, comment (b).

(foreign) state as opposed to a sum of money that is payable to a private person, be it punitive in nature.[61]

The situation in the Philippines seems comparable to that of the United States.[62] It is admitted in literature, as is the case for the application of foreign laws,[63] that foreign judgments that are penal in nature would not be recognised and enforced.[64] In addition, punitive damages are generally available under Philippine domestic law.[65] Therefore, "*[a]s a matter of general principle, if exemplary or punitive damages are available under the domestic law of the country of the court addressed then there should not be any reason why the court addressed should refuse to enforce foreign judgments awarding such damages in a similar context [...]*".[66] Such a statement is in line with the scholarly opinion in the Philippines. Indeed, it has been considered that the recognition and enforcement of such damages "*cannot be considered as contrary to public policy*" since punitive damages (exemplary or corrective) are available under certain conditions in the Philippines.[67]

---

61 On the English approach, see A. Mills, 'Recognition of Punitive Damages in the United Kingdom', in S. Bariatti *et al.* (Eds.), *Punitive Damages and Private International Law: State of Art and Future Developments*, Assago, Wolters Kluwer Italia, 2019, pp. 184 ff. For a summary in the Asian context, see Y. Un Oppusunggu, 'Principle 9 – Public Policy', in A. Chong (Ed.), *Asian Principles for the Recognition and Enforcement of Foreign Judgments*, Singapore, Asian Business Law Institute, 2020, p. 124 and the references cited therein. However, the author presents Australian law as having a different position from the one followed mainly in common law jurisdictions.

62 Cf. L.J. Dhooge, '*The Loewen Group v. United States:* Punitive Damage Awards as Expropriation Pursuant to the North American Free Trade Agreement', *Journal of Legal Studies in Business*, Vol. 8, 2001, p. 68 indicating that "*the recovery of punitive damages in the Philippines much more closely resembles that in the United States*".

63 J.R. Salonga, *Private International Law*, Manila, Regina Publishing Company, 2nd ed., 1961, pp. 77 ff.

64 *Ibid*, p. 390.

65 See e.g. Title XVIII (Damages), Chapter III (Other Kinds of Damages), Section 5 (Exemplary or Corrective Damages) articles 2229-2235 of the Civil Code of the Philippines. See. e.g. *Mariano Mendoza vs. Leonora Gomez*, G.R. No. 160110 (18 June 2014).

66 Y. Un Oppusunggu, 'Principle 9 – Public Policy', in A. Chong (Ed.), *Asian Principles for the Recognition and Enforcement of Foreign Judgments*, Singapore, Asian Business Law Institute, 2020, 124.

67 E. Aguiling-Pangalangan, 'Republic of the Philippines', in A. Chong (Ed.), *Recognition and Enforcement of Foreign Judgments in Asia*, Singapore, Asian Business Law Institute, 2017, p. 154. See e.g. (in a different context) *Manufacturers Hanover Trust Co. and/or Chemical Bank v. Rafael MA. Guerrero*, G.R. No. 136804 (19 February 2003). This case concerned a complaint for damages arising out of relationship between the appellant bank (Y) and its depositor (X). X sought, *inter alia*, the payment of exemplary damages as well as attorney's fees in addition to actual damages in application of Philippine law. Y invoked the application of New York law as the law governing the deposit contract. It argued that the X was entitled only to actual damages under New York law and that, in the State of New York, exemplary or punitive damages were not allowed for a breach of contract even when the defendant acted with malice. The Supreme Court, however, upheld the ruling of the Court of Appeals, rejecting Y's claim on the ground that New York law was not properly ascertained.

4 Recognition and enforcement of punitive damages in Japan

Like the previous section, this section will introduce the relevant cases (4.1) and the academic debate over the recognition and enforcement of punitive damages in Japan (4.2).

4.1 Case law

4.1.1 The Mansei Kyōgyō case[68]

This case concerned the enforcement of a California judgment obtained in an action relating to a breach of a lease agreement. Based on the fraudulent acts of the appellees (a Japanese company and its former president), the California courts ordered the payment in favor of the appellant (an American partnership) of compensatory damages (about 425.000 USD), litigation costs (about 40.000 USD), as well as punitive damages (1.125.000 USD). The central question in this case concerned the compatibility of punitive damages with the public policy of Japan. The courts in particular addressed the following issues. The first concerned the nature of punitive damages, i.e. whether punitive damages were 'penal' in nature and, therefore, should not be subject to the regime of the international circulation of judgments. Assuming that punitive damages were 'civil' in nature, the second concerned the consistency of punitive damages with public policy, i.e. considering their function and aim, whether punitive damages should be regarded as inconsistent with the public policy in Japan. As shown below, although Japanese courts reached the same conclusion (i.e. rejection of the petition to enforce the punitive part of the California judgment),[69] their reasoning differed.

First, in its judgment of 18 February 1991,[70] the Tokyo District Court considered that, although "*the purpose of punitive damages was similar to that of fines*", it was "*not appropriate to regard them as punishment*". The court, however, considered that the findings made by the foreign court "*clearly lack[ed] in factual and logical relevance with other findings*" made therein, and concluded that the awarding of such an "*enormous sum*" in punitive damages on the basis of "*such weak grounds*" (the alleged fraudulent acts) violated Japanese public policy.[71] On appeal, the Tokyo High Court took a different approach. In its ruling of

68 For a detailed overview of this case in English, see N.T. Braslow, 'The Recognition and Enforcement of Common Law Punitive Damages in Civil Law System: Some Reflections on the Japanese Experience', *Arizona Journal of International and Comparative Law*, Vol. 16, 1999, pp. 285 ff.

69 It should be noted that the compensatory part of the judgments and costs were held to be enforceable.

70 *Hanrei Jihō*, No. 1376, 1991, p. 79, *Hanrei Taimuzu*, No. 760, 1991, p. 250. For an English translation, see *Japanese Annual of International Law*, No. 35, 1992, p. 177. For a comment on this case in English, see D.F. Henderson, 'Comparative Law in The Japanese Courts: Punitive Damages', *Law in Japan*, Vol. 24, 1991, pp. 98 ff.

71 Commentators in Japan, opponents and proponents of punitive damages, have severely criticised the District Court's reasoning as it entailed violation of the principle of the prohibition of *révision au fond*. See

28 June 1993,[72] the court considered that punitive damages were akin to fines under Japanese law and should be considered as having a penal rather than a civil character. The Court concluded that punitive damages did not fit within the definition of 'judgment of a foreign court' entitled to enforcement under Japanese law.[73]

The Supreme Court, in its landmark ruling of 11 July 1997,[74] took a less clear position. Unlike the Tokyo High Court, the Court did not frontally address the question of whether foreign judgments awarding punitive damages qualify as civil in nature. By directly examining the compatibility of punitive damages with Japanese public policy, the Supreme Court seems to have implicitly supported the position of the Tokyo District Court. On the other hand, when examining the consistency of punitive damages with public policy, the Court emphasised the deterrence function of punitive damages (sanctioning the wrongdoer and preventing future wrongs) and its similarity with criminal law. It also contrasted this punitive function with the function of the tort system in Japan, which essentially purports to restore the actual loss caused to the victim. Based on the fundamental difference in nature and function of punitive damages compared to compensatory damages allowed under Japanese law, the Supreme Court considered that punitive damages were incompatible with the basic principles of the Japanese civil law system.[75]

---

e.g. Yasushi Nakanishi *et al.*, *Kokusai Shihō [Private International Law]*, Japan, Yūhikaku, 3rd ed., 2022, p. 184. Compare with D.F. Henderson, 'Comparative Law in The Japanese Courts: Punitive Damages', *Law in Japan*, Vol. 24, 1991, pp. 103-104, considering that the examination engaged by the District Court was "*perilously close to a retrial on the merits*".

72 *Hanrei Jihō*, No. 1471, 1993, p. 89, *Hanrei Taimuzu*, No. 823, 1993, p. 126. For an English translation, see *Japanese Annual of International Law*, No. 37, 1994, p. 155.

73 It should be indicated that the High Court – after considering that punitive damages are "*akin to a fine in its penal character*" – cautiously indicated that even if the American judgement ordering punitive damages could be considered as "*a judgment of foreign court*" concerning civil matters under Japanese law, "*it could not cross the threshold of public policy*" in Japan. In other words, due to their penal nature, punitive damages should be treated as alien to Japanese law.

74 *Minshū*, Vol. 51(6), 1997, p. 2573. An English translation of this ruling is available at https://www.courts.go.jp/app/hanrei_en/detail?id=316. See also, *Japanese Annual of International Law*, No. 41, 1998, p. 104. For comments in English on this ruling, see C. Heath, 'Punitive Damages', *International Review of Intellectual Property and Competition* Law, Vol. 30, 1999, p. 480; K. A. Jung, 'How Punitive Damage Awards Affect U.S. Business in the International Arena: The *Northcon I v. Mansei Kyogo Co.* Decision', *Wisconsin International Law Journal*, Vol. 17(2), 1999, pp. 489 ff.; T. Kono, 'Case No. 67', in M. Bälz *et al.* (Eds.), *Business Law in Japan – Cases and Comments*, The Netherlands, Kluwer Law International, 2012, pp. 739 ff.; *idem*, 'Case No. 46', in C. Heath & A. Furuta (Eds.), *Japanese Patent Law – Cases and Comments*, The Netherlands, Kluwer Law International, 2019), pp. 497 ff.

75 From this point of view, the Supreme Court's ruling seems to be in line with the view expressed by the High Court.

4.1.2 The Hondaya Inc. case[76]

The case concerned the enforcement of a California court's default judgment obtained against the defendant (Y) for infringing the plaintiffs' trade secret. The California court ordered Y to pay about 275.500 USD, divided into 90.000 USD as punitive damages and 184.990 USD as compensatory damages, as well as other related additional fees. After the plaintiffs initially obtained partial satisfaction (134.873 USD) of the awarded damages through compulsory execution in the United States, they moved to enforce the remaining part (i.e. 140.635 USD) in Japan.

Y challenged the petition for enforcement on the ground that, among other things, punitive damages were incompatible with Japanese public policy and therefore had no effect in Japan, and therefore, the payment made in the United States (134.873 USD) should be appropriated to satisfy the compensatory part of the foreign judgment. The plaintiffs, on the other hand, argued that the judgment did not violate public policy as the amount they sought to obtain in Japan was confined within the scope of compensatory damages. Therefore, the question that Japanese courts had to consider was as follows. Considering the incompatibility of punitive damages with Japanese public policy, to which part should the amount paid in the U.S. be appropriated: the compensatory part or the punitive part?[77] Here, the courts' reasoning and conclusions diverged.

The Osaka District Court considered that the punitive damages ordered by the California court were effectively punitive in nature and, as such, against public policy and had no effect in Japan.[78] According to the court, the payment made in the U.S. should correspond to the part *other than* the punitive portion of the damages, otherwise the final result would not substantially differ from the recognition of the effect of punitive damages in Japan. The District Court finally ruled that the enforcement petition was to be admitted to the extent of the remaining amount (i.e. only 50.635 USD) after deducting the amount already paid (134.873 USD) and the punitive damages part (90.000 USD). The case continued its way up to the Supreme Court, which, in a first appeal, decided to remand the case to the Osaka High court for further examination without the issue of punitive damages being raised or examined.[79]

---

76 For an overview in English on this case, see B. Elbalti, 'The Supreme Court of Japan on Punitive Damages...' available at https://conflictoflaws.net/2021/the-supreme-court-of-japan-on-punitive-damages/.

77 The issue was crucial because if one considers that the money recovered abroad satisfied the punitive damages part of the judgment, this means that the plaintiffs would be entitled to seek the enforcement of the remaining compensatory part of the award (i.e. 140.635 USD) in Japan. If, however, one considers that the defendant was not required to pay more than 184.990 USD – due to punitive damages' inconsistency with the public policy in Japan – the plaintiffs would be entitled to revover only 50.635 USD since they already obtained the payment of 134.873 USD in the United States.

78 Osaka District Court Judgment of 12 October 2016, *Minshū*, Vol. 73(1), 2019, p. 17.

79 The High Court and the Supreme Court did not address the question of punitive damages. The High Court decided to reject the enforcement of the California default judgment on the ground of a violation of procedural public policy. The Supreme Court quashed the High Court's ruling because it was not sufficiently

Before the Osaka High Court, as the court of remand, the issue of punitive damages was brought back to the centre of the debate. In this respect, like the Osaka District Court, the Osaka High Court considered that the 90.000 USD award was punitive in nature and, therefore, incompatible with public policy in Japan.[80] However, unlike the Osaka District Court, the High Court considered that since the obligation to pay punitive damages *in* California could not be denied, the payment made abroad through the compulsory execution procedure should be appropriated to the satisfaction of the amount ordered by the California court as a whole. Therefore, since the remaining part (i.e. 140.635 USD) did not exceed the total amount of the foreign judgment, excluding the punitive damages part (i.e. 185.500 USD), the High Court considered that the enforcement of the judgment was not contrary to public policy. Unhappy with this ruling, Y appealed to the Supreme Court one more time.

In its ruling of 25 May 2021,[81] the Supreme Court ruled as follows. Since punitive damages have no effect in Japan, there exist no obligation to pay such damages when deciding the effect of a satisfaction of an obligation resulting from a foreign judgment. The Supreme Court then agreed with the Osaka District Court in considering that, due to their incompatibility with Japanese public policy, there was no obligation on the defendant's part to pay punitive damages and that the defendant's obligation under the foreign judgment was limited to 185.500 USD. Therefore, since Y had already paid 134.873 USD in the compulsory execution procedure in the rendering state, the plaintiffs were entitled to claim only the difference of 50.635 USD.

4.2 Academic debate

As indicated above, the issue of the recognition and enforcement of punitive damages has been actively debated in Japan for a long time. A scrutiny of the various academic opinions shows that Japanese scholars have diverged on two issues.[82] The first issue concerns whether punitive damages should be considered penal sanctions and, therefore, should be automatically excluded from the recognition regime. Put differently, whether judgments

justified. Supreme Court Ruling of 18 January 2019. An English translation of this ruling is available at https://www.courts.go.jp/app/hanrei_en/detail?id=1628. For brief analyses of this case in English, see K. Yamamoto and K. Kato, 'Case Comment', *Waseda Bulletin of Comparative Law*, Vol. 29, 2021, pp. 115-121.

80 Osaka Hight Court, Judgment of 4 October 2019, *Minshū*, Vol. 75(6), 2022, p. 2949; C. Nakamura, 'Failure of Service of Judgment Documents and Public Policy Control at the Stage of Recognition and Enforcement of Foreign Judgments', *Japanese Yearbook of International Law*, Vol. 65, 2022, pp. 336 ff.

81 *Minshū*, Vol. 75(6), 2022, p. 2935. An English translation of this ruling is available at https://www.courts.go.jp/app/hanrei_en/detail?id=1830.

82 For a succinct and detailed overview of the different opinions, see M. Haga, *Gaikoku Hanketsu no Shōnin [The Recognition of Foreign Judgments]*, Japan, Keio University Press, 2018, pp. 228 ff.

awarding punitive damages can be regarded as 'concerning private law disputes' at all for the purpose of the recognition and enforcement of foreign judgments.[83] The affirmative answer is the prevailing one.[84]

The second issue concerns whether recognising punitive damages is incompatible with public policy.[85] Here again, opinions diverge. One view considers that, taking into account the various contexts in which punitive damages can be awarded and their different functions, a case-by-case approach should be favoured based on which the recognition of punitive damages would be allowed taking into account, *inter alia*, the amount of damages or the compensatory function of punitive damages.[86] This point of view seems to gain more and more support in literature[87] as well as in legislative proposals.[88] For others, taking into account their nature (criminal versus civil) and function (punitive/sanctioning

83 See T. Kono, 'Case No. 67', in M. Bälz *et al.* (Eds.), *Business Law in Japan – Cases and Comments*, The Netherlands, Kluwer Law International, 2012, pp. 742-743; *idem*, 'Case No. 46', in C. Heath & A. Furuta (Eds.), *Japanese Patent Law – Cases and Comments*, The Netherlands, Kluwer Law International, 2019, p. 500. Cf., B. Elbalti, 'Foreign Judgments Recognition and Enforcement in Civil and Commercial Matters in Japan', *Osaka University Law Review*, Vol. 66, 2019, pp. 7-8.

84 See e.g. K. Nishioka & Y. Nishitani, *Japanese Private International Law*, Great Britain, Hart Publishing, 2021, p. 208, indicating that "*the prevailing view is that foreign judgments awarding punitive damages generally qualify as civil and commercial matters although their recognition may well be refused for breaching public policy.*"

85 T. Kono, 'Case No. 67', in M. Bälz *et al.* (Eds.), *Business Law in Japan – Cases and Comments*, The Netherlands, Kluwer Law International, 2012, p. 743; *idem*, 'Case No. 46', in C. Heath & A. Furuta (Eds.), *Japanese Patent Law – Cases and Comments*, The Netherlands, Kluwer Law International, 2019, p. 500.

86 See e.g. M. Takeshita, 'The Recognition of Foreign Judgments by the Japanese Courts', *Japanese Annual of International Law*, Vol. 39, p. 68, indicating that "*[…] an award of punitive damages […] might involve, for example, fees for attorneys and solatium, both of which are recoverable in the name of compensatory damages in tort cases. It follows that, as far as its compensatory components are concerned, a foreign judgment for punitive damages is not repugnant to the ordre public, and on the other hand, that ordre public is operative to the extent that an award of punitive damages was determined exclusively in terms of punishment and deterrence*".

87 See e.g. J. Yokoyama, *Private International Law in Japan*, The Netherlands, Kluwer Law, 2nd ed., 2019, p. 164 (suggesting that punitive damages may include some aspects – such as costs and expenses – that are classified as compensatory under Japanese law and that in such case, the examination of such an aspect is possible when they are specifically mentioned in the award). Cf. T. Kono, 'Case No. 67', in M. Bälz *et al.* (Eds.), *Business Law in Japan – Cases and Comments*, The Netherlands, Kluwer Law International, 2012, p. 743.

88 See the Legislative Proposal on Jurisdiction, Choice of Law, Recognition and Enforcement of Foreign Judgments in Intellectual Property of the Transparency of Japanese Law Project adopted by the Japanese Transparency Group (October 2009) as outlined in T. Kono, N. Tada & M. Shin, 'Recognition and Enforcement of Foreign Judgments relating to IP Rights and Unfair Competition: The Transparency Proposal', in J. Basedow *et al.* (Eds.), *Intellectual Property in the Global Arena*, Germany, Mohr Siebeck, 2010, p. 325. The authors explain at p. 325 that "*[t]he Transparency Proposal takes a position that punitive damages […] will not always be contrary to public policy. A part of punitive damages might be acceptable in Japan. This is an issue to be resolved in a flexible manner on the case-by-case basis*".

versus compensatory), punitive damages are contrary to Japanese public policy and, therefore, should be *categorically* ruled out.[89] This seems to be the prevailing view.[90]

In addition, the *Hondaya Inc.* case and the position taken by the Supreme Court have brought into the debate a new delicate question of the effect of partial payment of damages, including punitive damages, as a result of a compulsory execution procedure in the rendering State.[91] Moreover, in this particular case, the Supreme Court did not only invoke public policy to assess the compatibility of the foreign judgment with public policy in Japan, but also it went far beyond to deny the existence of the obligation to pay punitive damages. The position taken by the Court, which seems to confuse the regularity of the foreign judgment with the existence of the obligation based on the foreign judgment, was severely criticised by eminent scholars in Japan.[92]

5 COMMENTS AND ASSESSMENT

5.1 *The Philippines*

Case law and literature in the Philippines are interesting in many regards. Indeed, it is striking that, in the cases introduced above, the Supreme Court passed over the question of punitive damages in silence. Even more remarkable is that neither the parties nor the courts seemed to have been preoccupied with the existence of punitive components in the foreign awards. In *Mijares v. Ranada*, for example, the considerable amount in terms of punitive damages should have brought the Court into questioning the consistency of the foreign judgment with public policy. It should be borne in mind, however, that this case presented many particularities. In fact, in this case, the Philippine government had actively engaged before the American courts so that the case would be decided in the United States.[93] The Republic of the Philippines had indeed submitted an *amicus curiae* brief urging the American courts to exercise jurisdiction over the human rights claims and to

89 See e.g. Y. Fujita, 'Shōgai Minji Jiken no Jitsumu to Mondai-ten [Practice and Issues of Foreign-Related Civil Cases]', *Jiyū to Seigi [Freedom and Justice]*, Vol. 31(11), 1980, p. 22 whose opinion is briefly introduced in N.T. Braslow, 'The Recognition and Enforcement of Common Law Punitive Damages in Civil Law System: Some Reflections on the Japanese Experience', *Arizona Journal of International and Comparative Law*, Vol. 16, 1999, p. 296.

90 The position of the Supreme Court is in line with this opinion. See e.g. N. Tada, 'Enforcement of Foreign Judgments in Japan regarding Business Activities', *Japanese Annual of International Law*, Vol. 46, 2003, p. 91, indicating that "*the conclusion of the Supreme Court is generally accepted by authors in Japan*".

91 See the overview of the case in 4.1.2 above.

92 See e.g., M. Dogauchi, 'Case Note', *Jurist*, No. 1570, 2022, p. 262 (in Japanese).

93 Cf. S. Schreiber & L. D. Weissbach, '*In Re Estate of Ferdinand E. Marcos Human Rights Litigation*: Personal Account of the Role of Special Master', *Loyola of Los Angeles Law Review*, Vol. 31, 1998, p. 476.

allow the cases to proceed on the merits.[94] Moreover, the Republic of the Philippines also filed a separate lawsuit before the American courts based on the Racketeer Influenced and Corrupt Organizations Act (RICO) and sought the recovery of 1.55 billion USD.[95] Considering these elements, it is not very surprising that the Supreme Court later did not question the enforceability of the American judgment.[96]

The same can be said with respect to legal literature. It is indeed striking that the issue has rarely been addressed in legal writings, be they journal articles, book chapters, or general books dealing with private international law. The situation gives the impression that punitive damages do not present serious issues, except probably where the foreign judgments are regarded as having a 'penal' character.

5.2 *Japan*

The situation in the Philippines can be contrasted with that of Japan. In its 2021 ruling, the Supreme Court reiterated its earlier categorical position on the incompatibility of punitive damages with Japanese public policy.[97] The position of the Supreme Court can be criticised. Indeed, it is generally admitted in Japan that public policy can be triggered only when two complementary requirements are met. These are: (1) the incompatibility of the effects of the foreign judgment with the legal order in Japan, and (2) the degree of the connection between the case in question and Japan.[98] However, by simply declaring that punitive damages are contrary to public policy, the Japanese Supreme Court left no room for taking into account the degree of the connection between the case in question and Japan or the different purposes that punitive damages can serve.[99] In this respect, it is regrettable that the Court failed to seise the opportunity in the *Hondaya Inc.* case to revise its position.[100]

94 American courts first dismissed the claims on the basis of Act of State doctrine. *In re Estate of Ferdinand Marcos*, 94 F.3d 539 (9th Cir. 1996).

95 *Ibid.* The case later ended with a settlement between the parties.

96 It is notable that, in this case, the Commission on Human Rights (an independent constitutional office created under article XIII, Section 17 of the Philippine Constitution), which was permitted to intervene in the proceeding, did urge the enforcement of the American judgment. See *Mijares et al. v. Ranada et al.*, G.R. 139325 (12 April 2005).

97 In its ruling of 25 May 2021 (*Minshū*, Vol. 75(6), 2022, p. 2935), Supreme Court stated that the part of the foreign judgment ordering punitive damages did not meet the public policy requirement and considered that part "*ineffective in Japan*".

98 See B. Elbalti, 'Foreign Judgments Recognition and Enforcement in Civil and Commercial Matters in Japan', *Osaka University Law Review*, Vol. 66, 2019, p. 21. On public policy in Japanese private international law, see D. Yokomizo, 'Public Policy (*Ordre Public*) in Japanese Conflict of Laws', in A. Bruns & M. Suzuki (Eds.), *Reactive Instruments of Social Governance*, Germany, Mohr Siebeck, 2019, pp. 169 ff.

99 Cf., e.g., Yokomizo, *ibid*, p. 181.

100 See B. Elbalti, 'The Supreme Court of Japan on Punitive Damages…' available at https://conflictoflaws.net/2021/the-supreme-court-of-japan-on-punitive-damages/.

The Supreme Court's position greatly impacted the practice in Japan. Some reported cases show that creditors who have been awarded punitive and compensatory damages abroad usually attempt to seek the enforcement of the compensatory part and give up on the enforcement of the punitive part. The case decided by the Tokyo District Court in 2008 concerning the enforcement of a California judgment is illustrative.[101] In this case, although the foreign court ordered the payment of 2.8 billion USD as actual and punitive damages, the judgment creditor sought only the enforcement of 40 million USD, which corresponded to the compensatory part of the foreign award. The District Court considered that, since the judgment creditor was only seeking the enforcement of the compensatory (and not punitive) part of the judgment, there was no violation of public policy.[102] In the *Hondaya Inc.* case, the plaintiffs did not attempt to enforce the punitive portion of the foreign judgment. In fact, although their argument did not convince the Supreme Court, the plaintiffs argued that the part of damages they sought to enforce in Japan corresponded to the compensatory part and not the punitive one. As a potential impact of the Supreme Court judgment in the *Hondaya Inc.* case, plaintiffs would be encouraged to enforce their judgments in Japan first before seeking to collect the remaining sum abroad.[103]

However, it should also be indicated that, notwithstanding the categorical Japanese courts' position on the enforcement of punitive damages, the simple fact that the awarded damages are qualified in the State of origin as 'punitive' will not automatically lead to the conclusion that such damages are against public policy. This is particularly true when the awarded damages correspond to actual damage sustained by the victim, irrespective of their punitive qualification.[104] Similarly, even when the damages are ordered based on a punitive evaluation, they can be recognised and enforced if they have a compensatory function. For example, the Supreme Court considered that the foreign judgment ordering the losing party who acted in bad faith to pay full litigation costs, including lawyer's fees based on a special statute to that effect, did not violate public policy in Japan despite the

101 See e.g. Tokyo District Court Judgment of 19 February 2008, LEX/DB25451563. For an English translation, see *Japanese Yearbook of International Law*, Vol. 53, 2010, p. 608.

102 See also the Supreme Court Ruling of 24 April 2014, *Minshū*, Vol. 68(4), 2014, p. 329. An English translation is available at https://www.courts.go.jp/app/hanrei_en/detail?id=1232. See also *Japanese Yearbook of International Law*, Vol. 58, 2015, p. 463. For comments on this case in English, see B. Elbalti, 'The Jurisdiction of Foreign Courts and the Recognition of Foreign Judgments Ordering Injunctions: The Supreme Court Judgment of April 24, 2014', *Japanese Yearbook of International Law*, Vol. 59, 2016, pp. 395 ff. (focusing on indirect jurisdiction).

103 See B. Elbalti, 'The Supreme Court of Japan on Punitive Damages…' available at https://conflictoflaws.net/2021/the-supreme-court-of-japan-on-punitive-damages/.

104 See e.g. Mito District Court Ryugasaki Branch Judgment of 29 October 1999, *Hanrei Taimuzu*, No. 1034, 2000, p. 270, accepting the enforcement of a Hawaiian default judgment ordering compensatory and punitive damages. In this case, although the court admitted that the Hawaiian judgment contained a punitive effect, it nevertheless considered that the ordered sum of money corresponded to the damage sustained by the plaintiff, and therefore not inconsistent with public policy.

fact the foreign ruling contained a punitive evaluation.[105] Therefore, it can be said that to the extent the amount corresponds to costs incurred by the judgment creditor, the awarded damages would be regarded as compatible with Japanese public policy.[106]

6 Concluding remarks

This chapter examined the recognition and enforcement of punitive damages in two Asian jurisdictions, notably the Philippines and Japan. As shown above, the situation in both jurisdictions is very different. In the Philippines, although the enforcement of foreign judgments awarding punitive damages has been brought before Philippine courts, the judges were not impressed by the considerable amount ordered by American courts as to trigger the scrutiny of punitive damages and their compatibility of with public policy. A similar attitude can be seen in the legal literature since the decided cases did not result in any particular reaction from legal scholars. This can be contrasted with the situation in Japan, where the courts, notably the Supreme Court, have adopted a traditional conservative approach and have relied on public policy to shut the door on punitive damages. In literature, the question has triggered an intense discussion among scholars who, based on different considerations, have reached different conclusions about how punitive damages should be treated.

The difference between the Philippines and Japan can be explained in part by the legal culture in which each of the two legal systems is rooted. Indeed, the fact that the Philippines is a mixed jurisdiction with a strong common law influence inherited from the United States explains the Philippine courts' attitude towards punitive damages, especially those rendered in the United States.[107] On the other hand, the prevailing civil law background in

105 See, e.g. Supreme Court Ruling of 28 April 1998, *Minshū*, Vol. 52(3), 1998, p. 853. An English translation is available at https://www.courts.go.jp/app/hanrei_en/detail?id=392. See also, *Japanese Annual of International Law*, No. 42, 1999, p. 155. For comments on this case in English, see T. Kono, 'Case No. 68', in M. Bälz *et al.* (Eds.), *Business Law in Japan – Cases and Comments*, The Netherlands, Kluwer Law International, 2012, pp. 745 ff.

106 *Cf.* Kono, *ibid*, p. 754.

107 See e.g. references cited *supra* footnote 57.

Japan and the influence of German legal doctrines[108] explain the attitude of Japanese courts and the majority opinion in literature.[109]

Finally, one can question the two approaches followed in both jurisdictions. Indeed, the categorical position of the Japanese Supreme Court can be regarded as unnecessarily rigid as it leaves no room for considering whether or not the awarded damages serve purposes other than purely punitive ones. The Philippine approach can be regarded as excessively liberal as it fails to protect against excessive non-compensatory awards. A wiser approach would consist in trying to find a middle way that takes into account the need to protect the parties' legitimate interests and expectations as well as the ideals of private international law as an instrument of coordination of legal diversity.

108 See e.g. N.T. Braslow, 'The Recognition and Enforcement of Common Law Punitive Damages in Civil Law System: Some Reflections on the Japanese Experience', *Arizona Journal of International and Comparative Law*, Vol. 16, 1999, p. 294, indicating that the Japanese Supreme Court in *Mansei Kyōgyō* case closely tracks the German approach (footnote 40) and pointing out the influence of German legal doctrine in Japan (p. 299). With regard to the punitive damages debate at the time of the Supreme Court's decision in the *Mansei Kyōgyō* case, the author also pointed out that Japanese commentators referred to German law (p. 299, footnote 65).

109 For an account comparing the common law approach with the civil law approach (including Japan) regarding the willingness to recognise and enforce foreign judgments, see A. Gray, 'Enforcement of Punitive Damages Awards in the Convention on Choice of Court Agreements', *Willamette Journal of International Law and Dispute Resolution*, Vol. 17(1), 2009, pp. 131 ff.

Enforcement of US Punitive Damages in Commonwealth Africa

*Abubakri Yekini** *and Adeola Adedeji-Adeyemi***

1 Introduction

The concept of punitive damages is part of common law legacy in Commonwealth Africa. Punitive damages are awarded to a plaintiff over and above what will compensate him for his loss, where the wrong done to him was aggravated by circumstances of violence, oppression, malice, fraud or wanton and wicked conduct on the part of the defendant. The purpose of punitive damages is twofold: to provide solace to the plaintiff for the mental anguish, humiliation, degradation, and other aggravations caused by the wrongdoing, and to punish the defendant for their reprehensible behaviour. In this way, punitive damages serve as a deterrent to others who may consider engaging in similar conduct in the future.[1]

The award of punitive damages has been controversial.[2] Per Lord Foster in *Fay v. Parker* "*[t]he idea is wrong. It is a monstrous heresy. It is an unsightly and unhealthy excrescence, defying the symmetry of the body of law*".[3] Their availability in civil claims does not enjoy universal acceptance.[4] The same is true for Commonwealth Africa. While some States

* Lecturer in Law, the University of Manchester Law School. The author can be reached via abubakri.yekini@manchester.ac.uk.

** Lecturer in Law, the University of Lagos, Lagos State, Nigeria.

1 *Guardian Newspapers Ltd v. Ajeh* (2005)12 NWLR at pp. 229-230, paras. G-A. In jurisdictions such as Nigeria and Kenya, the availability of punitive damages is indisputable. See *Elochin v. Mbadiwe* (1986) 1 NWLR(Pt) 47, *Kabo Air Ltd v. Mohammed* (2014) LPELR 23614 (Nigeria). For Kenya, see *D K Njagi Marete v. Teachers Service Commission* [2020] eKLR (Civil Appeal 316 of 2013); *Godfrey Julius Ndumba Mbogori & Another v. Nairobi City County* [2018] eKLR (Civil Appeal 55 of 2012); *Leonard Gethoi Kamweti v. National Bank of Kenya Limited* [2020] eKLR (Cause 237 of 2014). However, in South Africa, it seems the courts are very reluctant in recognising their availability. See *Fose v. The Minister of Safety and Security* 1997 (3) SA 786 (CC) 823-828; See also *Innes v. Visser* (1936) WLD 44; *Lynch v. Agnew* (1929) TPD 974 978; *Esselen v. Argus Printing and Publishing Co Ltd* 1992 3 SA 764 (T) 771.

2 E. Weinrib, 'Punishment and Disgorgement as Contract Remedies', *Chicago-Kent Law Review*, Vol. 78, No. 1, 2003, p. 84.

3 Per Foster J in *Fay v. Parker* (1872) 53 NH 342 at p. 382.

4 See C. I. Nagy, 'Recognition and Enforcement of US Judgments Involving Punitive Damages in Continental Europe', *Nederlands Internationaal Privaatrecht*, Vol. 30, 2012, p. 11 (where he states that "*the recognition and enforcement of US punitive judgments has been a highly controversial issue, both globally and in Europe*").

such as Nigeria award punitive damages,[5] it is restrictively applied in other States such as Kenya.[6] Yet, it is disputed whether they are available to claimants in South Africa.[7]

In today's interconnected world, the propriety of punitive damages will continue to be an issue in courts across various jurisdictions, either under the forum law or in enforcement proceedings. The focus of this chapter is to explore the topic of punitive damages with a view to gaining a deeper understanding of the legal intricacies surrounding the enforcement of punitive damages, particularly United States (hereafter: US) punitive judgments, in Commonwealth Africa. Section 2 of the chapter examines the composition of Commonwealth Africa, its legal landscape, the diversity of its legal systems and the theoretical basis for enforcing foreign judgments in the area. Section 3 discusses the enforcement of US punitive judgments in Commonwealth African states under the common law action and under statutory enforcement schemes. The section further looks at the prospect of US punitive damages under the 2017 Commonwealth Model Law on Recognition and Enforcement of Foreign Judgments. Section 4 concludes the chapter.

2 COMMONWEALTH AFRICA: THE LEGAL LANDSCAPE

2.1 *Commonwealth Africa*

The Commonwealth originally represents a friendly association of former British colonies. It started as "the British Commonwealth of Nations" in the late nineteenth century comprising the dominions of Canada, Australia, New Zealand and South Africa. In the early to mid-twentieth century, other British colonies in Asia and Africa – India, Pakistan, Nigeria, Ghana, Cameroon, and Malaysia amongst others – joined the association after gaining independence from Great Britain.[8] Thus, the association changed its name from the British Commonwealth of Nations to 'the Commonwealth'.

Commonwealth Africa comprises the members of the association from Africa. Although it used to represent the former British colonies from Africa and mainly the common law jurisdictions of Africa, the same may not be true today. Commonwealth

---

5 See *Guardian Newspapers Ltd v. Ajeh* (2005)12 NWLR at 229-230, paras. G-A; *Elochin v. Mbadiwe* (1986) 1 NWLR(Pt) 47; *Kabo Air Ltd v. Mohammed* (2014) LPELR 23614.

6 *Leonard Gethoi Kamweti v. National Bank of Kenya Limited* [2020] eKLR, *D K Njagi Marete v. Teachers Service Commission*, [2020] eKLR, Godfrey *Julius Ndumba Mbogori & Another v. Nairobi City County* [2018] eKLR.

7 See *Fose v. The Minister of Safety and Security* 1997 (3) SA 786 (CC) 823-828; See also *Innes v. Visser* (1936) WLD 44; *Lynch v. Agnew* (1929) TPD 974 978; *Esselen v. Argus Printing and Publishing Co Ltd* 1992 (3) SA 764 (T) 771.

8 A. Yekini, *The Hague Judgments Convention and Commonwealth Model Law: A Pragmatic Perspective*, London, Hart Publishing, 2021, pp. 78-79.

Africa now represents a diverse group of independent states in Africa bound together by certain shared goals and values.[9] Geographically, it consists of 21 African states from sub-Saharan Africa. These countries are Botswana, Cameroon, Gabon, The Gambia, Ghana, Kenya, the Kingdom of Eswatini, Lesotho, Malawi, Mauritius, Mozambique, Namibia, Nigeria, Rwanda, Seychelles, Sierra Leone, South Africa, Togo, Uganda, the United Republic of Tanzania and Zambia.

Commonwealth Africa is a highly diverse region. As against the popular assumption that Commonwealth Africa comprises common law jurisdictions because of their erstwhile affiliation with Great Britain, what is apparent today is that there is increasing visibility of civil law tradition. The admission of Mozambique to the Commonwealth in 1995, Rwanda in 2009, and Gabon and Togo in June 2022 further strengthens the presence of the civil law system in Commonwealth Africa.[10] Yet, there are other states with a combination of common, and civil law traditions (e.g. Seychelles), or common/civil law together with customary and Islamic law (e.g. Mozambique and Tanzania).

2.2 *Legal landscape*

The diverse legal traditions of Commonwealth Africa and invariably the judgments recognition and enforcement laws and policies are rooted in the colonial history of the region. Before the advent of colonialism, the various countries were controlled and governed by a number of kingdoms and empires. Indigenous laws regulated cross-border trading activities amongst the peoples of the various kingdoms of sub-Saharan Africa.[11]

Another layer of legal diversity was added when Europe came in contact with Africa. The reformation of the traditional legal systems and the introduction of European legal traditions are some of the lasting legacies of colonialism. The States colonised by Great Britain – Anglophone Africa – inherited the common law of England, the doctrines of Equity and the English statutes of general application. The French pursued a policy of assimilation in their colonies and the Napoleonic Code was either introduced to the Francophone states or the Code became the inspiration for national laws.[12] In most of

9 The Commonwealth Charter (2013) https://thecommonwealth.org/charter (accessed 22 October 2022).

10 Commonwealth Secretariat, 'Togo's flag raised at Marlborough House to mark admission into the Commonwealth', https://thecommonwealth.org/news/togos-flag-raised-marlborough-house-mark-admission-commonwealth (accessed 22 October 2022).

11 I.O. Ojo & E. O. Ekhator, 'Precolonial Legal System in Africa: An Assessment of Indigenous Laws of Benin before 1897', *Journal of Benin and Edo Studies*, Vol. 5, 2020, pp. 38-73.

12 M. Sesay, *Domination Through Law: The Internationalization of Legal Norms in Postcolonial Africa*, Maryland, Rowman & Littlefield Publishers, 2021, p. 66; L.M Arguelles, 'Mixed Jurisdictions: The Road Ahead' in V.V. Palmer, & M.Y. Mattar (Eds.), *Mixed Legal Systems, East and West*, London, Taylor & Francis, 2016, pp. 34-35.

these states, the legal system is still a reflection of the inherited colonial laws and legal traditions with some modifications to reflect indigenous circumstances.[13]

The extant judgments recognition systems in Commonwealth Africa are built on theoretical foundations like those of western states. A few Anglophone countries in Commonwealth Africa recognise and enforce foreign judgments based on the doctrine of comity.[14] Theoretically, judgments from any foreign country, including the United States, are enforceable provided such judgments do not offend the sovereignty and fundamental policy of the receiving state. Kenya and Uganda seem to be the only countries in Commonwealth Africa whose courts have applied comity as a basis for recognition of judgments. Coincidentally, in the Ugandan case of *Christopher Sales v. Attorney General*,[15] a US judgment was sought to be enforced despite the absence of any bilateral judgments' recognition scheme between the two countries. The receiving court heavily relied on the US case of *Hilton v. Guyot*[16] in arriving at its conclusion. Similarly, comity was cited in the Kenyan case of *Jayesh Hasmukh Shah vs Navin Haria & Anor.*[17] Scholars like Roodt have suggested that foreign judgments may be enforced in South Africa based on comity.[18] However, this opinion is open to question as there is no reported case backing such a position.

The theory of obligation is the prominent theoretical basis for the recognition of foreign judgments in most common law jurisdictions in Commonwealth Africa. Foreign judgments are seen as creating an obligation which can be enforced by the judgment creditor in the receiving state. It is a common law action on debt which is available for liquidated judgment sums. A judgment creditor files a fresh action pleading the foreign judgment as evidence of the debt. Through a summary judgments procedure, judgment creditors can quickly get judgments enforced as foreign judgments constitute proof of issues or claims decided in the judgments. The inherent value in the doctrines of comity and obligation is that receiving courts are open and disposed to recognise most foreign judgments save those that violate the public policy of the receiving state.

Foreign judgments are also enforceable in Commonwealth Africa on a reciprocal basis. This entails the existence of bilateral or multilateral treaties or some form of

---

13 F. Joireman, 'Inherited Legal Systems and Effective Rule of Law: Africa and the Colonial Legacy', *The Journal of Modern African Studies*, Vol. 39, 2001, p. 576; M. Berinzon & R.C. Briggs, 'Legal Families Without the Laws', *The American Journal of Comparative Law*, Vol. 64, 2016, p. 345.

14 Comity has been described as a principle of deference and recognition of acts of foreign states. See *Morguard Investments Ltd v. De Savoye* [1990] 3 SCR 1077.

15 [2013] UGHCCD 15.

16 159 US 113 (1895).

17 Civil Appeal 147 of 2009.

18 C. Roodt, 'Recognition and enforcement of foreign judgments: still a Hobson's choice among competing theories?', *The Comparative and International Law Journal of Southern Africa, Vol. 38, No. 1, 2005*, pp. 20-21; C.F. Forsyth, *Private International Law*, 4th ed, Cape Town, Juta & Co Ltd., 2003, p. 409.

international judicial cooperation (e.g. court-to-court agreements). Most common law jurisdictions have statutory reciprocal regimes for the recognition and enforcement of judgments. The statutory schemes provide a simple registration process for the enforcement of foreign judgments from reciprocating states. It should be noted that no such reciprocal arrangement exists between any country in Commonwealth Africa and the United States. However, Nigeria enforces judgments from the United States under a reciprocal framework even though the US is not listed under the statute.[19]

Reciprocity forms the basis for the enforcement of judgments in the civil law jurisdictions of Commonwealth Africa. In the absence of treaties, foreign judgments are subjected to exequatur proceedings as provided in the respective Codes. A typical illustration of the enforcement framework is provided in article 204 of the Rwandan Code of Procedure: "*Except where international agreements provide otherwise, judgements ruled by foreign courts and foreign deeds issued by foreign officials shall not be subject to execution in Rwanda, unless they are rendered enforceable by the competent Court.*"[20]

The conditions for the grant of exequatur vary from one jurisdiction to the other. For instance, section 7 of the Cameroonian Law No. 2007/001 of 2007[21] simply requires the receiving court to ensure that the foreign court had jurisdiction, parties were duly served or represented, and the decision was not contrary to public policy or a final decision of the receiving court. This Law, just like some other Codes, is silent on whether reciprocal enforcement of judgments of the receiving state is a requirement for the grant of exequatur.

3 ENFORCEMENT OF FOREIGN PUNITIVE JUDGMENTS IN COMMONWEALTH AFRICA

3.1 *Anglophone Commonwealth Africa – common law action*

As discussed in the preceding section, common law is the predominant legal tradition in the Anglophone region of Commonwealth Africa. Not only is common law predominant, but their courts are also greatly influenced by the developments of the common law by the English courts. This is not to say the English common law is binding on these courts. Since

19 This emanated from an erroneous interpretation of the reciprocal statutes. The error travelled through to the Supreme Court and was confirmed by the apex court. See A. Yekini, 'Foreign judgments in Nigerian courts in the last decade: a dawn of liberalization', *Nederlands Internationaal Privaatrecht*, No. 2, 2017, p. 205.

20 Law No. 21/2012 of 14 June 2012, Law relating to the civil, commercial, labour, and administrative procedure, Official Gazette no. 29 of 16 July 2012.

21 Law No. 2007/001 of 19 April 2007 to institute a Judge in charge of Litigation related to the execution of judgements and lay down conditions for the enforcement in Cameroon of foreign court decisions.

independence, these countries have become republics, and English decisions are only of persuasive effect. Nevertheless, the courts are accustomed to following the English common law. The United States has no reciprocal enforcement regime with any African state, and neither is there any treaty relation. Apart from Nigeria, where US foreign judgments can be enforced under the statutory reciprocal regime, in most states, such judgments can only be enforced by common law action.

The requirements for enforcement of judgments via common law action are similar in most Anglophone states. These requirements are derived from the common law rules developed by the common law courts in England in cases such as *Schibsby v. Westenholz,*[22] *Godard v. Gray,*[23] and *Emanuel v. Symon*[24] amongst others.[25] In an enforcement action, common law courts would rarely disturb the findings of foreign courts or review the merits of the judgment under any guide. This is a well-established principle across the common law jurisdictions in Africa from South Africa,[26] to Nigeria,[27] Kenya,[28] and others. A corollary of this principle is that a foreign court might arrive at a decision contrary to that which the court addressed would have reached. Thus, common law courts would ordinarily not be moved by the fact that a judgment creditor was awarded a judgment sum far above what he would have obtained if the matter was litigated in the forum.

The major obstacles to enforcing foreign judgments under common law action are lack of international jurisdiction, breach of a right to a fair trial and public policy.[29] Of these obstacles, public policy seems to be engaged with punitive damages. Unlike civil law jurisdictions where punitive damages are largely unknown in their laws and thus deemed contrary to public policy, such is not the case in most common law jurisdictions. The common law courts do award punitive damages in deserving cases and there is nothing inherently against public policy in awarding punitive damages.[30] In *SA Consortium Textiles*

22 (1870) LR 6 QB 155.

23 (1870) LR 6 QB 288.

24 [1908] 1 KB 302 (CA).

25 For a restatement of the common law rules, see *Adams & Ors v. Cape Industrials Plc* (1990) Ch. 433.

26 See *Elan Boulevard (Pty) Ltd v. Fnyn Investments (Pty) Ltd and Others* [2018] ZASCA 165; *Jones v. Krok* [1995] 2 All SA 30.

27 *Overseas Union Insurance Ltd & Ors v. Marine & General Assurance Co Ltd* (2001) 9 NWLR (Pt. 717) 92; *Teleglobe America Inc. v. Twenty First Century Tech. Ltd.* (2008) 17 NWLR (Pt. 1115) 108; *WittBusch Ltd. v. Dale Power Systems Plc.* (2007) 17 NWLR (Pt. 1062) 1; *Conoil v. Vitol S.A.* (2018) 9 NWLR (Pt. 1625) 463.

28 See *Jayesh Hasmukh Shah v. Navin Haria & another* [2016] eKLR (Civil Appeal 147 of 2009); *Raw Bank PLC v. Yusuf Shaa Mohamed Omar & another* [2020] eKLR (Civil Suit 10 of 2014); *ABSA Bank Uganda Limited (Formerly Known as Barclays Bank of Uganda Limited) v. Uchumi Supermarkets PLC* [2021] KEHC 14 (KLR); *Ssebagala & Sons Electric Ltd v. Kenya National Shipping Lines Ltd* [2002] eKLR (civ case 1723 of 2000).

29 A. Yekini, *The Hague Judgments Convention and Commonwealth Model Law: A Pragmatic Perspective*, London, Hart Publishing, 2021, p. 186; T.J. Monestier, 'Foreign Judgments at Common Law: Rethinking the Enforcement Rules', *Dalhousie Law Journal*, Vol. 28, No. 1, 2005, pp. 174-178.

30 In the United Kingdom, the House of Lords limited the award of punitive damages to cases where it is provided by statutes, or where the defendant's conduct is calculated to make a profit for himself *"which*

v. Sun & Sand Agencies Limited, Lord Denning also wondered whether English courts could describe foreign punitive judgments as contrary to public policy when English courts equally award such judgments.[31] To the best of the writers' knowledge, there are no known foreign judgments from the United States or elsewhere that have been denied recognition and enforcement in England strictly under common law principles.[32]

The common law courts do not sit on appeals over foreign judgments. They also take cognisance of the diversity of procedural laws and the outcomes of civil litigation. The recognition rules prioritise the connection between a foreign court and the subject matter. A judgment rendered by a foreign court that had international jurisdiction would hardly be disturbed simply because the outcome or award would be different if the matter were to be decided by the court addressed. While it can be safely assumed that foreign punitive judgments may not necessarily be contrary to public policy in most Anglophone states based on the reasoning of Lord Denning cited above, it would not be out of place to argue that, if the size of the award is outrageous, public policy concerns may be triggered.

The law in South Africa deserves special attention. The question of whether a punitive foreign judgment is contrary to public policy has been debated in South Africa. Most South African private international law scholars agree that South African courts should decline to enforce foreign punitive judgments on public policy grounds.[33] There, however, appears to be no convincing and authoritative position from the courts. In *Jones v. Krok*, a judgment creditor sought to enforce a US judgment awarding the sum of USD 13.670.987 as compensatory damages and USD 12.000.000 as punitive damages.[34] The trial court ruled that the judgment was unenforceable because it was contrary to South African public policy. The lower court did not only reject the punitive damages, it further held that the purportedly compensatory part was also not enforceable because it "rested upon the same foundations as those which support the assessment and award of punitive damages". On appeal to the Supreme Court, Corbett CJ held that:

---

might well exceed the compensation payable to the plaintiff". See *Rookes v. Barnard and Others* [1964] A.C. 1129. Kenyan courts seem to have restricted the award of punitive damages to the categories allowed in the *dicta* of Lord Devlin in *Rookes v. Barnard*. See *D K Njagi Marete v. Teachers Service Commission* [2020] eKLR (Civil Appeal 316 of 2013); *Godfrey Julius Ndumba Mbogori & Another v. Nairobi City County* [2018] eKLR (Civil Appeal 55 of 2012); *Leonard Gethoi Kamweti v. National Bank of Kenya Limited* [2020] eKLR (Cause 237 of 2014). In *Elochin v. Mbadiwe* (1986) N.W.L.R (Pt. 14) 47, the Nigerian Supreme Court pronounced that *Rookes v. Barnard* was only a persuasive authority. The apex court rejected the limitations introduced by the English House of Lords.

31 [1978] QB 279 at 309.

32 Potter LJ in *Lewis v. Eliades* (No 2) [2004] 1 W.L.R. 692 indeed raised this question. His Lordship wondered whether punitive judgments would be enforceable under common law.

33 South African Law Reform Commission, 'Project 121: Consolidated Legislation Relating to International Judicial Cooperation in Civil Matters: Report', December 2006, pp. 74-75.

34 [1995] 2 All SA 30 (A).

> *"In my view, there was no valid basis on the papers for these findings by the Court a quo; and, in any event, they seem to involve entering into the merits of the case adjudicated upon by the US Court, which as I have pointed out is not permissible. Accordingly, public policy afforded no ground for denying the appellant relief in respect of the amount of US $13.670.987. The award of US $12.000.000 does pertinently raise the question of whether or not our courts will enforce an award of punitive damages made by a foreign court, but in all the circumstances I prefer not to deal with this question at this stage."*[35]

This case presented the Supreme Court with a golden opportunity to rule on whether foreign punitive judgments are contrary to public policy, but the Court declined to take a stance. At the rehearing of the case, Kirk-Cohen J enforced the compensatory part and rejected the punitive part.[36] The court reasoned that punitive damages are not inherently unconscionable. However, the court found that in this instance the amount was exorbitant and therefore contrary to public policy.[37]

In the more recent case of *Danielson v. Human and Another*, the sum of USD 859.595,51 which was trebled to USD 2.578.786,53 was awarded by a US court for breach of certain provisions of the Racketeer Influenced and Corrupt Organizations Act (RICO).[38] In an application to enforce the US judgment before a South African court, the question of public policy was also presented to the court. In a reasoned judgment, Cloete J thus held:

> *"It seems to me that the treble damage provision is designed to compensate a plaintiff for his entire loss suffered (including those components which of their nature are difficult to quantify). It is not strictly punitive in the sense that its purpose is to, in addition, punish the defendant because of his reprehensible behaviour. As was held by Kirk-Cohen J in Jones v. Krok supra, the mere fact that awards are made by a foreign court on a basis not recognised in South Africa does not mean that they are necessarily contrary to public policy. Put differently, that a particular formula to fully compensate a plaintiff for actual loss suffered is not familiar to South African legal practice is not for that reason alone justification for the conclusion that the damages are impermissibly punitive in nature. I thus find that the recognition and enforcement of the judgment of the American court is not precluded by public policy."*[39]

35 *Ibid*, para 53.

36 *Jones v. Krok* 1996 1 SA 504 (T).

37 *Ibid*, 516.

38 [2016] ZAWCHC 92.

39 [2016] ZAWCHC 92, paras 37-38.

It does appear that Cloete J was persuaded by the expert opinion of Blakey who distinguished between RICO treble damages which are remedial in nature (aimed at fully compensating a victim for harm suffered), limited to three times the actual damage, and assessed by the court and punitive/exemplary damages which are often assessed by a jury and often awarded under state laws.[40] The takeaway from these cases is that the question of whether foreign punitive judgments are contrary to public policy and therefore unenforceable appears not to be settled under South African law. The answer would likely depend on the characterisation of the foreign punitive judgments (whether remedial or punitive) and the reasonableness of the value.

Apart from public policy grounds, foreign judgments are also unenforceable under common law action if the foreign judgments border on the enforcement of foreign penal law. The question to be asked is whether US punitive judgments fall under the "foreign penal laws" ground. Treble damages are punitive in nature. In the words of the Nigerian Court of Appeal in *U.B.N. Ltd. v. Oredein*:[41]

> *"Exemplary damages convey a punitive element because its object is to punish the defendant. A plaintiff cannot recover exemplary damages unless he is the victim of the punishable behaviour. Because of the punitive nature of the damages, courts of law do not award exemplary damages unless in clearly deserving cases."*[42]

It may be argued that punitive damages are not enforceable because their objective sits well within the general framework of criminal law. This argument seems unsustainable considering how common law courts have interpreted "foreign penal laws".[43] US punitive damages awarded to private litigants in purely private law actions would not be considered as foreign penal law notwithstanding that punitive damages are penal in nature. This view is supported by English court decisions. In *SA Consortium General Textiles v. Sun and Sand Agencies Ltd*, Lord Denning concluded that punitive damages awarded to a private litigant, and not the state, cannot be characterised as a penalty.[44] Potter LJ came to the same conclusion in *Lewis v. Eliades (No 2)*.[45]

Many countries in Commonwealth Africa are accustomed to following English court decisions even though those decisions are only persuasive. In the absence of any clear-cut common law principle or rule barring the enforcement of foreign punitive judgments, one

40 *Ibid*, paras 29-34.
41 (1992) 6 NWLR (Pt. 247) 355.
42 *Ibid*, p. 379.
43 See the rule in *Huntington v. Attrill* [1893] AC 150.
44 [1978] QB 279 at 309.
45 [2004] 1 W.L.R. 692 at para 50.

can conclude that US treble/punitive damages may be enforceable in Anglophone Commonwealth Africa if the judgment meets the conditions for recognition and enforcement of foreign judgments under common law. At the risk of sounding repetitive, the key conditions include the existence of international jurisdiction, a fair trial, and the non-violation of the public policy of the forum or of some overriding mandatory rules.[46] Only South Africa has a rule concerning overriding mandatory rules in place. US punitive judgments may be treated differently in South Africa because of a statute blocking the enforcement of foreign punitive damages. As mentioned in the preceding paragraph, even though US judgments can only be enforced through a common law action (because there is no bilateral/multilateral relationship in place), an overriding mandatory statute prohibiting the enforcement of such judgments is a potent defence for judgments debtors.

In 1978, the South African parliament passed the Protection of Businesses Act.[47] It has been suggested the Act was enacted during the Apartheid era to protect South African businesses from the reach of US antitrust laws and other foreign laws and judgments awarding multiple damages.[48] However, the scope of this Act is limited to foreign judgments concerning "*the production, importation, exportation, refinement, possession, use or sale of or ownership to any matter or material*". In other words, the underlying transaction must be connected with mining and minerals. In 1984 the Act was amended to prohibit the enforcement of foreign multiple or punitive judgments (damages) in South Africa.[49] Section 1A (2) of the 1984 amendment states that:

> *"'multiple or punitive damages' means that part of the amount awarded as damages which exceeds the amount determined by the court as compensation for the damage or loss actually sustained by the person to whom the damages have been awarded."*

There have been different attempts at invoking the Protection of Businesses Act to deny recognition to foreign judgments in South Africa, including US punitive judgments. However, judgment debtors were not successful because of the limited scope of the Act. *Danielson v. Human and Another* was one such case.[50] One of the issues argued in the

46 See *Jones v. Krok* [1994] ZASCA 177; 1995 (1) SA 677 (A) at 685B-D; *Purser v. Sales* [2000] ZASCA 135; 2001 (3) SA 445 (SCA) paras 11-12; *Elan Boulevard (Pty) Limited v. Mahomed* (12451/2014) [2016] ZAKZDHC 49.

47 No. 99 of 1978.

48 See *Trademore (Pty) Ltd v. Minister of Trade and Industry and Another* (49321/2017) [2019] ZAGPPHC 591, para 42; *International Fruit Genetics LLC v. Redelinghuys* [2017] ZAWCHC 6. See also South African Law Reform Commission, 'Project 121: Consolidated Legislation Relating to International Judicial Cooperation in Civil Matters: Report', December 2006.

49 Protection of Businesses Amendment Act 71 of 1984.

50 [2016] ZAWCHC 92 ; 2017 (1) SA 141 (WCC).

enforcement proceeding was whether the enforcement of the US punitive judgment was barred by the statute. The court had no difficulty in concluding that the subject matter falls outside the scope of the Act and as such the Act does not apply.[51] *Elan Boulevard (Pty) Ltd v. Fnyn Investments (Pty) Ltd* and other decisions further reiterate that the scope of the Act is limited to transactions bothering on only raw materials.[52] As other scholars have noted, there has not been any successful attempt at blocking the enforcement of foreign punitive judgments under this Act.[53] This can be contrasted with a similar blocking statute in the United Kingdom – the Protection of Trading Interests Act 1980 – but with no such restriction in material scope. The UK Act was successfully used to deny recognition and enforcement to US punitive judgments in *Service Temps Inc v. MacLeod*[54] and *SAS Institute Inc v. World Programming Ltd.*[55]

3.2 *Anglophone Commonwealth Africa – statutory schemes*

There are two statutory reciprocal regimes for the recognition and enforcement of foreign judgments. These statutes are modelled after the UK's Administration of Justice Act 1920 (AJA) and Foreign Judgments (Reciprocal Enforcement) Act 1933. These frameworks were aimed at facilitating the liberalisation of foreign judgments within the Commonwealth. The first variant applies to judgments between the United Kingdom and respective Commonwealth states. The 1933 variant was meant to replace the 1920 version and is potentially applicable to any non-Commonwealth states. While some states have just one statute in place, several Commonwealth African states maintain both statutes. Be that as it may, most states have extended the statutory reciprocal schemes to only a handful of states. None of the Commonwealth African states have extended the reciprocal scheme to the United States. Therefore, US punitive judgments would hardly be governed by the statutory schemes.

Nigeria stands as an exception. While the reciprocal statute has not been extended to the United States, the Nigerian Court of Appeal has ruled that US judgments can be registered under the statutory scheme.[56] In *Overseas Union Insurance Ltd & Ors v. Marine & General Assurance Co Ltd* the Nigerian Court of Appeal noted that when an application

51 *Ibid.*, paras 20-21.

52 [2018] ZASCA 165. See also *Tradex Ocean Transportation SA v. MV Silvergate (or Astyanax)* 1994 (4) SA 119; *Richman v. Ben Tovim* 2007 (2) SA 283 (SCA).

53 R. Oppong, *Private International Law in Africa*, London, Cambridge University Press, 2015, p. 342; S. Khanderia, 'The Hague Conference on Private International Law's Proposed Draft Text on the Recognition and Enforcement of Foreign Judgments: Should South Africa Endorse it?', *Journal of African Law*, Vol. 63, No. 3, 2019, p. 422.

54 2014 S.L.T. 375.

55 [2018] EWHC 3452 (Comm).

56 *Teleglobe America Inc. v. Twenty First Century Tech. Ltd.* (2008) 17 NWLR (Pt. 1115) 108.

for enforcement is brought under the statute, courts should be guided by the provisions of the statute.[57] The same position was reiterated in *Hyppolite v. Egharevba* where it was emphasised that the grounds for setting aside foreign judgments are those provided under section 6(l)(a)(i) to (vi) of the Act.[58] Under this section, the award of multiple damages is not one of the grounds for denial of recognition and enforcement of foreign judgments. In *Witt & Busch Ltd. v. Dale Power Systems Plc*, the Supreme Court re-echoed the well-known principle that Nigerian courts will not sit as appellate courts over judgments of foreign courts.[59] The apex court further noted that a judgment creditor is entitled to have its judgment enforced once it meets the requirements of the statute. Thus, the position under the Act may not be different from that of common law action.

It should be mentioned that while both variants of the Commonwealth statutory reciprocal regimes do prohibit recognition of punitive judgments, the Kenyan Foreign Judgments (Reciprocal Enforcement) Act 1984 was amended by Act No. 18 of 2018 to prohibit the enforcement of exemplary, multiple or punitive damages.[60] Section 1 of the Act defines multiple damages as an 'amount payable under a judgment which has been arrived at by multiplying by any factor a sum assessed as compensation for loss or damage sustained by a person in whose favour the judgment was given'.

3.3 *Francophone Commonwealth Africa – exequatur*

Most civil law jurisdictions do not accept the philosophical basis of punitive damages. Damages are meant to redress the actual loss or harm suffered by a victim and nothing more. Although scholars have identified some traces of what can be described as punitive damages in some of the civil law countries,[61] treble, multiple and other similar forms of punitive damages as commonly awarded in the United States may be considered a violation of public policy especially when the value of the award is disproportionate to the harm suffered.[62]

The law and practice of judgments recognition and enforcement in francophone Commonwealth countries are derived from Continental legal traditions, especially the

57 (2001) 9 NWLR (Pt. 717) 92.

58 (1998) 11 NWLR (Pt. 575) 598.

59 (2007) 17 NWLR (Pt. 1062) 1.

60 See s.3(b) Act No. 18 of 2018.

61 For instance, see C. Vanleenhove, *Punitive Damages in Private International Law*, Cambridge-Antwerp-Portland, Intersentia, 2016, pp. 147-206.

62 See A. Sprengel, 'Enforcement of Foreign Judgments: France' in M. Moedritzer & K.C. Whittaker (Eds.), *Enforcement of Foreign Judgments in 29 jurisdictions worldwide*, London, Law Business Research Ltd, 2014, p. 48 (citing Court of Cassation, First Civil Chamber decision of 1 December 2010 in Appeal No. 09-13303). See further Court of Cassation, Criminal Chamber decision in Appeal No. 13-83.884 (2014); Court of Cassation, First Civil Chamber decision in Appeal No 16-26.012 (2018).

French legal tradition. US punitive judgments may be viewed as contrary to public policy since their courts rarely award such judgments. Indeed, such is the case in Cameroon where one commentator suggested that US punitive damages would hardly be awarded by Cameroonian courts except in intentional tort cases.[63] While the Cameroonian judgments enforcement statute does not include punitive damages as one of the refusal grounds for recognition, section 7(b) provides the public policy exception.[64] It is highly unlikely that exequatur would be granted to US punitive judgments because of this public policy ground.

Article 44 of the Rwandan Law No. 30 of 2018 which deals with the enforcement of foreign judgments contains similar provisions as those of Cameroon. The first condition for the grant of exequatur is an inquiry into whether the foreign judgment contravenes Rwandan public policy or any Rwandan law principle. While the position of the French courts on US punitive damages, especially those that are proportionate, appears to have changed recently,[65] it is doubtful whether these recent developments in judicial practice in France would be followed in francophone Commonwealth Africa.

3.4 *Prospect under the Commonwealth Model Law?*

Judgment recognition and enforcement frameworks in the Commonwealth have stagnated for decades. There have been various calls and attempts geared toward modernising the subject matter. After failed attempts,[66] Commonwealth Law Ministers met in The Bahamas in 2017 to consider and adopt a brand-new Model Law on the enforcement of foreign judgments. While no Commonwealth state in Africa has thus far adopted this model law, it is important to take note of the improvements introduced in the Model Law, especially as it affects the enforcement of foreign punitive damages, since the model law can potentially apply in the Commonwealth states in the nearest future.

The drafters of the Model Law intend that it should be applied to all foreign judgments without the need for establishing reciprocity. This is a significant departure from the extant statutory frameworks. The Law seeks to promote justice for private citizens instead of concerns of state interest and policy. Therefore, if this Model Law is adopted by any

63 S.D. Galega, 'Strict Liability for Defective Products in Cameroon? Some Illuminating Lessons from Abroad', *Journal of African Law*, Vol. 48, No. 2, 2004, p. 239.

64 Law No. 2007/001 of 19 April 2007 to institute a Judge in charge of Litigation related to the execution of judgements and lay down conditions for the enforcement in Cameroon of foreign court decisions.

65 C. Vanleenhove, *Punitive Damages in Private International Law*, Cambridge-Antwerp-Portland, Intersentia, 2016, pp. 130-139 (discussing the French Supreme Court decision in *Schlenzka & Langhorne v. Fountaine Pajot S.A* and other relevant cases).

66 See generally J.D. McClean & K.W Patchett, *The Recognition and Enforcement of Judgments and Orders and the Service of Process within the Commonwealth*, London, Commonwealth Secretariat, 1977.

Commonwealth state in Africa, US judgments will become registrable under the statutory framework.

Section 3 of the Law deals with punitive judgments. Under this section, a court addressed can sever the punitive part of a foreign judgment and enforce the compensatory part in the circumstance that punitive damages are contrary to the forum's public policy. This development aligns with what is obtainable under the Hague and EU frameworks. This can potentially settle the controversy surrounding the enforcement of US punitive damages, especially where the judgment contains different heads for compensatory and punitive damages. The Model Law may be of little or no help where there is no differentiation between compensatory and punitive damages as it is practically impossible to apply the severance provision since the court addressed would have no clue as to how the US court arrived at the lump sum. A practical application of section 3 of the Model Law can be seen under the Australian statutory enforcement scheme. Under section 6(13) of the Australian Foreign Judgments Act 1991, a court addressed has the discretion to sever an unenforceable part of a foreign judgment and grant recognition to the enforceable part.[67] In *Schnabel v. Lui*, the court addressed was asked to enforce a US judgment which included both compensatory and punitive damages.[68] The court severed the punitive part and enforced the compensatory part.

It is also worth mentioning that section 14 of the Model Law has an interesting provision which empowers the court addressed to limit the enforcement of multiple or punitive damages to a comparable value under the forum law. This is a pragmatic solution to the conundrum arising out of the enforcement of punitive damages, especially in cases where the compensatory and punitive parts are not separated. Rather than rejecting the foreign judgment in its entirety, the court addressed can reduce the award up to the amount that is awardable in the forum. Read together with section 3, US punitive judgments should hardly be denied recognition under the Model Law.

4 Conclusion

There are divergent approaches to the question of the availability of punitive damages. The divergence is not unconnected with the understanding of legal scholars, judges and policymakers on the fundamental objective of damages on the one hand and of the distinction between civil and criminal law on the other hand. While the objective of criminal law is to punish offenders and deter them from repeating reprehensible conduct,

67 Although, section 1 of the Act defines a judgment to include any award or damages awarded in criminal proceedings.

68 [2002] NSWSC 15.

civil law seeks to compensate victims for the harm suffered and to put them back in the position they were before the harm suffered.

Over the years, courts have awarded damages in civil claims to punish the defendant. This led to the award of exemplary and punitive damages in purely civil actions. While this is a common practice in several Commonwealth jurisdictions, the same is considered contrary to public policy in most civil law jurisdictions because the award of punitive damages blurs the distinction between the objectives of civil and criminal law. The award of punitive damages is not the only problematic issue. In Commonwealth jurisdictions that award this kind of damages, there is considerable debate about what should be the appropriate and reasonable value.

With such divergence under national laws, the question of whether foreign punitive damages judgments are enforceable becomes trickier. In the absence of specific precedents, the answer can only be speculative. In the common law jurisdictions of Commonwealth Africa such as Ghana, Nigeria, and Kenya, US punitive judgments are potentially enforceable under common law action on judgment debt if the US judgment meets the conditions for recognition. The potential refusal ground is public policy. It has been argued that since the courts in these states do award punitive damages in civil claims, foreign judgments rendered on foundations recognised under the laws of these states should hardly be refused recognition. It is however open to question whether the court addressed would be willing to enforce US punitive damages whose value appears to be unreasonably too high. This is certainly the case for South Africa where a trebled US RICO judgment was enforced in one case and non-RICO punitive damages were not recognised in another case.

Punitive damages are hardly available in the civil law jurisdictions in Commonwealth Africa. Highly influenced by Continental legal traditions, punitive damages are considered to be contrary to public policy irrespective of the value of the judgment. Since public policy is engaged, a court addressed would hardly grant an exequatur to enforcement requests.

Probably, the solutions brought by the Commonwealth Model Law on the Recognition and Enforcement of Foreign Judgments may be adopted by the courts in the nearest future. The Model Law allows courts to sever punitive awards from other compensatory damages where these awards are distinct. The decision in *Jones v. Krok* reflects this approach. Alternatively, in cases where the court addressed is only concerned about the reasonableness of the value of the award, the Model Law permits the court addressed to enforce the foreign judgments to the extent of the value considered reasonable under the forum law.

Punitive damages in Argentina and Mexico

Rethinking the scope of the public policy exception

María Guadalupe Martínez Alles[*]

1 Introduction

In the modern continental tradition, discussions on the place of punishment in private law have been stirred in recent decades by intense debates over the (in)convenience of introducing punitive damages and their (in)compatibility with existing civil law legal systems.[1] Punitive damages, understood as extra-compensatory awards imposed by judges at the request of the plaintiff in order to punish the defendant and deter her (and perhaps third parties) from engaging in similarly reprehensible misbehaviour in the future, are certainly a controversial institution. By incorporating punishment into private law, punitive damages raise many varied questions, some conceptual, and others that involve their practical implementation.[2]

In general, scholars have resisted the punitive institution and, as the discussion has progressed, different types of arguments have been employed to justify its rejection. One of the main arguments against punitive damages argues that their eminently punitive nature is proper to the criminal law (public law) and that they are therefore alien to tort law (private law).[3] They are rejected because punitive damages depart from the traditional corrective function of tort law, which stipulates that the amount of compensation should not exceed the harm caused to the victim and that the judge should disregard the

* Assistant Professor of Private Law at IE University, Spain.

1 L. Meurkens & E. Nordin, *The Power of Punitive Damages. Is Europe Missing Out?*, Cambridge, Intersentia, 2012. In this compilation on punitive damages in Europe, it becomes clear that the (in)compatibility of punitive damages with existing civil liability systems is the most prominent dispute in the debates over its incorporation in modern continental tort law.

2 For a comprehensive analysis of the theoretical and practical implications of the introduction of punitive damages in Argentina, see M.G. Martínez Alles, '¿Para Qué Sirven los Daños Punitivos? Modelos de Sanción Privada, Sanción Social y Disuasión Óptima', *Revista de Responsabilidad Civil y Seguros*, Vol. XIV, No. 5, 2012, pp. 55-100. For an analysis of the retributive dimension of punitive damages, see M.G. Martínez Alles, 'Moral Outrage and Betrayal Aversion: The Psychology of Punitive Damages', *Journal of Tort Law*, Vol. 11, No. 2, 2018, pp. 245-303.

3 J. Bustamante Alsina, 'Los Llamados "Daños Punitivos" son Extraños a Nuestro Sistema de Responsabilidad Civil', *La Ley*, Vol. B, 1994, p. 860. For common law scholars arguing that punitive damages should be abolished because they are in serious tension with tort law, see e.g. A. Beever, 'The Structure of Aggravated and Exemplary Damages', *Oxford Journal of Legal Studies*, Vol. 23, 2003, pp. 87-110.

seriousness of the defendant's conduct when determining the proper amount of compensation.[4] Accordingly, the condoned practice of punitive damages in private law is understood to cause more dysfunction than good by "ridiculously mixing the civil with the criminal and the administrative law."[5] At the same time, disallowing punitive damages has led some to seek or even invent other more appropriate institutions to fulfil the functions of punitive damages.[6] This perspective understands punitive damages as a threat to the traditional distinction between "public law" and "private law".

Despite this attitude of generalised resistance, recent relevant movements in the opposite direction can also be observed. In Latin America, countries such as Argentina, Chile and Mexico have grown receptive to introducing punitive damages into their domestic legal systems. In 2008, Argentina became the first civil law jurisdiction to introduce punitive damages under the rubric of consumer law.[7] Chile joined in this trend by introducing the sanction in the framework of its Consumer Protection Law passed in 2018.[8] The case of Mexico presents certain particularities, starting with their unusual origin. The Mexican Supreme Court of Justice directly introduced punitive damages under the umbrella of non-pecuniary damages in 2014.[9] In continental Europe, similar signs can also be identified. Although perhaps more timid than the Latin American developments, they indicate an increasingly receptive attitude to the punitive institution.[10] In fact, the discussion has recently been revitalized by the recognition that the determination of the extent of damages that are legally recognized as compensable in each European jurisdiction ultimately belongs to their domestic spheres, meaning that no obstacle, at least in principle, precludes the incorporation of punitive damages in the different jurisdictions of the European Union.[11] This is the logic followed in France where, within the framework of the

4 P.S. Coderch, 'Punitive damages', *InDret*, Vol. 1, 2000, pp. 1-17, p. 3; J. Mayo, 'La Inconsistencia de los Daños Punitivos', *La Ley*, Vol. B, 2009, pp. 1269-70.

5 J. Mayo & L.D. Crovi, 'Penas Civiles y Daños Punitivos', *Revista de Derecho de Daños*, Vol. II, 2011, p. 19.

6 A.J. Bueres & J.S. Picasso, 'La Función de la Responsabilidad Civil y los Daños Punitivos', *Revista de Derecho de Daños*, Vol. II, 2011, pp. 65-75, p. 73 (following this line of thinking, the authors share the conclusion of a report issued by the French Senate, which states "*that the development of class actions is revealed as a much more appropriate instrument to achieve the goals that are theoretically associated with punitive damages*").

7 Articles 8*bis* and 52*bis*, Law N° 24.240 (text according to Law N° 26.361, B.O. 7/4/2008).

8 Article 53 (c), Law N° 21.081, 13/09/2018 (although it should be noted that the law does not expressly refer to it as "punitive damages"). On this point, see S. Gamonal Contreras & A. Pino Emhart, 'La Dignidad Humana en el Derecho Privado. Una Lectura desde el Concepto de Dignidad Como Estatus', *Revista de Derecho Privado*, Vol. 43, 2022, pp. 45-72, p. 60 (arguing that the new regulation has elements that bear some resemblance to (English) aggravated damages rather than punitive damages).

9 Amparo Directo 30/2013, Primera Sala, Suprema Corte de Justicia de la Nación, 26/02/2014, pp. 87-91.

10 On this point, see R.C. Meurkens, *Punitive Damages: The Civil Remedy in American Law, Lessons and Caveats for Continental Europe*, Deventer, Wolters Kluwer, 2014, chapter 8 and 9.

11 E. Büyüksagis, I. Ebert, D. Fairgrieve, R.C. Meurkens & F. Quarta, 'Punitive Damages in Europe and Plea for the Recognition of Legal Pluralism', *European Business Law Review*, Vol. 1, 2016, pp. 137-57 (arguing, based upon scholarly work and case law from Germany, Italy, the Netherlands, France and Switzerland, that

recent *Projet de Réforme de la Responsabilité Civile*, a form of punishment (*amende civile*) was introduced in order to combat lucrative forms of illicit behaviour.[12]

In parallel, the European approach to recognising and enforcing foreign punitive judgments has recently shifted from invoking the "public policy exception"[13] out of hand as a trump card that completely overrules such foreign judgments, towards a more nuanced reconstruction of that exception, one that considers a range of relevant questions previously ignored.[14] For instance, the Italian Court of Cassation radically modified its position in 2017 when it recognised that the execution of a punitive award ordered by a foreign court is not necessarily contrary to the *public order*, since the sanctioning function is no longer incompatible with Italian private law, which was the predominant argument only a few years ago.[15] Indeed, the Court of Cassation pointed out examples of Italian legal provisions that serve punitive aims, therefore concluding that the idea of punishment in private law can no longer be considered foreign. Notwithstanding, the Italian Court of Cassation did not wholly abandon the "public policy exception". It instead offered a reading which narrows the exception's scope down to, for the most part, questions concerning "proportionality" and "excessiveness". In this way, Italy joined the growing trend in continental Europe (that Spain and France had already joined) of acknowledging the compatibility of punitive damages with their legal systems and, by consequence, narrowing the scope of the classic "public policy exception" to cases where foreign punitive awards fail to satisfy several criteria before they can be enforced domestically, with particular emphasis on whether the punitive award is deemed excessive.[16]

From these developments, it can be inferred that the overall attitude and sentiment towards the proper place for punishment in private law is a dynamic, evolving feature of

---

"*extra-compensatory damages are frequently applied by national judges, albeit not always in an overt manner, and that such a phenomenon should not be deemed a priori in conflict with the principles of European law*".).

12 Projet de Réforme de la Responsabilité Civile, article 1266-1 (2017). For analysis of the proposal, see S. Rowan, 'Punishment and Private Law: Some Comparative Observations', in E. Bant, W. Courtney, J. Goudkamp & J.M. Paterson (Eds.), *Punishment and Private Law*, Oxford, Hart Publishing, 2021, pp. 63-82.

13 In this chapter, "public policy" refers to "international public policy" as policy with an exceptional character that must be construed narrowly and applied with circumspection compared with the "domestic public policy", which can in principle encompass a broad range of legal and moral prescriptions.

14 For an overview of the current situation in Europe, see S. Bariatti, L. Fumagalli & Z. Crespi Reghizzi (Eds.), *Punitive Damages and Private International Law: State of the Art and Future Developments* (Vol. 83 Studi e Pubblicazioni della Rivista di Diritto Internazionale Privato e Processuale), Italy, Wolters Kluwer, 2019.

15 Axo Sport S.P.A. v. Nosa Inc., Corte di Cassazione, 5 July 2017, no. 16601/2017.

16 For an in-depth analysis of these cases, see C. Vanleenhove, *Punitive Damages in Private International Law: Lessons for the European Union*, Antwerp-Cambridge-Portland, Intersentia, 2016, pp. 124-36 and 139-44. For an analysis of the question of proportionality raised by the Spanish Supreme Court, see M. Requejo Isidro, 'Punitive Damages: How Do They Look Like When Seen from Abroad?', in L. Meurkens & E. Nordin (Eds.), *The Power of Punitive Damages: Is Europe Missing Out? Common Law and Civil Law Perspectives*, Intersentia, 2012, pp. 327-328.

most civil law jurisdictions.[17] At the same time, acknowledging this observed phenomenon implies recognising that the "public policy exception" is also conceptually dynamic and fluid, generally informed and constructed on the basis of the domestic understandings on the proper place of punishment in private law. This interconnectedness calls for more refined and context-dependent scholarship on the recognition and enforcement of foreign punitive judgments. This scholarship should be capable of acknowledging the need for an understanding of the domestic debates over the punitive function of private law for the sake of more meaningfully addressing the particular scope that the "public policy exception" should take in different jurisdictions.[18] The changing landscape of the discussions on the proper place for punishment in private law taking place in each jurisdiction affects the scope of the "public policy exception", which means that outright rejection could eventually become an unreasonable (incoherent, unconvincing) response in jurisdictions that start to recognise that punishment, either overtly or covertly, does actually play a role in their law of torts. To clarify, I am not suggesting direct causation but rather correlation, as evidence shows that jurisdictions which become more receptive to the punitive function of private law within their own legal systems tend to shy away from invoking the complete "public policy exception" (i.e. "punitive damages oppose public policy"). Receptivity to punitive elements, it should be emphasised, does not necessarily require express introduction of punitive damages. Recognising punitive-like instruments within their private law has corresponded with a shift in approach from outright rejection of foreign punitive judgments to focusing instead on the factors behind the punitive award, mostly in terms of proportionality, and how they jibe with domestic criteria.[19]

Against the shifting European landscape, looking at Argentina and Mexico is worthwhile, since both have recently introduced punitive damages in their legal systems, posing a challenge to the classic response to requests for the enforcement of foreign punitive judgments simply because punitive damages are against the public order. Instead, much more complex and nuanced questioning is called for: under which circumstances

17 Note that common law jurisdictions are not exempt. For instance, an ongoing discussion in English law questions the restrictiveness of the classic "categories test" originally introduced in *Rookes v. Barnard*, subsequently arguing for expansion in the scope of application of exemplary damages. For scholarly work along these lines, see J. Goudkamp & E. Katsampouka, 'Punitive damages: Ten Misconceptions', in E. Bant, W. Courtney, J. Goudkamp & J.M. Paterson (Eds.), *Punishment and Private Law*, Oxford, Hart Publishing, 2021, pp. 187-223.

18 On the connectivity function of private international law, see M. Pertegás Sender, 'Connectivity in Private International Law', Inaugural speech at Maastricht University, 2019, available at https://cris.maastrichtuniversity.nl/en/publications/connectivity-in-private-international-law.

19 This general attitude can be observed in the following cases: Axo Sport S.P.A. v. Nosa Inc., Corte di Cassazione, 5 July 2017, no. 16601/2017 (Italy); Miller Import Corp. v. Alabastres Alfredo S.L., Tribunal Supremo, 13 November 2001, Exequatur no. 2039/1999, AEDIPR 2003, 914 (Spain); Schlenzka & Langhorne v. Fountaine Pajot S.A., Cour de Cassation 1re Civ. 1 December 2010, no. 09-13303, D 2011, 423 (France).

would the enforcement of punitive damages compromise the "public order" of those particular jurisdictions? Since I was unable to identify representative cases dealing with the enforcement of foreign punitive judgments after punitive damages were introduced in the Mexican and Argentinean legal systems, I will concentrate on offering a thorough understanding of the contours of the punitive institution in those two jurisdictions from the internal perspective of tort law and its practice, largely assuming the above-mentioned interconnectedness between domestic tort law and private international law. It is my understanding that providing first-hand insights on the internal debates on punitive damages and its specific legal features in those countries will provide a helpful framework for private international law scholars who study requests for the enforcement of foreign punitive judgments in Argentina and Mexico (and perhaps other national jurisdictions as well) in the years to come.

The structure of the chapter is as follows. Section 2 describes the current physiognomy of modern tort law in Latin America, identifying the current scholarly landscape of its punitive dimension. Section 3 explores the distinctive history and process by which punitive damages were introduced in Argentina and Mexico. It reveals that even though both jurisdictions were principally inspired by the American experience and literature on punitive damages, they have nonetheless diverged significantly from each other in several aspects. They followed different institutional procedures for the introduction of punitive damages and ended up with differences in the concrete legal criteria for domestic application. Moreover, the large degree of uncertainty around practical matters important for implementation (for instance, the precise scope within which punitive damages can be applied, the legal requirements for imposing them and the methods adopted to quantify them or caps or limits on its amounts) strongly suggests that punitive damages are a dynamic, constantly evolving institution. Section 4 considers the domestic legal features of punitive damages identified in Argentina and Mexico that pose new questions for further inquiry as regards future changes in the potential scope of the "public policy exception" in those jurisdictions and offers tentative thoughts on directions for further exploration before a brief conclusion will be provided in section 5.

2 The contours of modern tort law in Latin America

Before engaging with the theoretical framework in which current discussions on the relationship between tort law and punishment take place and, in particular, on the space for punitive damages in Latin American legal systems, it is important to understand the landscape of modern tort law. In Latin America, the current theoretical debate on tort law basically revolves around two issues. The first is the discussion behind the growing acknowledgment that the dominant theoretical framework which exclusively understands tort law as a private compensatory mechanism can no longer be sustained. The second debate, related to the first, concerns the determination of the circumstances that call for deterrent (preventive) and punitive functions of tort law as well as the specific justification according to those circumstances. In other words, the current debate focuses, first, on the tension among the three primary functions of compensation, deterrence and punishment and, second, on the need to conceptually identify, relate, distinguish and demarcate them.[20]

It turns out that tort law is less oriented towards reparation than is usually claimed.[21] Similarly, the blameworthiness of defendants' conduct is considered to a much greater extent than is generally admitted.[22] The theorised compensatory orientation is further undermined by repeated analyses that demonstrate the general failure of the law of torts to genuinely compensate victims of serious harms. The vast majority of such harms are irreparable (whether prolonged pain and suffering, severe or irremediable physical injury, gross invasion of individual dignity or privacy, and so on), making accurate quantification in purely monetary terms virtually impossible. The objective of restoring the victim to the same (or close to the same) situation she was in before the harm occurred is therefore delusional in the vast majority of cases.[23] For example, in cases of harm to one's image or privacy arising from social network posts, the appropriate response, most will agree, will not exclusively involve monetary compensation. Rather, and overwhelmingly, plaintiffs demand a response that prevents the harm from persisting or being compounded (by, for instance, requesting the judge to order the removal of the offensive content). Similarly, apologies are also often more appropriate responses to certain types of harm than monetary awards.[24] The classic rectificatory monetary response, however sufficient and appropriate in many instances (for example, simple car or other accidents where the

20 M.G. Martínez Alles, 'La Dimensión Retributiva del Derecho de Daños. La Perspectiva de la Víctima', in J.A. Garcia Amado & D.M. Papayannis (Eds.), *Dañar, Incumplir y Reparar. Ensayos de Filosofía del Derecho Privado*, Lima, Palestra Editores, 2020, pp. 107-132; D. M. Papayannis, 'Responsabilidad Civil (Funciones)', *Eunomía: Revista en Cultura de la Legalidad*, Vol. 22, 2022, pp. 307-327; E. Barros Bourie, *Tratado de Responsabilidad Extracontractual*, Santiago, Editorial Jurídica de Chile, 2006.

21 G. Keating, 'Is the Role of Tort to Repair Wrongful Losses?', in D. Nolan & A. Robertson (Eds.), *Rights and Private Law*, Oxford, Hart Publishing, 2012, pp. 367-405; A. Vargas Tinoco, 'El Valor de No Dañar: De la Responsabilidad Civil a la Prevención', in D. M. Papayannis & E. Pereira Fredes (Eds.), *Filosofía del Derecho Privado*, Marcial Pons, 2018, pp. 327-358.

22 E. Pereira Fredes, 'Un Alegato a Favor de las Consideraciones Punitivas en el Derecho Privado', *Revista de Derecho Escuela de Postgrado*, Vol. 7, 2015, pp. 61-78 (arguing that the judicial practice of awarding damages in Chile often runs contrary to the principle of rectification).

23 S. Hershovitz, 'Tort as a Substitute for Revenge', in J. Oberdiek (Ed.), *Philosophical Foundations of Tort Law*, Oxford, Oxford University Press, 2014, p. 93; A. Pino Emhart, 'Restaurar para Corregir. La Dimensión Restaurativa de la Justicia Correctiva en la Responsabilidad Extracontractual', in D.M. Papayannis & E. Pereira Fredes (Eds.), *Filosofía del Derecho Privado*, Marcial Pons, 2018, pp. 359-375.

24 A. Vargas Tinoco, 'Reparar o Reconocer. Algunas Consideraciones sobre la Justificación de Medidas No Pecuniarias ante el Daño en el Derecho Privado', in J.A. Garcia Amado & D.M. Papayannis (Eds.), *Dañar, Incumplir y Reparar. Ensayos de Filosofía del Derecho Privado*, Lima, Palestra Editores, 2020, pp. 57-106.

damage is solely pecuniary), is highly unsatisfactory in a significant number of tortious cases. This demonstrates, at the very least, a crucial shortcoming of the principle extolling rectification as the exclusive objective of tort law.

Returning to another point mentioned above, the blameworthiness of the defendant's conduct has been demonstrated to carry more weight in tort law decisions and with greater regularity than is assumed.[25] Judgments for compensatory awards, such as those often handed down in cases involving non-pecuniary damages, include extra-compensatory (punitive) elements meant to respond to the seriousness (or reprehensibility) of the defendant's conduct. Such judgments make clear the inadequacy of a purely rectificatory response to satisfy the demands of justice for victims of aggravated conducts. At the end of the day and no matter how they are framed, those so-called "compensatory" responses do "more than compensation". Indeed, scholars have identified an established practice of awarding "generous" compensatory damages when the judges seem to address the outrageous behaviour of the defendant – as illustrated by large awards for "pain and suffering," which according to theory should be strictly compensatory.[26]

All of the above reveals not only the crisis that the pretension to exclusivity of the rectificatory principle is going through, but also the covert presence of the ideas of punishment and deterrence already operating in the law of torts. The sharp division between "public law" and "private law" is much less clear in practice than it is theoretically vaunted.[27] The logic and operation of modern tort law in Latin America has, as we have seen in the examples discussed, become much more complex. Compensation, deterrence and punishment often coexist (even if covertly), comprising an ongoing challenge for tort scholars to identify and define the conceptual aspects of each function and to elucidate their relative autonomy, overlap and coordination with the others. As will become evident, distinct legal systems in Latin America provide different spaces for these functions, both

25 M.G. Martínez Alles, 'Tort Remedies as Meaningful Responses to Wrongdoing', in P. Miller & J. Oberdiek (Eds.), *Civil Wrongs and Justice in Private Law*, Oxford, Oxford University Press, 2020, pp. 231-252.

26 Examples of Latin American countries where this practice has been observed by scholars include among others: Argentina, see M.G. Martínez Alles, '¿Para Qué Sirven los Daños Punitivos? Modelos de Sanción Privada, Sanción Social y Disuasión Óptima', *Revista de Responsabilidad Civil y Seguros*, Vol. XIV, No. 5, 2012, pp. 55-100 (identifying the use of non-pecuniary awards as a punitive mechanism employed by judges); Chile, see C. Domínguez Hidalgo, *El Daño Moral*, Santiago: Editorial Jurídica de Chile, 2000, p. 91 (noting how Chilean judges award damages for pain and suffering to punish the defendant) and Brazil, see A.G. Corrêa de Andrade, *Indenização Punitiva*, Roncarati, 2008 (discussing the use of emotional damages as a punitive tool by judges in Brazil).

27 T. Honoré, 'The Morality of Tort Law – Questions and Answers', in D.G. Owen (Ed.), *Philosophical Foundations of Tort Law*, Oxford, Oxford University Press, 1997, p. 74 (arguing that both tort law and criminal law aim to eliminate or reduce undesirable behaviours, contemplate sanctions to be imposed on those whose behaviours are undesirable and raise complex questions about the conditions for imposing sanctions and the degree of responsibility of the perpetrators of unlawful acts).

because of the specific arrangements in the given legal community and the policy orientation of the faction in power.[28]

3 Understanding punitive damages in Argentina and Mexico

Argentina and Mexico have both recently introduced punitive damages in their legal systems, as has been mentioned, and their introduction in each case was heavily influenced by the Anglo-American scholarship and relevant case law on the punitive institution.[29] Legal scholarship and the reasoning of the judges imposing punitive awards in both jurisdictions often directly refer to American sources and U.S. Supreme Court decisions.[30] Notwithstanding, Argentina and Mexico have followed fundamentally different institutional paths to introduce punitive damages in their own legal systems, as did the domestic debates on the place of punishment in private law. The specific legal features and practical implementation aspects of their punitive awards are distinctive too. A closer look at each facet follows.

3.1 *Argentina: The Consumer Protection Statute*

For the last three decades, Argentinean scholars have actively discussed the place of punishment in tort law.[31] The debates have focused on a variety of issues concerning the (dis)advantages of recognising punitive damages, the relative autonomy of punitive damages vis-à-vis compensatory damages, the desired legal requirements for their

---

28 For example, in Argentina, after the recent reform of the Civil Code (which entered into force in August 2015 and, for the first time, systematically regulates tort law requirements from article 1708 onwards) compensation and deterrence are autonomous functions that coexist simultaneously in any given tort litigation.

29 For the influence of the United States experience and scholarship on punitive damages in the debates in civil law systems, see M.G. Martínez Alles, 'Punitive Damages: Reorienting the Debate in Civil Law Systems', *Journal of European Tort Law*, Vol. 10, No. 1, 2019, pp. 63-81.

30 For examples of references to the U.S. jurisprudence in Mexico, see Amparo Directo 30/2013, p. 87, notes 125-26 (explicitly referring to Anglo-American scholarship on punitive damages in the judgment); concurrent opinion of Justice José Ramón Cossío Díaz, pp. 13-14, notes 5-7 (pointing out to the need to refer to the system of origin, the United States, to elucidate questions such as the scope of their availability, their method for quantification and their limits); Amparo Directo 50/2015, Primera Sala, Suprema Corte de Justicia de la Nación, pp. 55-63 (referring to punitive damages in the United States to exclude their availability against the state); p. 61 (referring to the U.S. precedent in Pacific Mutual Life Insurance Co. v. Haslip as guidance for quantification of the punitive award). For similar examples in Argentina, see M.G. Martínez Alles, '¿Para Qué Sirven los Daños Punitivos? Modelos de Sanción Privada, Sanción Social y Disuasión Óptima', *Revista de Responsabilidad Civil y Seguros*, Vol. XIV, No. 5, 2012, pp. 55-100.

31 For the leading scholarly work that ignited the debate over punitive damages in Argentina, see D. Pizarro, 'Daños Punitivos', in A. Kemelmajer de Carlucci & C. Parellada (Eds.), *Derecho de Daños: Libro Homenaje al Profesor Félix Trigo Represas*, Vol. II, Buenos Aires, La Rocca, 1993, p. 287.

imposition, and several practical aspects surrounding implementation (insurability, limits or caps, how to determine the level of reprehensibility of the defendant's conduct, whether to divide the award between the victim and the state, and so on). The scholarly work on the topic is vast and comprehensive – for instance, the few existent books on punitive damages in Latin America have mostly been written by Argentinean scholars.[32]

This long process of debate within scholarly and judicial circles paved the way for Argentina's Congress to introduce punitive damages in the Consumer Protection Statute.[33] A judicial decision in the context of consumer law in Argentina might therefore simultaneously contain compensatory, deterrent and punitive elements. For an idea of such a combination, I will explain a 2015 case tried in Argentina, a simple individual lawsuit against a cell phone company.[34] A single consumer sued a cell phone company seeking reimbursement for fees improperly charged under the rubric of "collection management activities." The lawsuit also requested the judge to order, by way of deterrence, the telephone company to cease this abusive practice and, finally, to award punitive damages due to the seriousness of the company's conduct.

The situation is different outside of the consumer law realm, for even though compensation and deterrence are autonomous functions that can coexist simultaneously in any given tort action, punitive damages are not available in general civil law litigation in Argentina.[35] The general sentiment seems to deem punitive damages acceptable in the circumscribed context of consumer disputes characterised by the asymmetric power dynamics between mass producers and individual consumers. Opening the door to punitive awards broadly available in more general private law disputes is much more controversial, not to mention cases involving civil liability of public and government officials. However reasoned or faulty this understanding is, it may explain the exclusion of punitive damages from the final version, although they were initially proposed by the drafting commission of the Argentinean Civil Code reformed in 2015.[36]

The Consumer Protection Statute regulates punitive damages through two main norms: article 52*bis*[37] stipulates the general rule and article 8*bis*[38] identifies specific types

---

32 See e.g. E. López Herrera, *Los Daños Punitivos*, Buenos Aires, Abeledo Perrot, 2008; A.D. Chamatropulos, *Los Daños Punitivos en la Argentina*, Buenos Aires, Errepar, 2009.

33 Articles 8*bis* and 52*bis*, Law N° 24.240 (text according to Law N° 26.361, B.O. 7/4/2008).

34 CcivCom. 6 Nom. (Córdoba), *Raspanti, Sebastián c. AMX Argentina S.A.* (26/Mar/2015).

35 Article 1708, Civil Code of Argentina (2015).

36 Articles 1714 and 1715 of the Project of Reform of Argentinean Civil Code (2014).

37 The general basic rule is expressed in article 52*bis*: "*Punitive Damages. To the provider that does not comply with its legal or contractual obligations vis-à-vis the consumer, at the request of the injured party, the judge may apply a civil fine in favour of the consumer, which will be graduated according to the seriousness of the conduct and other circumstances of the case, regardless of other compensation that corresponds to the consumer.*"

38 Article 8*bis* states that providers' behaviour revealing undignified or inequitable treatment or that places consumers in embarrassing, humiliating or intimidating situations, may be subject to the imposition of

of abusive conducts susceptible to the imposition of punitive damages. The overall regulation establishes three dimensions for punishment in consumer law: (i) legal requirements (the circumstances under which can punitive damages be imposed); (ii) factors relevant for the amount of the award (guidelines for its determination and maximum amounts); and (iii) implementation issues (two in particular that relate to legal standing and who receives the award). As regards (i), currently overwhelming consensus follows a holistic interpretation of the Consumer Protection Statute that qualifies the reprehensibility of the provider's conduct as the grounds for punitive damages.[39] Regarding the amount of the punitive award (ii), the seriousness of the conduct displayed by the defendant is the primary consideration, and it is capped at five million Argentinean pesos.[40] This legal cap has been heavily criticised for disregarding the pervasive and severe inflationary feature of the Argentinean currency. To overcome it, a draft proposal to update the legal cap to account for inflation without constant legislative intervention is currently under discussion.[41] The most well-known objection to legal caps is that they sometimes impede the award from performing the double function of punishment and deterrence. In those particular cases, legal systems could solve the dilemma by issuing guidelines on quantification that ensure the punitive award is proportionate to the reprehensibility of the defendant's conduct without imposing a predefined legal limit. Finally, as regards implementation issues (iii), the legal standing to sue for punitive damages is exclusively given to affected consumers who are also the sole recipients of the punitive award.[42]

After almost a decade of punitive damages awards, the practice remains incipient in Argentina. The awards are in general modest. Only recently have we seen instances of higher amounts (although still far below the legal limit).[43] At the same time, a recent proposal that would instigate a comprehensive reform of the Consumer Protection Statute, including the modification of the current regulation of punitive damages, is under

---

punitive damages, without prejudice to the compensation that corresponds to the consumer.

39 On the development of this discussion in Argentina, see F.G. Santarelli & A.D. Chamatropulos (Eds.), *Comentarios al Anteproyecto de Ley de Defensa del Consumidor: Homenaje a Rubén S. Stiglitz*, Buenos Aires, La Ley, 2019.

40 Taking into account the exchange rate as of 1 August 2022, the Argentinean peso is equivalent to 0,0075 USD, so the limit of punitive damages under the Argentinean Consumer Protection Law is equivalent to USD 37.700. Note that the legal cap was recently reformed as follows: "*The amount of the fine cannot be more than [2.100 basic baskets]*" (article 119, Law Nº 27.701 B.O. 1/12/2022). This means that the limit of punitive damages as of 1 December 2022 is equivalent to USD 1.837.000.

41 Project of Reform of the Consumer Protection Law (2018) articles 118 and 157, inc. 2.: "*The amount of the fine cannot be more than [5.000 minimum wages], or ten times the total amount of the profit obtained by the supplier as a result of the illicit act, if the latter is greater*".

42 Article 52*bis*, Law Nº 26.361.

43 See, for instance, Cámara Primera de Apelación en lo Civil y Comercial Departamental, Sala II, *Castelli, María Cecilia vs. Banco Galicia y Buenos Aires S.A.*

discussion.[44] If implemented, it would introduce innovations in the practice of the adjudication of punitive damages in Argentina that would certainly lead to new questions and further developments in the years to come.

3.2 *Mexico: The Mayan Palace Case*

Mexico has followed quite a different path. Punitive damages were directly introduced by the Supreme Court of Justice, not by the Mexican legislature.[45] This happened in 2014, when the Supreme Court of Mexico imposed punitive damages in its judgment on a wrongful death case (referred to as "The Mayan Palace Case"). As part of the compensation that may be awarded to victims of serious torts, the Court ordered the defendant to pay $30.000.000 Mexican pesos in punitive damages.[46] However, unlike Argentina where punitive damages have been discussed for some time, the Mexican scholarly debate over the (un)desirability of punitive damages and, more broadly, the place of punishment in private law, was mostly absent prior to 2014. Tort litigation itself, historically considered unattractive by Mexican jurists, is a very recent phenomenon in Mexico and, as a consequence, the law of torts has only drawn significant scholarly attention in the last decade or two.[47]

---

44 For instance, the main aspect of the proposed reform that could impact the current practice of awarding punitive damages in Argentina is that it confers judges two main prerogatives: (i) to impose punitive damages ex officio (article 118, inc. 1); and (ii) to decide in a reasoned judgment the recipient of the punitive award (article 118, inc. 3).

45 Amparo Directo 30/2013, Primera Sala, Suprema Corte de Justicia de la Nación, 26/02/2014 (Mexico). Briefly, the facts of the case were the following: the victim and his friends were kayaking in the Mayan Palace Resort's artificial lake, which was available for all hotel guests, when the victim's kayak turned over. Unfortunately, an underwater water pump that had not received maintenance for many years had caused the artificial lake to become electrified. Twenty minutes passed before Resort employees shut down the electricity to allow for the victim to be rescued from the pool. The victim had died by then. Regarding the analysis of the defendant's behaviour, the Court found that the conduct was highly reprehensible, not just towards the victim, but also in regard to the other guests staying at the Resort since it had also placed them at risk of serious injury. The Court also considered that the Resort did not have any sort of protocols in place to address emergency situations (such as the one in which a guest loses his life) as evidenced by the twenty minutes it took for the staff to shut the electricity down, and the need to request first-aid from other guests as no qualified hotel employees were on hand. The Court further noted that another twenty minutes passed after the victim had been removed from the artificial lake before he was taken to the Resort's infirmary.

46 Amparo Directo 30/2013, p. 124. Taking into account the exchange rate as of 1 August 2022, the Mexican peso is equivalent to 0,049 USD, so the amount of the punitive award ordered by the Supreme Court of Mexico is equivalent to USD 1.475.000.

47 See e.g. E. Muñoz & R. Vázquez Cabello, *El Renacimiento del Derecho de Daños en México: Un Análisis Comparativo*, México, Tirant lo Blanch, 2019; C. De la Rosa Xochitiotzi (Ed.), *Derecho de Daños: Ideas para Iniciar el diálogo*, México, Suprema Corte de Justicia de la Nación, 2022.

It was in this context that the Mexican Supreme Court introduced punitive damages as the "punitive aspect (or facet)" for non-pecuniary awards, justifying them under the constitutional principle of "fair (or just) reparation".[48] A majority of the Ministers of the Mexican Supreme Court agreed that the principle of "fair (or just) reparation" requires compensation that satisfies the victim's requirement of justice, and on that basis introduced a punitive component into the traditionally compensatory non-pecuniary award in order to respond to the reprehensibility of the defendant's conduct.[49] This concept of "fair reparation" derives from a broad interpretation of article 63.1 of the American Convention on Human Rights, which states that, in cases involving the violation of a right or freedom protected by the Convention, the injured party must be restored to full enjoyment of the violated right or freedom. It also states that, if appropriate, "fair reparation" should be paid to the injured party.[50] This interpretation is reinforced by the constitutional rank that, according to articles 1 and 133 of the Mexican Constitution, the Constitution itself and international treaties concerning human rights enjoy. In other words, the legal authority and rank of the American Convention on Human Rights is on a par with the Mexican Constitution. Granted, the Mexican Supreme Court's interpretation that punishment in tort law is justified under the principle of "fair reparation" is contested.[51] One relevant question is whether courts in civil law legal systems can legitimately introduce punishment in private law without any prior legal provision establishing such punitive elements.[52]

In any case, the main point is that the judgment granted non-pecuniary awards of a mixed nature: compensatory and punitive. By contrast, the discussion in Argentina over mixed-natured (punitive and compensatory) non-pecuniary awards only came up at the very beginning of the debate on whether to introduce punitive damages, and was quickly dismissed by overwhelming consensus. The consensus held that non-pecuniary awards were compensatory in nature (and, as such, responsive to the impact of the wrongdoing on the individual plaintiff) while punitive damages were inherently punitive (and, as such,

48 Amparo Directo 30/2013, pp. 126-31.

49 Amparo Directo 30/2013, pp. 121-22.

50 Amparo Directo 30/2013, pp. 120-24.

51 On the impact of decisions of constitutional courts on tort law (or what is usually referred in Latin America as "the constitutionalization of private law") in Chile and Mexico, see C. Pizarro Wilson, 'Notas sobre la Intervención de los Tribunales Constitucionales en la Construcción del Derecho de Daños', in C. De la Rosa Xochitiotzi (Ed.), *Derecho de Daños: Ideas para Iniciar el Diálogo*, México, Suprema Corte de Justicia de la Nación, 2022, pp. 98-126.

52 Amparo Directo en Revision 5612/2017, pp. 24-25 (arguing that, due to the sanctioning nature of punitive damages, they require previous legislative recognition to be imposed as such: regulation determining the scope of their availability, the legal requirements for its application, the standards to prevent excessive punishment, etc.).

responsive to the level of reprehensibility of the defendant's conduct). As a consequence, both types of awards were to be treated as essentially distinct heads of damages.[53]

A tentative explanation for the particular path that Mexico followed would focus on the explicit and transparent acknowledgment of the Supreme Court regarding the global recourse in civil law systems to non-pecuniary awards as a covert means to punish reprehensible defendants.[54] The underlying dilemma for the Court was whether continuing to impose punishment covertly under the label of compensatory damages was to be preferred over the explicit recognition of the punitive motive and, by consequence, a separate treatment with corresponding substantive and procedural safeguards that any given legal system ought to require before imposing punishment.

Another possible reading would regard maintaining punishment parasitically within classic compensatory damages (such as non-pecuniary awards), rather than introducing them as an autonomous head of damages, as less disruptive of the underlying principles of Mexican tort law. Under this reading, the Supreme Court could justify (even if contested) interpreting punitive awards under the umbrella of the constitutional principle of "fair reparation". The Supreme Court might have been following this line of thinking when it proposed a teleological interpretation of the law (in particular, of article 1916 of the Civil Code of the Federal District of Mexico, which regulates non-pecuniary damages), concluding that reparation is not limited to compensation but also may call for sanctioning the wrongdoer.[55] Either way, one important aspect of the judgment is that it signals the significance of distinguishing and rendering transparent the part of the award that the defendant is ordered to pay to compensate for the harm caused to the victim and the part imposed as a sanction for reprehensible conduct towards the victim. Without the explicit distinction between the two, damages awards in cases of reprehensible behaviour could be treated merely as a "price" to be paid for reprehensible conduct, one which fails to convey the moral condemnation of the serious behaviour in particular.[56]

---

53 On this point, see D. Pizarro, 'Daños Punitivos', in A. Kemelmajer de Carlucci & C. Parellada (Eds.), *Derecho de Daños: Libro Homenaje al Profesor Félix Trigo Represas*, Vol. II, Buenos Aires, La Rocca, 1993, p. 287.

54 For an overview of this phenomenon in civil law jurisdictions, see M.G. Martínez Alles, 'Punitive Damages: Reorienting the Debate in Civil Law Systems', *Journal of European Tort Law*, Vol. 10, No. 1, 2019, pp. 63-81.

55 Amparo Directo 30/2013, p. 90.

56 I have offered reasons for distinguishing punishment from deterrence and punishment from compensation in M.G. Martínez Alles, 'La Dimensión Sancionadora del Derecho de Daños: Los Daños Punitivos', in D.M. Papayannis (Ed.), *Manual de Daños Extracontractuales*, México, Suprema Corte de Justicia de la Nación, 2022; and M.G. Martínez Alles, 'Tort Remedies as Meaningful Responses to Wrongdoing', in P. Miller & J. Oberdiek (Eds.), *Civil Wrongs and Justice in Private Law*, Oxford, Oxford University Press, 2020, pp. 231-252.

As no Mexican legal provision regulates punitive damages, the institution is mainly evolving through case law,[57] which, only recently, has been complemented by the work of tort law scholars.[58] It is thus difficult to predict the exact direction punitive damages will take in Mexico.[59] Up until now, for example, the Supreme Court has repeatedly insisted that punitive damages cannot be imposed on the state.[60] Yet uncertainty over many other aspects of practical implementation persists: (i) the relative autonomy of punitive awards from non-pecuniary awards and (ii) the lack of clear guidelines on the required level of reprehensibility of the defendant's conduct and on the relevant elements to take into account when determining the amount of the punitive award.

Regarding the distance that separates punitive awards from non-pecuniary awards (i), since punitive awards were introduced into the Mexican legal system as a subset or derivative of non-pecuniary damages this could make them dependent on compensatory awards (that is, they might only be available when non-pecuniary awards have been recognized and adjudicated). Moreover, two categories of non-pecuniary awards theoretically now coexist in Mexican tort law: pure compensatory non-pecuniary damages in cases of negligent behaviour, and mixed (compensatory and punitive) non-pecuniary damages in cases involving reprehensible behaviour.[61] One main objection to maintaining this coexistence could be that punitive damages would still be adjudicated under the rubric of non-pecuniary damages, so, even in cases where they are conceptually separated from compensatory facets of non-pecuniary awards and given differentiated treatment, they will only be available when grounds are found for non-pecuniary damages. In other words, punitive damages would not be available in tortious situations that involve particularly reprehensible conducts deserving of sanction but in which only pecuniary damages are manifested or where, for some reason, the claim for non-pecuniary damages is not granted. In short, linking the punitive claim to the compensatory claim for non-pecuniary damages not only dilutes the conceptual distinction between punishment and compensation, it also limits the scope of application of punitive damages, undercutting its primary sanctioning function.[62]

---

57 For a compilation of the relevant case law, see C. De la Rosa Xochitiotzi & V.F. Márquez Rojas, *Derecho de Daños: Responsabilidad Extracontractual*, México, Suprema Corte de Justicia de la Nación, 2020.

58 See e.g. E. Muñoz & R. Vázquez Cabello, 'Elementos, Umbral y Quantum de los Daños Punitivos en el Derecho Mexicano', in C. De la Rosa Xochitiotzi (Ed.), *Derecho de Daños: Ideas para Iniciar el Diálogo*, México, Suprema Corte de Justicia de la Nación, 2021, pp. 1-64.

59 For instance, see Amparo en Revisión 1133/2019 (in which the Supreme Court – featuring a different composition – introduces uncertainty as to whether punitive damages are really justified under the constitutional principle of fair (or just) compensation).

60 Amparo Directo 50/2015, Primera Sala, Suprema Corte de Justicia de la Nación; Amparo en Revision 1133/2019, pp. 1114-1116.

61 See generally Amparo Directo en Revisión 358/2022.

62 See generally Amparo en Revisión 1133/2019 (pointing out the significance of the distinction between punishment and compensation).

Furthermore, the lack of clear guidelines on the required level of reprehensibility of the defendant's conduct and on the relevant elements to be taken into consideration when setting the amount of the punitive award (ii) is problematic. The Mexican Supreme Court has broadly considered as relevant factors the wealth of the defendant, the severity of the injury and the reprehensibility of the defendant's behaviour. However, it has not yet offered more concrete guidelines on quantification, which leaves open the critical question of how much punishment would be proportionate.[63] As is easily observed, the current status of punitive damages in Mexico is fluid, dynamic and, to some extent, uncertain.

4 The scope of the "public policy exception": open questions

The classic "public policy exception" raised in many civil law systems to straightforwardly reject domestic enforcement of foreign punitive judgments has usually followed the line that domestic tort law provides for extra-contractual compensation but is not meant to punish the defendant, as state-sanctioned punishment clearly pertains to criminal rather than private law. However, as described above, the introduction in Argentina and Mexico of punitive damages in their domestic private law systems not only complicates the categorical use of the public policy exception, but also invites us to think about the potential scope of the exception in a much more sophisticated manner. Indeed, the longstanding attitude of outright rejection no longer appears reasonable in a context in which the place of punishment is explicitly recognised in domestic private law.[64] On the other hand, just because punitive damages have been domestically recognised does not necessarily mean that the enforcement of foreign punitive judgments should be straightforwardly executed.[65] For instance, in terms of substance, Argentina could object to the enforcement of foreign punitive judgments awarded in disputes that are unrelated to provider-consumer relationships. The attempt to introduce punitive damages more broadly in the recent Argentinean Civil Code was, after all, unsuccessful. Similarly, Mexico could object to the enforcement of foreign punitive judgments that are not predicated on the award of non-pecuniary damages (i.e. punitive awards imposed as an independent

63 Amparo Directo 30/2013, pp. 118, 124.

64 On this point, see C. Vanleenhove, *Punitive Damages in Private International Law: Lessons for the European Union*, Antwerp-Cambridge-Portland, Intersentia, 2016, pp. 158-59 (arguing that punitive-like remedies in the private law of a given legal system makes it a legal hypocrisy to declare punitive damages directly and categorically unenforceable using the shield of the public policy exception).

65 An illustrative example are those common law jurisdictions, such as the United States and the United Kingdom (except for Scotland), where punitive damages are firmly recognized as such since the very beginning but nonetheless differ significantly in the substantive scope of their availability. See M.G. Martínez Alles, 'La Dimensión Sancionadora del Derecho de Daños. Los Daños Punitivos', in D.M. Papayannis (Ed.), *Manual de Derecho de Daños Extracontractuales*, Mexico, Suprema Corte de Justica de la Nación-Marcial Pons, 2022, pp. 633-635.

head of damages), assuming the current legal reasoning of the Supreme Court is eventually consolidated (which remains uncertain). Moreover, according to the Hague Choice of Court Convention (which is in force, inter alia, in Mexico and the European Union, and which the United States has signed but not yet ratified), Mexico is to enforce the "compensatory" aspect of foreign punitive awards (typically those parts of the punitive award that are meant to cover legal costs such as American contingency fees). Yet it may reject the recognition and enforcement of the "extra-compensatory" aspect (i.e. the punitive element) of the foreign punitive award.[66] As this provision was signed almost a decade before punitive damages were explicitly introduced in Mexico, it is unclear whether the recognition of punishment as one of the functions of tort law will affect the prerogative granted by the treaty to reject the enforcement of the "punishment aspect" of the foreign punitive award from now on.[67] Admittedly, these are speculations that concern substantive understandings that certainly depend on (or are influenced by) the particular trajectory that the practice of punitive damages follows in those countries in the years to come. Nonetheless, they are all relevant aspects to consider when thinking about the potential scope that the public policy exception could take in those jurisdictions.

The main focus of the potential content of the public policy exception will probably centre on the analysis of whether the amount of the foreign punitive award is considered proportionate or excessive. In the case of Argentina, as mentioned above, the Consumer Protection Statute currently imposes a legal cap (a maximum amount of $5.000.000 Argentinean pesos), because punitive damages are understood as a penalty and, as such, they should be limited by the legislator.[68] The question is therefore whether a foreign punitive award exceeding this limited amount (which probably means most judgments, considering the devaluation of the Argentinean peso at current exchange rates) would be considered directly unenforceable in Argentina, or whether partial recognition of the foreign punitive award up to the legal limit would be allowed.[69] One possible development

66 Article 11 of the Hague Choice of Court Convention (2005): "*Damages: (1) Recognition or enforcement of a judgment may be refused if, and to the extent that, the judgment awards damages, including exemplary or punitive damages, that do not compensate a party for actual loss or harm suffered. (2) The court addressed shall take into account whether and to what extent the damages awarded by the court of origin serve to cover costs and expenses relating to the proceedings.*"

67 Note that the 2019 Hague Judgments Convention on the Recognition and Enforcement of Foreign Judgments in Civil and Commercial Matter has a similar provision regarding punitive awards – perhaps the opportunity to reconsider this issue may provide guidance for the stance towards enforcement of foreign punitive awards to be taken in Mexico. See generally M. Pertegás Sender & P. Beaumont, 'Institutional and Framework Issues – Hague Conference on Private International Law', in P. Beaumont & J. Holliday (Eds.), *A Guide to Global Private International Law*, Oxford, Hart Publishing, 2022, pp. 91-103.

68 Evidence of such a rationale for introducing a cap on punitive awards is found in the legislative reports which served as basis for the introduction of punitive damages in the Consumer Protection Statute in 2008.

69 Note that the question whether revising the amount of the punitive award through an excessiveness analysis is a "revision on the merits", that is in principle not permissible by private international law, is an important but altogether different question that exceeds the reach of this chapter. Besides, private international law

that could affect the excessiveness test is the recent proposal being discussed in Argentina, referred to earlier, to change the method of determining the legal maximum of punitive awards. Concretely, the projected reform proposes the introduction of two alternative mechanisms: (i) an amount equal to 5000 times the national minimum monthly salary;[70] or (ii) ten times the profit obtained by the supplier as a result of the wrongful act, whichever is greater.[71] It is not clear whether the proposal will be approved; however, if successful, it will certainly raise new questions about the proper proportional punishment since the legal limit itself says little about the content of the principle of "sanction proportionality" in any particular case.

In the case of Mexico, since there is no legislative limit and the Supreme Court has not yet offered concrete guidelines for quantification, discerning the proportionate level of punishment is even more challenging. To clarify, the Mexican Supreme Court found that the wealth of the defendant, together with the severity of the injury and the reprehensibility of the defendant's behaviour, are to be considered as relevant criteria to determine the proper amount of the punitive award, which is certainly a good starting point. However, these factors do not in themselves provide much guidance regarding the appropriate punitive award in particular circumstances. Moreover, regarding the imposition of caps[72] or ratios, the Supreme Court of Mexico incidentally alluded to the 9:1 ratio (of punitive damages to compensatory damages) established by the United States Supreme Court in *State Farm Mutual Automobile Insurance v. Campbell*, qualifying it as hardly satisfying the due process standards in the United States. To clarify, the allusion is just an *obiter dictum* reference to the American case law without binding force in Mexico,[73] however the main function of sanctioning behaviour requires that the amount of the punitive award be proportional to the seriousness of the conduct displayed by the defendant. As a consequence, the amount of punitive damages should not necessarily be a function of the amount of compensatory damages. On the contrary, it should be understood that the

---

scholars are divided on this particular issue. For an account of this discussion, see C. Vanleenhove, 'A Normative Framework for the Enforcement of U.S. Punitive Damages in the European Union: Transforming the Traditional "¡No pasarán!"', *Vermont Law Review*, Vol. 41, 2016, pp. 398-401 (arguing that a reduction of the punitive award of the kind described in the text – i.e. following a 1:1 ratio punitive-to-compensatory damages – would not amount to a review of the judgment as to its merits since the requested court would neither be "*giving its opinion about the merits of the foreign case*", nor "*questioning whether the foreign decision was correct in fact and/or in law*".)

70 For an approximation, 5000 minimum wages in Argentina as of 1 August 2022 was equivalent to USD 1.715.000.

71 Project of Reform of the Consumer Protection Law (2018), article 118.

72 It is important to note that over the past few years, the Mexican Supreme Court and the Federal Judiciary had been removing the caps on compensation for non-pecuniary awards, which in many Mexican states are still limited to one-third of pecuniary damages. The Federal Judiciary has consistently ruled that the cap is unconstitutional because it does not allow for "*fair (or just) compensation*".

73 Amparo Directo 30/2013, pp. 13-14, notes 5-7 (concurrent opinion, Justice José Ramón Cossío Díaz).

appropriate amount of punitive damages will necessarily depend on the particular characteristics of the defendant's conduct (the level of indifference or disregard for the rights of others, intentionality, gross negligence, etc.). The greater the reprehensibility of the defendant's conduct, the greater the punitive award.

In addition to the reprehensibility of the defendant's conduct and the seriousness of the offense, another parameter that the judges considered in assessing the amount of the punitive award is the defendant's wealth (i.e. her ability to pay) to ensure that the award represents a genuine sanction and effectively deters her from similar behaviour in the future.[74] In this line of reasoning, a ratio in relation to compensatory damages (e.g., "the amount of punitive damages cannot be more than 10 times the compensatory award" or any other ratio that is proposed) would establish a pragmatic arbitrary line that not only dilutes the conceptual distinction between punishment and compensation but also comes up short in terms of the criteria for a genuinely proportionate sanction in any particular case. As the methodological procedure for the assessment of punitive awards slowly develops in Mexico, the excessiveness test for the domestic enforcement of foreign punitive awards could thus take many potential different forms as the practice of punitive damage awards evolves in the years to come.

Private international law scholars have suggested, mainly through references to European jurisdictions where punitive damages have not yet been explicitly recognised but are covertly present in legal institutions that either resemble punitive damages or pursue punitive aims, the following guidelines: a 1:1 ratio of punitive to compensatory awards as a starting point for the European courts' proportionality test, and a 9:1 ratio of punitive to compensatory awards as the upper limit for the former (particularly in the case of punitive damage awards from United States courts), thus allowing some flexibility to account for the particular circumstances of the case at hand and the nature of the interests involved.[75] It is unclear, however, whether such guidelines would be endorsed in countries like Mexico and Argentina that have instituted their own domestic practice of awarding punitive damages and, consequently, the procedure for determining the appropriate punishment in their jurisdictions, which might well differ from the foreign country's idea of what comprises proportional sanctions. Furthermore, as already mentioned, the emphasis on the relative relationship between punitive and compensatory awards, even if pragmatic, is misguiding since the question of sanction proportionality of the punitive award is relative to the seriousness of the defendant's behaviour, not to the harm caused to the victim (i.e. compensatory damages). Ultimately, it will be up to each jurisdiction to

74 See generally Amparo Directo 30/2013.

75 For more on this proposal, see C. Vanleenhove, 'A Normative Framework for the Enforcement of U.S. Punitive Damages in the European Union: Transforming the Traditional "¡No pasarán!"', *Vermont Law Review*, Vol. 41, 2016, pp. 377-401.

offer their own understanding of the principle of sanction proportionality that will guide their treatment of the quest for enforcement.

5 Conclusion

The current status of punitive damages in Latin America, particularly in Argentina and Mexico, is tending towards acceptance and incorporation, yet remains highly fluid and dynamic. Because of the unresolved uncertainties regarding implementation and inherent tensions between the punitive institution and other established elements of those countries' legal systems, it could follow any of various directions and take different forms in the years to come. It seems likely, however, that the developments in Mexico and Argentina will ultimately influence the attitude towards recognition and enforcement of foreign punitive awards in Latin America more generally and, in particular, how the scope of the public policy exception will be refined.

Recognition and enforcement of foreign punitive damages decisions in Brazil

*Erico Bomfim de Carvalho**

1 Introduction

There is a vibrant international debate, particularly in civil law countries, regarding the compatibility of foreign punitive damages with public policy. While some EU Member States have refused to enforce punitive damages decisions based on the public policy exception, others have established that those decisions would only be contrary to public policy if the punitive damages awarded are deemed excessive or disproportionate.[1]

As a civil law jurisdiction, compensatory damages are usually the sole remedy available to Brazilian domestic claimants seeking to redress an injury or harm suffered. For that reason, scholars and commentators have always discussed whether the recognition or enforcement of a foreign judgment awarding exemplary or punitive damages - that do not compensate a party for actual loss or harm suffered and are unavailable under Brazilian law - would be compatible with public policy. However, in *Apotex v. Kalinka*, a groundbreaking decision published on 16 May 2022, the Brazilian Superior Court of Justice (*Superior Tribunal de Justiça - STJ*) ruled, for the very first time, that the public policy exception does not proscribe the recognition or enforcement of a foreign punitive damages decision.[2]

Given the STJ's exclusive authority to entertain all recognition requests,[3] this chapter briefly analyses the Court's historical approach to public policy and punitive damages in the context of recognition proceedings, with a particular emphasis on the *Apotex v. Kalinka* decision.

---

* Partner of Advocacia Velloso in Brasília (Brazil). Erico advises and represents clients in complex commercial disputes and private international law matters before the Brazilian Superior Court of Justice and the Brazilian Supreme Court. He holds an LL.M. from Columbia Law School (2016), where he was a Harlan Fiske Stone Scholar, a student editor of the American Review of International Arbitration - ARIA, and a recipient of the Parker School Certificate for Achievement in Foreign and Comparative Law (erico@velloso.adv.br).

1 See C. Vanleenhove, 'A normative framework for the enforcement of U.S. punitive damages in the European Union: transforming the traditional '¡No Pasarán!'', *Vermont Law Review*, Vol. 41, No. 2, 2016, pp. 347-403, available at: https://papers.ssrn.com/sol3/papers.cfm?abstract_id=2915209 (accessed on 12 October 2022).

2 *Apotex v. Kalinka*, STJ HDE 586/CA, Min. Raul Araújo, DJe 16/05/2022.

3 Constituição Federal de 1988, article 105, I, "i".

2 RECOGNITION AND ENFORCEMENT OF FOREIGN DECISIONS IN BRAZIL

2.1 General rules

The STJ, the higher non-constitutional Court in Brazil, has jurisdiction over all applications for recognition of a foreign decision. This is an essential and commendable feature of the Brazilian legal system. Concentrating the requests in a single high court has led to a more consistent interpretation of the legal requirements for recognition and enhanced legal certainty.[4]

At the outset, a distinction must be drawn between the "recognition" of a foreign decision and its "enforcement". While the recognition makes the decision valid and binding upon the parties,[5] the enforcement corresponds to a forced execution of the decision.[6] That distinction is necessary, given that in Brazil recognition and enforcement proceedings are inherently separated. In fact, the STJ is only responsible for deciding on the requests for recognition of a foreign decision (*homologação de decisão estrangeira*), i.e. to give legal force and effect to a foreign decision in Brazil. If, and only if, recognition is granted, the prevailing party may seek the enforcement of that decision by filing another request (*cumprimento de sentença*) before a federal court. In other words, a foreign decision - as well as a non-judicial decision with jurisdictional nature - only becomes enforceable in Brazil after being subjected to recognition proceedings before the STJ. That is what happened in the *Apotex v. Kalinka* case, further examined below in section 3. Apotex obtained the recognition of the decision before the STJ and will now have to file an enforcement action before a competent federal court.[7]

The following requirements are indispensable for recognition purposes: (i) a competent authority issued the foreign decision; (ii) the foreign decision has been preceded by adequate service of process, even if the Court finds that the party defaulted; (iii) the foreign decision is effective in the country where it was rendered; (iv) the foreign decision does not violate res judicata; (v) the foreign decision is accompanied by an official translation, unless expressly exempted by a treaty; and (vi) the foreign decision is not manifestly incompatible with public policy.[8] A foreign decision will also not be recognised

4 B.W. Rechsteiner, *Direito Internacional Privado: teoria e prática*, São Paulo, Saraiva Educação, 20th ed., 2019, p. 319.

5 N. Blackaby, *Redfern and Hunter on International Arbitration*, Oxford/New York, Oxford University Press, 6th ed., 2015, p. 611.

6 E. Gaillard & G.A. Bermann (eds.), *UNCITRAL Secretariat Guide on the Convention on the Recognition and Enforcement of Foreign Arbitral Awards*, Leiden/London, Brill Nijhoff, 2017, pp. 13-14.

7 Most certainly, the enforcement action will be filed in a Federal Court in São Paulo, the State where Kalinka took up residence.

8 *Código de Processo Civil* [Brazilian Code of Civil Procedure], article 963.

in Brazil if offensive to national sovereignty and good morals. Since 2014, the STJ Bylaws have been amended to include the violation of human dignity as a new ground for denying the recognition of a foreign decision.[9] However, the scattered references to national sovereignty, good morals, and human dignity are unnecessary and troublesome, as all those requirements unequivocally fall under the international public policy umbrella.

Those are the main requirements for processing recognition requests in Brazil, but there are also specific requirements detailed in multilateral treaties and conventions. For example, the requirements for recognition and enforcement of foreign arbitral awards are outlined in the Brazilian Arbitration Act[10] and the New York Convention on the Recognition and Enforcement of Foreign Arbitral Awards (NY Convention), ratified in 2002.[11]

Brazil has long adopted the Italian system of *giudizio di delibazione*, which limits the scope of recognition requests to its formal requirements.[12] That does not mean the judicial inquiry is restricted to a simple administrative review of sworn translations and consular seals. Assigning the highest federal court in Brazil with such a clerical task would be meaningless. Although a review of the merits of the underlying dispute is not possible, the STJ must examine if the formal requirements are met and, more importantly, ensure that the foreign decision is not offensive to substantive and procedural public policy.[13]

2.2 *Public policy exception*

Article 17 of the LINDB[14] establishes the public policy exception. It states that laws, acts, and court decisions from other countries, as well as any statements of intent, shall not be effective in Brazil if they offend national sovereignty (*soberania nacional*), public policy (*ordem pública*), and good morals (*bons costumes*). A more difficult task is to define public policy, a somewhat fluid concept with evolving interpretations over time.[15] It can be said,

---

9 According to article 216-F of the STJ Bylaws (*Regimento Interno do STJ*), a foreign judgment that violates national sovereignty, human dignity or public policy will not be recognised.

10 Lei Ordinária 9,307/1996.

11 The STJ rarely applies the NY Convention. The court prioritises the grounds for denying the recognition of foreign arbitral awards set forth in the Brazilian Arbitration Act.

12 J. Dolinger, 'Brazilian Confirmation of Foreign Judgments', *The International Lawyer*, Vol. 19, No. 3, 1985, p. 854.

13 The Superior Court of Justices established that a review of the merits of the foreign decision is not possible, except when there is an infringement of national sovereignty, public policy, or good morals. In these cases, the Court "*has broad discretion to review the foreign decision before recognizing its effectiveness in the national territory*". *Abengoa v. Ometto*, STJ SEC 9412/US, DJe 30/05/2017.

14 *Decreto-Lei 4,657/1942, Lei de Introdução às Normas de Direito Brasileiro* [LINDB] [Law of Introduction to the Norms of Brazilian Law].

15 B.W. Rechsteiner, *Direito Internacional Privado: teoria e prática*, São Paulo, Saraiva Educação, 20th ed., 2019, p. 203.

however, that public policy is formed by the "most fundamental principles of Justice"[16] or the "basic moral values"[17] of a nation. Anything considered shocking to the average person's mentality at a given time and place should be considered offensive to that nation's public policy.[18] For example, the Brazilian Supreme Court (*Supremo Tribunal Federal – STF*)[19] has displayed a significant shift in its approach to recognising foreign divorce judgments.[20] At one point, the recognition of a foreign divorce judgment was considered offensive to public policy if both spouses were Brazilians. If one of the spouses was a foreign person, the recognition could be granted, but the foreigner could not acquire a new marriage in Brazil. That was the mindset at the time. Only after 1977, when divorce became legal in Brazil, the public policy exception ceased to be used as an obstacle to deny the recognition of foreign divorce judgments.

Brazilian commentators agree that the public policy exception must be narrowly construed and that a recognition request should only be denied when there is a "severe incompatibility" between the foreign decision and Brazil's most basic notions of morality and justice.[21] In other words, the public policy offense must be flagrant and violate the Brazilian legal order's most fundamental and universal values.[22] It should not be used to deny the effectiveness of foreign decisions that are substantively or procedurally different from Brazilian law but only to avoid internalising decisions that are manifestly incongruent with the national legal system.[23] In that sense, article 960 of the Code of Civil Procedure requires the presence of a "manifest" violation – as opposed to a "simple" violation – to public policy for the STJ to deny the recognition of a foreign decision.

The STJ also interprets the public policy exception narrowly. It is rare for a recognition request to be denied on that basis. The *Abengoa v. Ometto* case is one of those exceptional cases where the recognition request of a foreign arbitral award was rejected on public

16 N. de Araújo, *Direito Internacional Privado: Teoria e Prática Brasileira*, São Paulo, Thomson Reuters, 9th ed., 2020, p. 93.

17 J. Dolinger & C. Tibúrcio, *Direito Internacional Privado*, Rio de Janeiro, Forense, 15th ed., 2020, p. 446.

18 *Ibid.*

19 The STF is the highest court in Brazil with the authority to interpret the Constitution. Its primary role is to ensure the constitutionality of laws and to resolve disputes related to constitutional matters. On the other hand, the STJ is the highest federal court for non-constitutional matters in Brazil. It is responsible for ensuring the uniform interpretation of federal laws nationwide. Eventually, if an STJ decision on a recognition case involves a constitutional matter, it may be subject to review by the STF through an extraordinary appeal ("*recurso extraordinário*"). However, the STF has never granted an extraordinary appeal on recognition cases.

20 Before 2004, the STF had exclusive authority to entertain all recognition requests.

21 B.W. Rechsteiner, *Direito Internacional Privado: teoria e prática*, São Paulo, Saraiva Educação, 20th ed., 2019, p. 205.

22 S. de Camargo, *Homologação de Sentenças Estrangeiras: Ordem Pública Processual e Jurisdições Anômalas*, São Paulo, Quartier Latin, 2019, p. 186.

23 J. Dolinger & C. Tibúrcio, *Direito Internacional Privado*, Rio de Janeiro, Forense, 15th ed., 2020, p. 461.

policy grounds due to the lack of impartiality of the presiding arbitrator.[24] It is noteworthy that when the recognition request was filed, an action to set aside the award had already been dismissed by the competent U.S. court at the seat of arbitration, due to a lack of evidence supporting the claim of bias on the part of the presiding arbitrator. Usually, the STJ would not re-examine the foreign award and would defer to the U.S. court's findings in the annulment action. However, in *Abengoa v. Ometto*, it was held that the STJ "*could not just turn a blind eye to the serious accusation of partiality*".

The STJ also held that the public policy analysis would not constitute a *révision au fond* of the foreign award because "*the impartiality of a judge is not a merits issue*". In the end, the STJ concluded that public policy barred the recognition request, given that the presiding arbitrator failed to disclose that the law firm in which he was a partner rendered legal services and received attorney fees from a company belonging to the same corporate group as one of the parties. That relationship gave rise to justifiable doubts about the presiding arbitrator's impartiality and was considered offensive to due process. The decision was 8-1 against the recognition of the foreign arbitral award.[25]

More recently, the STJ has also denied the recognition of two U.S. court decisions on public policy grounds.[26] The foreign decisions in question authorised Brazilian-born applicants who had taken residence in the United States to change their names. However, the STJ denied both recognition requests based on the argument that Brazilian law only permits adding or suppressing names and surnames in exceptional circumstances. As these extraordinary circumstances were absent, the STJ concluded that recognition would result in an "*evident offense to national sovereignty and public order*". From our perspective, the denial of both recognition requests was unjustified. A mere name change that is not offensive or unlawful could not represent a "manifest" offense to public policy or national sovereignty. Additionally, since the applicants in both cases were residents of the United States, the STJ decisions ignored the law of the jurisdiction with the closest connection to the parties and the implications the denial will have on their lives and self-identity.

There is another interesting matter on which the STJ still has not issued a final decision: whether a foreign judgment ordering the payment of a gambling debt would be entitled to

---

24 *Abengoa v. Ometto*, STJ SEC 9412/US, DJe 30/05/2017.

25 In his dissent, Justice Felix Fischer argued that the strictest notion of public policy as set forth in article V(2)(b) of the NY Convention should be adopted. He noted that the mere insinuation of partiality is not enough to deny recognition and enforcement of a foreign arbitral award. According to Justice Fischer, the partiality of an arbitrator/judge only amounts to a public policy violation when there are compelling indicia of partiality. Justice Fischer recognised that there are procedures in place, even under Brazilian Law, that allow courts to vacate an award when there is evident partiality or corruption. Ometto had followed those procedures and, nevertheless, was not able to prove to a U.S. Court the alleged partiality of the chair arbitrator. He also mentioned that the U.S. courts had refused to vacate the arbitral award and that their decisions, although not binding, must be considered as persuasive.

26 AgInt na HDE 6217/EX, Min. Maria Thereza de Assis Moura, DJe de 16/12/2022 and AgInt nos EDcl na HDE 4371/EX, Ministro Humberto Martins, Corte Especial, DJe de 15/10/2021.

recognition in Brazil or, conversely, whether it would be contrary to public policy. Brazil has strict laws regarding gambling. Only estate and federal lotteries and horse racing bets are currently regulated. Moreover, debts resulting from gambling or betting are not enforceable.[27] As a result, foreign gambling debts have been met with great resistance. At first, the STF rejected letters rogatories from U.S. courts requesting judicial assistance for summoning Brazilian nationals to defend themselves from a gambling debt collection.[28] In 2001, however, Justice Marco Aurélio adopted a more liberal approach.[29] He granted four exequaturs under the argument that the gambling contracts were valid according to the laws of the country in which they were entered. Additionally, refusing service of process would result in unjust enrichment of the gambling debtor.[30]

In 2008, the STJ also confirmed that allowing service of process of a person domiciled in Brazil to defend against a gambling debt claim filed in another country, where such actions are lawful, does not infringe public policy.[31] The concurring opinion authored by Justice José Delgado asserted that the STJ was only allowing for the debtor to be summoned in Brazil, "*a simple act of international cooperation*". Nevertheless, he cautioned that "*the recognition of a foreign gambling debt judgment would be offensive to public policy*".

Unfortunately, both the STF and the STJ never had the chance to address the issue of whether a foreign judgment ordering the payment of a gambling debt would be entitled to recognition in Brazil.[32] However, the STJ recently allowed the collection of a foreign gambling debt to be processed in Brazil. In *Wynn Las Vegas LLC v. Carlos Eduardo de Athayde Buono*,[33] the STJ ruled that the collection of gambling debts incurred by a Brazilian

27 Articles 814 to 817 of the Brazilian Civil Code.

28 For example STF CR 5332 AgR/EU, Min. Octavio Gallotti, DJ 02/06/1993; STF CR 7424/EU, Min. Celso de Mello, DJ 01/08/1996; and STF CR 7426/EU, Min. Sepúlveda Pertence, DJ 15/10/1996.

29 Before 2004, the STF had exclusive authority for hearing recognition and enforcement cases and letter rogatories. With the amendment of the Brazilian Constitution in that same year, the competence for hearing these cases was transferred from the Supreme Court to the Superior Court of Justice.

30 CR 9897/EU, Min. Marco Aurélio, DJ 04/02/2002; CR 9970/EU, Min. Marco Aurélio, DJ 01/04/2002; CR 10415/EU, Min. Marco Aurélio, DJ 03/02/2003; and CR 10416/EU, Min. Marco Aurélio, DJ 03/02/2003. Later, Justice Mauricio Corrêa reversed the last two decisions on internal appeal. He also denied a third exequatur on public policy grounds (CR 10853/EU, Min. Maurício Corrêa, DJ 05/11/2003).

31 STJ CR 3198/US, Min. Humberto Gomes de Barros, DJ 11/09/2008.

32 In *Trump Taj Mahal Associates v. Miguel Nicolau Duailibe Neto*, the STF was asked to recognise a foreign gambling debt judgment from the United States. During the judgment session, four of the 11 Supreme Court Justices voted to deny the recognition request on public policy grounds under the argument that gambling debts are not enforceable in Brazil. However, the judgment session was suspended after Justice Marco Aurélio asked more time to write his opinion. Justice Marco Aurélio never had the chance to present his vote as the parties settled before the new judgment session was scheduled and the case was dismissed with prejudice (*Trump Taj Mahal Associates v. Miguel Nicolau Duailibe Neto*, STF SEC 5440/EU, Min. Sepúlveda Pertence).

33 *Wynn Las Vegas LLC v. Carlos Eduardo de Athayde Buono*, STJ REsp 1628974/SP, Min. Ricardo Villas Bôas Cueva, DJ 25/08/2017.

citizen at a casino abroad is not offensive to public policy.[34] The case arose from a lawsuit filed in Brazil by Wynn Las Vegas seeking the payment of five "markers", a counter-check offered to the casino in exchange for gambling chips. According to the STJ's decision, "*those who visit a foreign country, enjoy its hospitality, and contract legally binding obligations cannot return to their home country expecting impunity*". That would amount to "*unjust enrichment*" and contravene public policy.

2.3 *Punitive damages*

Punitive damages are not available under Brazilian law.[35] Article 944 of the Civil Code establishes that the purpose of compensation is primarily to repair the harm suffered, meaning that indemnity should not exceed the extent of the damage suffered. That provision was largely influenced by the French law principle of full reparation (*réparation intégrale*), which emphasises the idea of reparation for the harm suffered by the victim, but nothing more (*tout le dommage, mais rien que le dommage*).[36] Article 944 of the Civil Code articulates a well-defined duty to compensate, and attempts to amend the provision have been unsuccessful.[37] Article 884 of the Civil Code also expressly prohibits "unjust enrichment". Therefore, given that the victim of an unlawful act only has the right to be compensated to the extent of the harm suffered, some commentators argue that a punitive damages award would unjustly enrich one of the parties at the expense of the other.[38]

Despite the unavailability of punitive damages in Brazil, some legal commentators have advocated their application in contractual relationships, particularly in cases of an intentional or grossly negligent breach of contract.[39] Others have proposed that "social damages" should at least have a punitive character as to promote social justice and prevent

---

34 In the past, procedural issues prevented the STJ from hearing the merits of two cases also involving the collection of gambling debts incurred by a Brazilian citizen at a casino abroad (*Baluma S.A. v. Vilson Ferreira da Costa*, STJ REsp 606171/CE, Min. Carlos Alberto Menezes Direito, DJ de 15/02/2005; and *Carnival Leisure Industries v. Wigberto Ferreira Tartuce*, STJ REsp 307104/DF, Min. Fernando Gonçalves, DJ de 23/08/2014).

35 The Superior Court of Justice has long established this position (for example STJ AgRg no Ag 850273/BA, Ministro Honildo Amaral de Mello Castro, DJe de 24/8/2010 and STJ REsp 1354536/SE, Ministro Luis Felipe Salomão, DJe de 05/05/2014).

36 R.F. Pinheiro & J.R.D.T. Trautwein. 'O princípio da reparação integral e a contraofensiva da culpabilidade: revisitando a cláusula de redução equitativa da indenização', *Revista de Informação Legislativa: RIL*, Vol. 57, 2020, p. 72.

37 In 2002, an Amendment Bill (PL 6.960/2002) was proposed in Congress with a provision stating that the compensation for moral damages should not only provide restitution to the injured party but also serve as a sufficient deterrent to the perpetrator. The amendment bill never became law and was archived.

38 D. Marinho Corrêa. *Danos Extrapatrimoniais: Interfaces entre Prevenção, Punição e Quantificação*, Londrina, Thoth, 2021, p. 137.

39 R. Marinangelo. *Indenização Punitiva e o Dano Extrapatrimonial na Disciplina dos Contratos*, Indaiatuba, Foco, 2021, Kindle Edition.

abusive behaviour.[40] Notwithstanding, there seems to be a growing recognition among commentators and courts in Brazil that the compensation for moral damages (*danos morais*)[41] should have a dual character: compensatory and punitive-pedagogical. While the compensatory aspect seeks to ensure that the victims are adequately compensated for their suffering, the punitive-pedagogical nature aims to punish the offenders for their wrongdoing and to dissuade others from engaging in similar behaviours.[42] In several instances, the STJ has also recognised this compensatory and punitive-pedagogical character of moral damages.[43]

Given the unavailability of punitive damages in Brazil, there were serious doubts as to whether the STJ would ever allow the recognition of a foreign punitive damages decision. Before *Apotex v. Kalinka*, the Court never had the chance to confront this issue.[44]

Aguinda v. Chevron was the first foreign punitive damages decision for which recognition was requested in Brazil. In *Aguinda v. Chevron*, the Ecuadorian judgment included an $8.6 billion punitive damages award against Chevron Corporation, equivalent to 100% of the compensatory damages already awarded.[45] In response, Chevron argued that the Ecuadorian judgment was offensive to public policy since punitive damages did not exist under Ecuadorian law and were unavailable in Brazil. Chevron also contended that the punitive damages were grossly disproportionate and that the award was offensive to due process. *Aguinda v. Chevron* was the perfect opportunity for the Court to decide on the enforceability of a foreign punitive damages decision. However, during the recognition proceedings in Brazil, the Ecuadorian National Court of Justice eliminated, on appeal, the punitive damages portion of the decision. That was only possible because the recognition request was filed in Brazil while an appeal was still pending before the Ecuadorian National Court of Justice. Therefore, before the STJ scheduled the judgment session to hear *Aguinda*

40 Y. Fisberg. *Dano Social: Reparação, Aspectos Processuais e Destinação*, São Paulo, Almedina Brasil, 2021, p. 12.

41 There is a clear distinction between objective and subjective moral damages in Brazil. While objective moral damages "*affect the moral status of a person in his community by hurting his reputation*", subjective moral damages are "*the subjective psychological or emotional harm suffered by a person, the pain and suffering that are essentially unknowable, but which demand unequivocal compensation*". See M. Reale, 'Moral Damages in Brazilian Law', *A Panorama of Brazilian Law*, 1992, p. 121, available at: https://www.e-publicacoes.uerj.br/index.php/pbl/article/view/34329/24247 (accessed 24 November 2022).

42 For example L.E. Fachin, 'Relação Obrigacional e Responsabilidade Solidária em Contrato Turnkey', *Revista dos Tribunais Online*, Vol. 1, 2012, pp. 137-156 and L.H.S. Franco, 'Notas sobre a Responsabilidade Civil na Atualidade e a sua Função Punitiva', *Revista dos Tribunais Online*, Vol. 951, 2015, pp. 105-138.

43 For example AgInt no AREsp 2149017/RJ, Ministro Francisco Falcão, DJe de 01/12/2022; REsp 1895272/DF, Ministro Marco Aurélio Bellizze, DJe de 29/4/2022; REsp 1645744/SP, Ministro Ricardo Villas Bôas Cueva, DJe de 13/6/2017; REsp 1405039/BA, Ministro Raul Araújo, DJe de 17/03/2015 and EDcl no AgRg no AREsp 540.533/PR, Ministro Moura Ribeiro, DJe 16/03/2015.

44 Y. Fisberg. *Dano Social: Reparação, Aspectos Processuais e Destinação*, São Paulo, Almedina Brasil, 2021, p. 220.

45 *Maria Aguinda Salazar et. al. v. Chevron Corporation*, STJ SEC 8542/EC, Ministro Luis Felipe Salomão, DJe 15/03/2018.

v. Chevron, the punitive damages portion of the Ecuadorian decision ceased to exist, and the issue became moot. In other words, the supervening mootness prevented the STJ from examining whether the $8.6 billion punitive damages award against Chevron could be recognised in Brazil.[46]

Abengoa v. Ometto is another remarkable case concerning the question whether damages not contemplated under Brazilian law would be entitled to recognition and enforcement.[47] The case originates from Ometto's sale of a Brazilian sugarcane and ethanol business to Abengoa. Following the completion of the transaction, Abengoa filed for two arbitrations with the ICC claiming, among other things, that Ometto misrepresented the crushing capacity of the acquired sugarcane mills. The arbitral tribunal, seated in New York, found Ometto liable. Given that the agreed mill purchase price was based on $100 per ton of crushing capacity, the Tribunal ordered Ometto to pay $100 million in damages to compensate for the shortfall of 1 million tons. Ometto attempted to set aside the arbitral awards in the U.S. District Court for the Southern District of New York (Judge Rakoff), citing partiality on the part of the presiding arbitrator and a manifest disregard of Brazilian law in the damages calculations. However, the District Court denied Ometto's motion to vacate both awards.

In contrast to the District Court's findings, the STJ denied Abengoa's subsequent recognition request on public policy grounds due to the lack of impartiality of the presiding arbitrator. Justice João Otávio de Noronha, writing for the majority, also recognised that the tribunal granted damages not contemplated under Brazilian law. Justice Noronha noted that the tribunal's decision should be based on the substantive laws of Brazil as agreed by the parties. Nevertheless, in awarding Abengoa $100 million for lost profits, the tribunal allowed for the recovery of prospective damages, which, according to Justice Noronha, are unavailable in Brazil. As a claimant may only recover against actual - not remote or speculative - damages, the STJ established that the tribunal issued a decision "*beyond the scope of the submission to arbitration*".[48] It is unknown whether the STJ would have reached a different result if the arbitration agreement had not provided for the application of Brazilian law.[49] Given the subsequent reasoning in *Apotex v. Kalinka*, confirming a foreign punitive damages award, I believe the STJ would also be tolerant to a foreign decision awarding prospective damages.

---

46 The STJ eventually rejected the recognition of the Ecuadorian judgment given the Court's lack of jurisdiction to entertain a recognition request against Chevron, a U.S. corporation with no assets in Brazil.

47 *Abengoa v. Ometto*, STJ SEC 9412/US, DJe 30/05/2017.

48 *Ibid.*

49 In his dissent, Justice Felix Fischer's argued that the tribunal grounded the damages awarded on article 944 of the Brazilian Civil Code, thus applying Brazilian law as provided by the arbitration agreement. Furthermore, an arbitral award should be allowed confirmation even if wrongly decided.

3 *Apotex v. Kalinka*: The Compatibility of Foreign Punitive Damages with Public Policy

Given the unavailability of punitive damages in Brazil, some commentators anticipated that a foreign judgment awarding punitive damages would not be entitled to recognition.[50] However, after decades of uncertainty, the STJ finally laid down in *Apotex v. Kalinka* that a foreign judgment awarding punitive damages should not be considered, *per se*, contrary to public policy.

3.1 *Canadian judgment*

In 2007, Apotex Inc. ("Apotex"), a Canadian-based pharmaceutical company, hired Dr. Peter Kalinka ("Kalinka") and his company, Tiburon Bio Consulting ("Tiburon"), to establish and oversee its Biopharmaceuticals Division.[51] Kalinka, the sole owner, director, and employee of Tiburon, a consulting firm incorporated under the laws of Germany, was initially hired as a consultant to develop biosimilar products. In 2012, he was appointed as Apotex's Vice-President of Biopharmaceuticals. According to the Consultancy and Employment Agreements between the parties, Kalinka and Tiburon owed a fiduciary duty to Apotex. As a result, they were not allowed to provide biosimilar consulting services to any other clients and should keep all information relating to Apotex and its biosimilar program confidential. In 2013, Kalinka's employment was terminated due to allegations of bribery. Apotex claimed that Kalinka and his company, Tiburon, received secret payments totalling at least €490.000 from a group of companies based in Budapest, Hungary (collectively, "Accelsiors"). In exchange, Apotex claimed that Kalinka and Tiburon awarded Accelsiors contracts worth approximately €13.1 million on behalf of Apotex. To conceal those illegal payments, Apotex alleged that Tiburon issued fraudulent invoices to Accelsiors for services that were never provided or carried out.

In 2014, Apotex commenced legal action against Kalinka and Tiburon before the Superior Court of Ontario, Canada, for breach of fiduciary duty, breach of duty of confidence, and breach of contract.[52] Apotex claimed that Kalinka's and Tiburon's breaches of their duties resulted in substantial damages as, at a minimum, the prices paid to Accelsiors were inflated by the amount of the bribes received. Consequently, Apotex sought €1.3 million in compensatory damages and the disgorgement of all profits made by Kalinka and Tiburon. In addition, given the "*wanton and contumelious disregard of their*

50 Y. Fisberg, *Dano Social: Reparação, Aspectos Processuais e Destinação*, São Paulo, Almedina Brasil, 2021, p. 220.

51 *Apotex Inc. v. Kalinka*, 2016 ONSC 5527, Court File CV-14-499221.

52 Apotex Statement of Claim, *Apotex Inc. v. Kalinka*, 2016 ONSC 5527, Court File CV-14-499221.

duties", Apotex also claimed punitive and exemplary damages.[53] In their joint statement of defence, Kalinka and Tiburon alleged that they fully complied with the Consultancy and Employment Agreements and performed their duties in good faith.[54] They also claimed that Accelsiors satisfactorily executed the agreed-upon services and that Apotex experienced substantial savings due to the Accelsiors contract. In their counterclaim, Tiburon sought compensatory damages for breach of the Consultancy Agreement, and Kalinka sought compensatory damages for Apotex's failure to pay the annual salary bonus, according to the terms of the Employment Agreement. They both sought punitive or aggravated damages, arguing that Apotex's conduct towards them was "*high-handed and outrageous*".[55]

On 2 September 2016, Justice Perell of the Ontario Superior Court granted Apotex summary judgment and ordered Kalinka and Tiburon to disgorge €324.100, corresponding to the amount received from contracting with Accelsiors after 1 April 2012.[56] Justice Perell found that the business done between Kalinka/Tiburon and Accelsiors during the currency of the Consultancy Agreement with Apotex was genuine and did not amount to fraud.[57] However, after Kalinka was appointed Apotex's Vice-President of Biopharmaceuticals on 1 April 2012, he was contractually prohibited from providing consulting services to anyone other than Apotex.[58] According to Justice Perell, after Kalinka became a full-time employee of Apotex, "*it was all of bribery, breach of fiduciary duty, and breach of contract to do business with Accelsiors*".[59]

Notwithstanding all those breaches, the Superior Court of Ontario dismissed Apotex's claim for punitive damages. The reasoning behind the dismissal was anchored in a set of principles established by the Canadian Supreme Court in the landmark case of *Whiten v. Pilot Insurance Co.*[60] Under *Whiten*, various factors must be considered to ensure that a punitive damages award is appropriate, including the analysis of the degree of misconduct, the harm caused, the availability of other remedies, the quantification of compensatory damages, and the adequacy of compensatory damages in achieving the goals of retribution, deterrence, and denunciation.[61] Applying the *Whiten* standards, the Ontario Superior Court concluded that there was no basis for the imposition of punitive damages against Kalinka. First, the Court asserted that there was no evidence that Apotex "*was actually*

53 *Ibid., para.* 22.
54 Peter Kalinka and Tiburon Bio Consulting Statement of Defence and Counterclaim, *Apotex Inc. v. Kalinka*, 2016 ONSC 5527, Court File CV-14-499221.
55 *Ibid., para.* 27.
56 *Apotex Inc. v. Kalinka*, 2016 ONSC 5527, Court File CV-14-499221.
57 *Ibid., para.* 5.
58 *Ibid., para.* 6.
59 *Ibid., para.* 6.
60 *Whiten v. Pilot Insurance Co.*, [2002] 1 S.C.R. 595.
61 *Ibid., para.* 43.

harmed" by the breach of contract.[62] Second, it was held that Kalinka's misconduct "*was more foolish than high-handed, malicious or arbitrary*".[63] Finally, the Court determined that Kalinka's "*reputation has been tarnished*" and that he was "*adequately punished*" by the disgorgement of his profits and the one-year unemployment period following his dismissal from Apotex.[64] In sum, absent harm, malice, or the need for additional punishment, Justice Perell saw no need for "*retribution, deterrence, and denunciation*" beyond a judgment for the disgorgement of all the profits received from Accelsiors amounting a total of €324.100.[65]

3.2 *Recognition proceedings before the STJ*

Apotex subsequently had to request the recognition of the Canadian judgment in Brazil,[66] where Kalinka had taken up residence.[67] In response, Kalinka and Tiburon jointly opposed the recognition request, arguing that Apotex's application did not meet some formal requirements.[68] Additionally, it was argued that the Canadian judgment violated public policy because: (i) the Superior Court of Ontario had relied in its judgment on illegally obtained evidence, in violation of due process; (ii) Kalinka was deprived of the profits obtained from the services rendered to Accelsiors, which constitutes an offense to human dignity; and also because (iii) Kalinka was ordered to disgorge the profits he received from Accelsiors despite the absence of any accompanying loss or harm to Apotex, a non-compensatory damage that violates Brazilian law.[69]

The Federal Prosecutor's Office (*Ministério Público Federal – MPF*) issued an opinion favouring the recognition. The MPF stressed that the formal requirements were met and that it would only be possible to examine the public policy offense with a *de novo* review

62 *Apotex Inc. v. Kalinka*, 2016 ONSC 5527, Court File CV-14-499221, *para.* 132.

63 *Ibid., para. 132.*

64 *Ibid., para. 132.*

65 *Ibid., para. 132.* Initially, Justice Perell granted Apotex judgment for €299.100 converted into Canadian dollars plus pre- and post-judgment interest. Later, Justice Perell recognised that he had omitted the existence of two invoices and granted Apotex's motion for reconsideration to order Kalinka and Tiburon to disgorge €324.100.

66 *Apotex v. Kalinka*, STJ HDE 586/CA, Min. Raul Araújo, DJe 16/05/2022.

67 As previously noted, the recognition and enforcement of a foreign decision in Brazil is a two-step process. First, the Superior Court of Justice is responsible for entertaining the recognition request, i.e. to give legal force and effect to a foreign decision in Brazil. Second, if recognition is granted, the prevailing party must seek the enforcement of the decision before a Federal Court.

68 Kalinka and Tiburon argued that the following formal requirements were not met: (i) the Superior Court of Ontario had no jurisdiction to hear the matter because at the time the service of process was made, Kalinka was already residing in Brazil; (ii) Apotex did not show that the foreign decision acquired *res judicata* effect; and (iii) the power of attorney granted to the Brazilian lawyers responsible for the recognition proceeding was invalid given that Apotex failed to present a copy of its by-laws.

69 *Apotex v. Kalinka*, STJ HDE 586/CA, Min. Raul Araújo, DJe 16/05/2022.

of the merits of the Canadian judgment. The MPF opinion was flawless. However, we understand that some degree of review is always necessary to ensure that the foreign decision is not offensive to international public policy. Naturally, a substantive review of the foreign decision, i.e. a *révision au fond*, is not possible. Nonetheless, since the offense to public policy must be "manifest" according to Brazilian legislation, at least a very limited and superficial review must occur.

On 2 February 2022, the Special Chamber (*Corte Especial*)[70] of the STJ heard the oral arguments and announced the Court's judgment. In his opinion, Raul Araújo, the reporting justice, stressed that all the formal requirements were met and that the Canadian decision was compatible with public policy.[71] According to Justice Raul Araújo, public policy should be understood as the "*most fundamental moral, religious, political, social, and economic values*" of the forum and must always be invoked "*with great caution*". Justice Raul Araújo underscored that nothing in the Canadian judgment was contrary to public policy.

First, Justice Raul Araújo dealt with the argument that the Superior Court of Ontario based its decision on illegally obtained evidence. It was stressed that "*the STJ is not allowed to conduct a substantive review of the evidence gathered during the fact-finding phase of the foreign proceedings*" as it should be evaluated in accordance with the procedural laws of Canada, not Brazil. Furthermore, the Canadian judgment was based on multiple pieces of evidence, including Kalinka's personal testimony, which led the Superior Court of Ontario to establish the breach of contract. In other words, a single piece of (allegedly) illegal evidence would not alter the Canadian judgment's outcome. Second, Justice Raul Araújo concluded that the Canadian judgment was not offensive to public policy since Kalinka was not illegally deprived of his profits. Justice Raul Araújo stated that the disgorgement of all the profits received from Accelsiors after 1 April 2012, i.e. when Kalinka was an Apotex employee, was appropriate given the breach of contract. Third, Justice Raul Araújo refuted Kalinka's and Tiburon's argument that the disgorgement had a non-compensatory nature and, therefore, would be incompatible with the Brazilian civil liability system. In doing so, he acknowledged that the Canadian judgment did not involve a tort action and that it "*expressly dismissed the punitive damages*" claim altogether.

After Justice Raul Araújo finished reading his opinion, there was a misunderstanding as to whether the Canadian judgment awarded punitive damages. Justice Herman Benjamin made an oral intervention highlighting the importance of the Apotex decision and also granting the recognition request. However, in opposition to Justice Raul Araújo's findings of fact, he stressed that this would be "*the very first time the Superior Court of Justice would grant recognition to a foreign judgment entirely based on punitive damages*".

70 The Special Chamber is composed by the 15 most senior Justices among the 33 members of the STJ.

71 *Apotex v. Kalinka*, STJ HDE 586/CA, Min. Raul Araújo, DJe 16/05/2022.

Justice Maria Isabel Gallotti also stated that the public policy exception could not be used to deny the recognition of a foreign punitive damages decision, even if that concept is alien to the Brazilian legal system. Justice Gallotti also noted that, in civil law matters, there is no requirement for "double criminality", as occurs in extradition cases, according to which the crime for which extradition is sought must be considered a punishable offense in both the requesting and the requested country. Furthermore, the Canadian judgment dealt with a breach of contract outside of Brazil, not a tort claim derived from a non-contractual obligation.[72]

Given those discussions, on 30 March 2022, the STJ held a second judgement session to examine the punitive damages issue. During that second judgment session, Justice Raul Araújo presented an amended version of his opinion to address Justices Herman Benjamin and Maria Isabel Gallotti's concerns. In a new and revised opinion, Justice Raul Araújo stressed, once again, that the Canadian judgment did not award any punitive damages to Apotex. Of greater significance, Justice Raul Araújo went further to conclude that "*even if mistakenly understood that the foreign judgment awarded punitive damages, the alleged public policy offense claim would not stand*". Citing Sergio Cavalieri Filho, a renowned commentator, Justice Raul Araújo emphasised that the Brazilian civil liability system recognises the punitive character of moral damages "*at least in certain circumstances*". For example, "*when the offender's behaviour is particularly reprehensible – either intentional or due to gross negligence – and, also, in cases where the offender profits from the illegal act or engages in multiple illegal conducts*". Two previous decisions from the STJ were also cited in support of the ruling. In both decisions, the STJ laid down that multiple factors must be considered when evaluating moral damages. These include the analysis of the proportionality of the damages, the nature of the violated right, the extent of the harm inflicted, and the financial status of the victim and the offender. Furthermore, when intentional conduct or gross negligence occurs, "*the assessment of moral damages must also assume a punitive and pedagogical character*". In conclusion, Justice Raul Araújo held that "*even if a punitive damages award existed, the foreign decision would not be incompatible with the Brazilian legal system, and there would be no transgression to public policy*".

The STJ's Special Chamber unanimously agreed with Justice Raul Araújo amended opinion. Justice Herman Benjamin even wrote a concurring opinion acknowledging that the Superior Court of Ontario dismissed Apotex's punitive damages claim and that the recognition request should be granted.

On a subsequent motion for clarification, Kalinka and Tiburon insisted on the argument that the disgorgement of profits would amount to a public policy offense given

72 It is not clear from this last passage whether a punitive damages decision arising from a tort claim would be treated differently, or if Justice Gallotti only wished to stress the contractual nature of the matter.

its non-compensatory nature. However, the STJ rejected that motion. The case became final on 24 February 2023 as no new appeal was filed.

4 Conclusion

After decades of academic debate, the STJ has finally established in *Apotex v. Kalinka* that a foreign decision awarding punitive damages should not be considered, *per se*, contrary to public policy. Yet, surprisingly, the case did not involve a foreign punitive damages award. Therefore, it is still unclear how the STJ will respond when confronted with a myriad of related issues: should the STJ be allowed to examine whether the punitive damages are excessive and disproportionate? Would a foreign judgment containing excessive and disproportionate punitive damages violate public policy? Which criteria should the Court use to evaluate the excessiveness of punitive damages? Is the STJ allowed to reduce the punitive damages to a reasonable amount without compromising the entire judgment? Those questions shall be answered in due time. For now, the *Apotex v. Kalinka* ruling resolves a longstanding uncertainty on the enforceability of foreign punitive damages in Brazil.

The repercussions are paramount and not limited to punitive damages cases. In *Apotex v. Kalinka*, the STJ indicates that the public policy exception examination must be carried out with extreme prudence, carefully balancing the fundamental values of the *lex fori*. The STJ also reaffirms that the public policy exception can only be invoked in exceptional circumstances, i.e. only when there is a manifest violation of the most fundamental principles of the Brazilian legal system. Finally, the ruling demonstrates the STJ's utmost respect for private international law principles and provides greater predictability and certainty concerning the recognition and enforcement of foreign judgments.

Towards an International Standard on the Recognition of Punitive Damages?

The role of the Hague Conference on Private International Law

Marta Pertegás Sender and Francesco Zappatore***

1 Introduction

The recognition and enforcement of punitive damages is a hard nut to crack for private international lawyers. Not only is the legal treatment of punitive damages strikingly diverse over the world's legal spectrum, there is also the common understanding that, in principle, judgments lack legal effects in another jurisdiction than the one in which they were rendered. These two key factors – a very diverse range of substantive solutions and the alleged lack of portability of foreign judgments – create significant obstacles for the development of uniform international standards in this specific area of international (tort) law.

Against that framework, it is in and of itself a success for the Hague Conference on Private International Law (the "Hague Conference" or "HCCH") to have successfully addressed punitive damages in recently concluded conventions on recognition and enforcement of judgments in civil and commercial cases.

This chapter assesses whether this work of the Hague Conference has led to international legal standards on the recognition and enforcement of judgments granting punitive damages. Section 2 describes how the relevant HCCH international conventions deal with such judgments, and reports on the status of the conventions under consideration. The authors consider whether, despite lacking the status of binding instruments in most jurisdictions, these conventions and the resulting internationally agreed rules constitute accepted legal practice. For this purpose, this chapter looks into the main characterising features of the treatment of punitive damages in two HCCH conventions. The conventions under review are the 2005 Choice of Court Convention and the 2019 Judgments Convention, both of which have not attained a wide number of ratifications at the time of writing this chapter (early 2023). Despite its lack of direct binding effect, what is known as

* Full Professor in Private International Law, Maastricht University and University of Antwerp; Visiting Professor, University of Johannesburg and Adjunct Professor, IE University.

** Postdoctoral Researcher in Private Law, University of Foggia Law School, Italy.

the "HCCH blueprint" on the recognition and enforcement of punitive damages is remarkable, if only because of the identical rules on punitive damages that these two conventions include.

Next, section 3 embarks on a comparative journey through a few European jurisdictions familiar to the authors. They refer to some of the leading cases on the enforcement of punitive damages judgments in this continent and compare such decisions with the earlier identified characterising features of the HCCH blueprint. The goal is to assess their potential status of an internationally accepted legal practice.

After this brief *tour d'horizon*, the authors conclude that there is little evidence that could support that the rules on punitive damages in recent HCCH work on recognition and enforcement have achieved the status of an international standard. The authors recommend reinforced attention for these provisions and would welcome their future application in relevant cases, either as a result of the conventions' ratification or, in the interim, as an interpretative guidance for the application of domestic rules on recognition and enforcement.

2 A carefully crafted and calibrated formulation

Other chapters in this book reveal how heterogeneous the substantive legal treatment of punitive damages can be in comparative tort law. The perfect scenario, one would argue, for the development of uniform private international law rules on punitive damages. Indeed, where uniform substantive rules on such damages appear unimaginable, common rules on international jurisdiction, on applicable law, and on the recognition and enforcement of judgments may mitigate legal uncertainty and provide a reasonable degree of legal foreseeability in international cases where punitive damages are granted.

However, a comprehensive set of PIL rules on punitive damages is lacking. Various PIL conventions deal with damages in particular sectors, such as traffic accidents, product liability or maritime torts, but they do not provide for specific rules in the case of punitive damages.[1] Interestingly, it is in the area of recognition and enforcement of foreign judgments where punitive damages have been prominently and consistently addressed in recent HCCH work. Both the 2005 Choice of Court Convention and the 2019 Judgments Convention contain identical rules for judgments on punitive damages. It is the result of a carefully crafted and calibrated formula adopted by consensus after lengthy negotiations in the lead-up to the 2005 Choice of Court Convention.

1 J. Von Hein, 'Damages', in G. Rühl, F. Ferrari, P. De Miguel Asensio & J. Basedow (eds.), *Encyclopedia of Private International Law*, Cheltenham, Edward Elgar Publishing, 2017, pp. 512-519.

2.1 *The HCCH blueprint on the international ordering of punitive damages*

Article 11 of the 2005 Choice of Court Convention and article 10 of the 2019 Judgments Convention contain identical provisions on damages. Both articles read as follows:

> "*Damages*
> *(1) Recognition or enforcement of a judgment may be refused if, and to the extent that, the judgment awards damages, including exemplary or punitive damages, that do not compensate a party for actual loss or harm suffered.*
> *(2) The court addressed shall take into account whether and to what extent the damages awarded by the court of origin serve to cover costs and expenses relating to the proceedings.*"

The Hartley-Dogauchi Report on the 2005 Choice of Court Convention duly reports on the painstaking negotiations and discussions leading to the adopted consensus formula.[2] A dedicated working group was set up to elaborate both the black letter rule of article 11 as well as a statement that, upon agreement by the 2005 Diplomatic Session, was inserted in the Explanatory Report. This is an explanatory statement agreed by a dedicated working group and then approved by the delegations, to give further context and facilitate the understanding and application of article 11 of the Choice of Court Convention. Years later, in the early negotiations that eventually led to the successful conclusion of the 2019 Judgments Convention, delegations agreed that the text of the 2005 Choice of Court Convention would provide the starting point for the drafting of the new treaty. This approach – copy-pasting the corresponding article of the previous convention – was a sensible one in particular for the discussion on punitive damages, as delegations vividly recalled the complicated drafting process of article 11 of the 2005 Choice of Court Convention. During the negotiations of the 2019 Judgments Convention, no delegation saw the need for a deviation and, as a result, an identical article on "Damages" was inserted in the 2019 Judgments Convention. The respective sections of the two relevant Explanatory Reports contain valuable additional information on this interesting drafting technique and the resulting alignment in formulation.[3]

---

2 See the Hartley/Dogauchi Report on the 2005 Choice of Court Convention, sections 203-205, available at Hague Conference on Private International Law, *Proceedings of the Twentieth Session*, Tome III (Choice of Court), pp. 833-834.

3 See the Hartley/Dogauchi Report on the 2005 Choice of Court Convention, sections 203-205 and the Garcimartín/Saumier Report on the 2019 Judgments Convention, sections 291-294. For more information about the earlier discussions on punitive damages, see a proposed article 33 on "Damages" in the Work. Doc. No. 98 of 19 June 2001, with the provisional outcome of the negotiations pertaining to the "Judgments Project" from 1992 to the first part of the Diplomatic Session of 2001 that did not produce a convention. See

For our current purposes, the two relevant articles, jointly referred to in this chapter as the "HCCH blueprint on punitive damages", possess three main characterising features.

The first is the distinction between the compensatory part of the judgment and the expressly punitive part of the judgment. The former is in principle enforceable under the respective conventions, while the latter may be enforceable, but there is no obligation to do so under the respective conventions. In other words, the "all or nothing approach" is not recommended: the court addressed should not refuse enforcement when domestic law ignores punitive damages and proceed with enforcement when punitive damages are known in the domestic law. Instead, the HCCH standard is based on the possibility of layering the foreign judgment and seeking partial enforcement.

As a corollary to this hybrid approach, the court addressed can calibrate what is compensatory and what is not. Damages intended to cover the costs and expenses of the proceedings can be factored in and should not be non-compensatory *per se*. Thus, as a second feature, the application of the HCCH blueprint allows for a combined assessment of the substantive part of the judgment (the award of damages) and the procedural costs (costs and expenses relating to the proceedings).

The third characterising feature of this HCCH blueprint is the specific treatment of punitive damages through a dedicated article on the nature and amount of damages. This *sui generis* solution was found to bridge the divergent positions on the use of the public policy exception for such cases. During the debate, certain delegations were of the view that the public policy exception could be used for damages that go beyond the actual loss, while others considered that their limited concept of public policy would not capture such cases and, as such, it would not allow for the application of the public policy exception under the respective conventions. This means that the public policy exception is not the preferred route for the specific treatment of punitive damages according to the HCCH standard.

Having described the relevant HCCH rules, we will next turn to their practical relevance by examining, in turn, whether they are either directly or indirectly applied in practice.

2.2 *Direct effect of the HCCH blueprint for punitive damages?*

At the time of writing, the direct effect of the HCCH rules described is rather limited. The authors are unaware of any reported judgment where the articles referred to have already been applied. This is mainly the consequence of the status of the conventions under

---

Hague Conference on Private International Law, *Proceedings of the Twentieth Session*, Tome II (Judgments), pp. 459-460.

review.[4] The 2019 Judgments Convention will enter into force on 1 September 2023 for Ukraine and the EU so it cannot have generated any case law to date. As to the 2005 Choice of Court Convention, it is in force since 2015 but only in a limited number of jurisdictions. Besides the limited geographical reach of this convention, there are, in our opinion, two other limiting factors. The first factor is that judgments awarding punitive damages will not typically arise from contractual transactions, while this is the most likely scenario for disputes between parties bound by a choice of court agreement. The second factor is that the limited number of jurisdictions where the 2005 Choice of Court Convention is currently in force are not known to be jurisdictions where damages of a non-compensatory nature or excessive damages can be awarded.

Lacking such direct effect, one could hastily conclude that the HCCH blueprint on punitive damages has not yet reached the stage of a generally accepted international standard. Before jumping to any such conclusions, the next section considers whether the characterising features of the HCCH blueprint mentioned above appear in a sample of significant judgments from EU jurisdictions familiar to the authors. Some of these cases are examined in further detail in the chapter submitted by Cedric Vanleenhove to this book. In this chapter, we take a specific angle and examine below whether any of the three characterising features of the HCCH blueprint are traceable in this case law.

3 A *Tour d'Horizon*: Is the HCCH Standard Applied or Influential in Practice?

3.1 *The use of the public policy exception*

Since the early stages of the preparatory work that led to the conventions under review, the use of the public policy exception was not met with approval.[5] In sharp contrast, European continental courts keep using this exception to date as the main safeguard for the (non-) enforcement of foreign punitive damages judgments. Reference can be made to German, Swiss and French cases.

4 For the most recent status of these conventions, see the specialised pages on the 2005 Choice of Court Convention and the 2019 Judgments Convention at https://www.hcch.net/en/instruments/conventions.

5 In the early negotiations of the Judgments Project, it became clear to the negotiators that reverting to the public policy exception for this type of cases was sub-optimal. See, e.g. C. Kessedjian, 'Report on the 1998 Special Commission', in Hague Conference on Private International Law, *Proceedings of the Twentieth Session*, Tome Rome? II (Judgments), pp. 125-126.

In Germany, the German Federal Court of Justice (*Bundesgerichtshof*) issued the first and most extensive decision in this area of law in 1992.[6] The case concerned a US decision that ordered the defendant to pay damages in the amount of USD 700.000 (including USD 400.000 in punitive damages) to a minor who had been sexually abused. During the proceedings, the perpetrator, who had dual US-German citizenship, relocated to Germany and the victim therefore applied for recognition and enforcement of the judgment in Germany.

The Court's ruling is of particular interest because of its thorough and extensive explanation as to why US punitive damages trigger the public policy exception found in article 328(1)4 of the *Zivilprozessordnung* (ZPO), i.e. the German Civil Code of Procedure.[7] The German Federal Court of Justice, first of all, stated that US damages suits were incompatible with the fundamental principles of German law, since the German private law system provides for compensation for the damages suffered, but does not intend an enrichment of the victim.[8] Moreover, the *Bundesgerichtshof* held that punishment and deterrence, the main objectives pursued by punitive damages, are aims of criminal law rather than of civil law.[9] Furthermore, it stated that the effect of accepting punitive damages

---

6 *Bundesgerichtshof* 4 June 1992, BGHZ 118, p. 312. Moreover, see H. Bungert, 'Enforcing U.S. Excessive and Punitive Damages Awards in Germany', *The International Lawyer*, Vol. 27, No. 4, 1993, pp. 1075-1076, according to whom "at least five important judgments have emerged during the past five years, accompanied by an increase of German and American law review commentary. In 1989, the *Landgericht* Berlin (District Court of Berlin) denied recognition of a Massachusetts award of $275.000 for pain and suffering and loss of earnings due to an industrial accident at a machine manufactured by the German defendant. In 1989 and 1992, the *Oberlandesgericht* Munchen (Munich Court of Appeals) held that a U.S. summons for punitive damages awards can be served upon a German defendant under the Hague Convention on the Service Abroad of Judicial and Extrajudicial Documents in Civil and Commercial Matters".

7 Article § 328 ZPO provides that: (1) The recognition of the judgment of a foreign court is excluded: 1. where the courts of the State to which the foreign court belongs have no jurisdiction under German law; 2. where the defendant, who has not appeared in the proceedings and relies on that fact, was not duly served with the document instituting the proceedings or was not served within sufficient time to enable him to arrange for his defence; 3. where the judgment is irreconcilable with a judgment rendered here, or with an earlier foreign judgment which is entitled to recognition, or where the proceeding which gave rise to the foreign judgment is irreconcilable with a proceeding instituted earlier here; 4. where the recognition of the judgment would produce a result which would be manifestly irreconcilable with fundamental principles of German law, especially where the recognition is irreconcilable with basic constitutional rights; 5. where reciprocity is not guaranteed. (2) The provision contained in sub-paragraph 5 shall not prevent recognition of the judgment where that judgment relates to a non-pecuniary claim and the German courts had no jurisdiction under German law, or where a matter concerning the status of children (§ 640) is at issue.

8 "*An American punitive damages judgement of not insignificant amount globally awarded along with damages for material and immaterial losses in so far generally cannot be declared enforceable in Germany*". Moreover, the German legal principle of awarding damages exclusively in order to reimburse the victim for what he has lost was held to be a fundamental principle of German law.

9 The Federal Court of Justice summarised the functions of punitive damages as follows: "*Punitive or exemplary damages are monies awarded beyond pure compensatory damages when the general elements of an offence are rendered more serious by intentional, malicious or reckless conduct (...). Punitive damages serve up to four main purposes: the offender shall be punished for his rough conduct so that possible acts of revenge by the victim become unnecessary. The offender and society in general shall be deterred from future anti-social*

would be that the claimant would act as a "private prosecutor" and this would be incompatible with the State's monopoly on penalisation and the relevant procedural safeguards.[10]

Then, the German Federal Court of Justice took its analysis one step further, by assessing whether punitive damages awards would pass the proportionality test. In fact, according to this principle, German courts must ensure that an award for damages does not exceed the amount needed to compensate the injured party. In this respect, the *Bundesgerichtshof*, by expressing its disapproval of sums of money imposed on top of the compensation for damages, found that, in the case before it, the punitive damages awarded were higher in amount than the sum of all the compensatory damages and, thus, the full enforcement would have been excessive.[11]

Lastly, the Court pointed out the differences between punitive damages and damages for pain and suffering, holding that the function of deterrence and punishment is not comparable to the aspect of satisfaction which has to be considered in damages for pain and suffering and damages for the infringement of personal rights.[12] Thus, the *Bundesgerichtshof* concluded that an award of punitive damages is fundamentally contrary to German public order and refused to recognise and enforce the US judgement.

---

behaviour so that the mere risk of a duty to compensate does not ensure a sufficient means to guide behaviour. The injured party shall be rewarded for the enforcement of law and order that is based on his commitment – to strengthening law and order in general. Ultimately, the victim shall receive a supplement to the compensation, which is perceived as insufficient, whereby inter alia a lack of social safeguard can have an impact; in this respect one can consider the counterbalancing effect on the claimant's non-recoverable extrajudicial costs".

10 The German Supreme Court noted that there are examples of contractual penalties that provide for punishment under civil law. However, since contractual penalties originate from a legal agreement between parties, the Court found them to be irrelevant to the case at hand. See C. Vanleenhove, 'The Current European Perspective on the Exequatur of U.S. Punitive Damages: Opening the Gate but Keeping a Guard', *Polish Yearbook of International Law*, Vol. 35, 2015, p. 244, according to whom "*this finding could have dismantled the civil/criminal distinction that the Court embraced and could have created an opening for punitive damages*".

11 See C. Vanleenhove, 'The Current European Perspective on the Exequatur of U.S. Punitive Damages: Opening the Gate but Keeping a Guard', *Polish Yearbook of International Law*, Vol. 35, 2015, p. 246, according to whom "*this statement may be interpreted such that the Bundesgerichtshof views a 1:1 ratio between compensatory and punitive damages as the maximum allowed*".

12 In fact, the Federal Court stated that: (1) for the determination of the damages for pain and suffering the level of the pain and suffering is the main aspect, (2) the aspect of satisfaction itself does not constitute a penal character of the damages for pain and suffering, and (3) the aspect of satisfaction would be connected to the aspect of compensation. Moreover, the *Bundesgerichtshof* held that the enforcement of the punitive damages award should be denied because its enforcement in Germany would put foreign creditors in a better position than domestic creditors, since the former would be able to gain access to the assets of German debtors to a considerably greater extent than the latter, even if the latter had suffered more damages. This leads, according to the Court, to a lack of equal treatment. See C. Vanleenhove, 'The Current European Perspective on the Exequatur of U.S. Punitive Damages: Opening the Gate but Keeping a Guard', *Polish Yearbook of International Law*, Vol. 35, 2015, p. 245, "*it thus seems that the Bundesgerichtshof attempted to protect German industry from US litigation*".

In Switzerland, the public policy exception features as the first ground for refusal of recognition and enforcement of foreign judgments in article 27 of the Swiss Private International Law Act. Academic writings refer to two notorious examples of Swiss case law concerning the recognition of US punitive damages judgments.[13] In a first case, in 1982, a lower court denied the recognition of a Texas punitive damages award. The ruling was issued on the argument that punitive damages were manifestly contrary to the principle of full compensation of the damage and no compensation of the victim beyond the actual harm.

A few years later, in 1989, a lower court in Basel granted recognition and enforcement of a US judgment awarding punitive damages.[14] In this instance, the court considered that, under the Swiss Civil Code, illicit profit must also be repaid in the circumstances of the case. Accordingly, the Basel court took the view that there was no incompatibility, rather a convergent approach, in a case relating to the disgorgement of an illegally gained profit.

Interestingly, France has adopted a more receptive and tolerant approach towards US punitive damages. In fact, the French Supreme Court (*Cour de Cassation*) has no objection to the concept itself. Instead of completely rejecting punitive damages, the Court focuses on the amount of punitive damages awarded by the foreign court.[15] This shows some similarities with the third characterising feature of the HCCH blueprint, according to which the nature and amount of the damages granted should be the primary consideration in deciding whether or not recognition and enforcement is possible.

This approach can be illustrated by reference to the French Supreme Court judgment in the *Schlenzka & Langhorne v. Fountaine Pajot S.A.* case.[16] In 2003, the California

13 See A. Stadler, 'Recognition of punitive damages in Germany and Switzerland', in S. Bariati, L. Fumagalli & Z. Crespi Reghizzi (Eds.), *Punitive Damages and Private International Law: State of the Art and Future Developments*, Milan, Wolters Kluwer, 2019, p. 150.

14 As reported in the book chapter by A. Stadler referred to in the previous footnote: Civil Court of Basel, 1 February 1989, *SF Inc vs TCS AG*.

15 See C. Vanleenhove, 'The Current European Perspective on the Exequatur of U.S. Punitive Damages: Opening the Gate but Keeping a Guard', *Polish Yearbook of International Law*, Vol. 35, 2015, p. 250, according to whom "*this more receptive stance increases the likelihood that the plaintiff will be able to enforce an American judgement containing punitive damages in its entirety against a defendant's assets in [...] France*".

16 Cass. Civ. 1st, 1 December 2010, *Schlenzka & Langhorne v. Fountaine Pajot S.A.*, no. 09-13303, *Recueil Dalloz*, 2011, p. 423. In France, before *Fountaine Pajot*, there had been only one decision dealing with the enforcement of a US judgment awarding punitive damages, in which the lower court refused to grant *exequatur* for two main reasons: (1) punitive damages are penal in nature and cannot be enforced in France, and (2) punitive damages violate the principle of full compensation (*principe de compensation intégrale*). Moreover, see B. West Janke & F.-X. Licari, 'Enforcing Punitive Damage Awards in France after Fountain Pajot', *American Journal of Comparative Law*, 2012, Vol. 60, p. 778, according to whom "*there were some faint hints in the jurisprudence that the Cour de cassation would recognize damages of a punitive nature. For example, French courts consistently enforce foreign sanctions based on contempt of court and penalty clauses (clauses pénales) in private contracts [...]. By contrast, French doctrine was much more prolix in admitting,*

Superior Court ruled in favour of the plaintiffs and awarded them USD 1.391.650,12 in actual damages. Moreover, the Court, holding that Fountaine Pajot's behaviour constituted fraud under California law, stated that an amount of USD 1.460.000 in punitive damages[17] would be suitable to punish and deter the French company. The American plaintiffs subsequently had to enforce the judgment in France, since Fountaine Pajot was located there.

Both the *tribunal de grande instance* and the French Court of Appeal refused to enforce the California judgement.[18] They held that the proper purpose of tort law is to return the victim to the *status quo* and, thus, the amount of damages should not be based on the wrongdoer's wealth or his fault, but it should be determined solely by the extent of the plaintiff's damages. Consequently, the Court of Appeal considered an award that punishes the tortfeasor to the benefit of the plaintiff as a windfall,[19] in violation of the French *ordre public international.*[20]

---

almost unanimously, the compatibility of foreign punitive damage awards with the French ordre public so long as the sum is not disproportionate or excessive".

17 The Court noted that the purpose of awarding punitive damages is not to bring financial ruin to the defendant, but, instead, to punish the defendant and deter it from engaging in such conduct in the future. Thus, it held that an award of 1.460.000 USD, "*which is approximately twenty percent of the net worth of the corporation*", was appropriate.

18 See Cour d'Appel Poitiers, 1re Chambre civile, 26 February 2009, *Schlenzka v. S.A. Fountaine Pajot*, no 07/02404, *137 JDI*, 2010, p. 1230.

19 See J.A. Breslo, 'Taking the Punitive Damage Windfall Away from the Plaintiff: An Analysis', *Northwestern University Law Review*, Vol. 86, 1992, p. 1130 ff. On the contrary, see B. West Janke & F.-X. Licari, 'Enforcing Punitive Damage Awards in France after Fountain Pajot', *American Journal of Comparative Law*, Vol. 60, 2012, p. 790, according to whom "*[...] in reality, there is not always a windfall or even full compensation for the plaintiff because there are many legal or factual obstacles to a veritable full compensation*"; R. Demogue, 'Validity of the Theory of Compensatory Damages', *Yale Law Journal*, Vol. 27, 1918, pp. 585-593, which supports punitive damages and regards them as a means to fully implement the principle of full compensation. In fact, many scholars believe that the American rule regarding attorneys' fees is a significant impediment to the principle of full compensation. Accordingly, since the plaintiff generally may not recover his attorney fees, paradoxically, punitive damages can sometimes operate to fill the gap and achieve full compensation.

20 See B. West Janke & F.-X. Licari, 'Enforcing Punitive Damage Awards in France after Fountain Pajot', *American Journal of Comparative Law*, Vol. 60, 2012, p. 791 ff., who "*regard the appellate court's determination as incorrect and incongruent with how the Cour de cassation has interpreted principles of compensation in light of the ordre public international*". According to the authors, the *Cour de Cassation* has rejected many decisions of lower courts that granted awards higher or lower than the damage actually suffered, by referring to the concept of *ordre public interne*, which involves purely domestic considerations. However, cases involving the recognition of foreign judgments deal with the *ordre public international*, which refers to "*a set of intangible and superior values, which combine the general (or public) interest, such as political, moral, and social rights. [It is a doctrine] whereby the courts will reject foreign laws or judgments when they are considered contrary to fundamental national cultural values*" (see M.L. Niboyet & G. de Geouffre de La Pradelle, *Droit International Privé no. 307*, L.G.D.J. Lextenso Editions, 2009, p. 63). As a consequence, a foreign law or a foreign judgment offending the *ordre public interne* is not sufficient to trigger the *ordre public international* exception.

Ultimately, the French Supreme Court ruled that "*the principle of awarding punitive damages is not, in itself, contrary to public policy; although this is not the case when the amount awarded is disproportional to the loss suffered and to the contractual breach of the debtor*".[21] Thus, this lack of proportionality of the award was contrary to the *ordre public international* and, as a consequence, the French Supreme Court rejected the entire judgment.

This judgment is particularly significant since punitive damages are not *per se* incompatible with the French public policy, as long as they are proportionate. Thus, the centre of the public policy analysis moves from the incompatibility of punitive damages themselves to an examination of their amount.[22] However, the Supreme Court did not provide guidelines on how to determine whether a foreign punitive damages award is proportionate. In fact, it just stated that punitive damages should not be disproportionate in relation to the injury suffered and the breach of the contractual obligations of the debtor. Consequently, the determination of the proportional nature of the award is at the discretion of the lower courts and may give rise to diverse outcomes.[23]

3.2 *"All or nothing approach"*

Despite the lack of explicit references, other judgments seem to have embraced the first feature of the HCCH blueprint. Instead of a categorical rejection of the foreign judgment, certain decisions in Spain, Italy and the Netherlands move away from the more conventional "all or nothing approach".

In Spain, the landmark judgment was rendered by the Spanish Supreme Court on 13 November 2001.[24] The Spanish Supreme Court considered whether a Texas judgment could obtain an *exequatur* pursuant to article 954 of the Spanish Code of Civil Procedure. In considering whether the conditions for *exequatur* were met, the Spanish Supreme Court referred to the punitive and sanctioning function of the damages awarded in Texas,

21 "*Le principe d'une condemnation à des dommages interest punitifs, n'est pas, en soi, contraire à l'ordre public, il en est autrement lorsque le montant alloué est disproportionné au regard du préjudice subi et des manquements aux obligations contractuelles du débiteur*".

22 See C. Vanleenhove, 'The Current European Perspective on the Exequatur of U.S. Punitive Damages: Opening the Gate but Keeping a Guard', *Polish Yearbook of International Law*, Vol. 35, 2015, p. 255, according to whom "*this revolutionary ruling makes it clear that objections against the enforcement of punitive damages based on the argument that they violate the divide between criminal and private law should be dismissed. This liberal, welcoming attitude on the part of France's Supreme Court appears [...] to be very progressive*". Moreover, this corresponds also to the attitude of the Spanish Supreme Court in *Miller Import Corp. v. Alabastros Alfredo, S.L.*

23 See C. Vanleenhove, 'The Current European Perspective on the Exequatur of U.S. Punitive Damages: Opening the Gate but Keeping a Guard', *Polish Yearbook of International Law*, Vol. 35, 2015, p. 255 ff.

24 Spanish Supreme Court (Tribunal Supremo), 13 November 2001, ATS 1803/2001 – ECLI:ES:TS:2001:1803.

as well as their deterrent function, and considered that such functions are not entirely remote from Spanish substantive and procedural law. Accordingly, in solving the "dilemma" whether or not such punitive damages are against Spanish public policy, the Spanish Supreme Court saw merit in applying a principle of proportionality, in line with judgments rendered in neighbouring countries in such circumstances. Without referring to particular jurisdictions, it seems quite likely that the Spanish Supreme Court was referring to judicial developments in Italy and France.

The developments in Italy are indeed noteworthy. To express it with the Italian Supreme Court wording itself:

> *"In the Italian juridical system, tort law is not exclusively given the task to restore the subject that suffered the injury, since it pursues punitive and deterrent functions as well, thus, punitive damages are not ontologically incompatible with the Italian juridical system. However, the exequatur of a foreign judgment awarding punitive damages is subject to the condition that it has been issued in a juridical system that guarantees the principle of legality and provides for limits as regards the amount, having only regard to the effects of the foreign act and to their compatibility with the public order".*[25]

This judgment is a complete shift from earlier decisions, where the Supreme Court had stated that foreign judgments awarding punitive damages are not compatible with Italian public order, since the exclusive task of tort law is compensation, whilst deterrence and punishment are alien.[26] There are three main reasons why the Supreme Court decided to change its approach: (i) an evolving notion of public policy, (ii) the changes introduced in Italian substantive law with regard to punitive damages, and (iii) the changes relating to the nature and functions of Italian tort law.

The first reason is quite essential. The Italian Supreme Court is currently of the view that the public policy exception is no longer the safeguard of the sum of fundamental principles that characterise a national community in a specific historical period but finds

25 Cass. Civ. Sez. Un., 5 July 2017, no. 16601, in *Danno e responsabilità*, 2017, p. 419 ff., which stated the following principle: "*Nel vigente ordinamento, alla responsabilità civile non è assegnato solo il compito di restaurare la sfera patrimoniale del soggetto che ha subìto la lesione, poiché sono interne al sistema la funzione di deterrenza e quella sanzionatoria del responsabile civile, sicché non è ontologicamente incompatibile con l'ordinamento italiano l'istituto, di origine statunitense, dei risarcimenti punitivi. Il riconoscimento di una sentenza straniera che contenga una pronuncia di tal genere deve, però, corrispondere alla condizione che essa sia stata resa nell'ordinamento straniero su basi normative che garantiscano la tipicità delle ipotesi di condanna, la prevedibilità della stessa ed i suoi limiti quantitativi, dovendosi avere riguardo, in sede di delibazione, unicamente agli effetti dell'atto straniero ed alla loro compatibilità con l'ordine pubblico*".

26 Cass., Sez. III, 17 January 2007, no. 1183, in *Foro it.*, 2007, I, p. 1460; Cass., Sez. I, 8 February 2012, no. 1781, *Foro it.*, 2012, 5, p. 1454 ff.

that it should reflect the fundamental principles derived from the Constitution, the Founding Treaties of the European Union, the Charter of Fundamental Rights of the European Union and, indirectly, the European Convention on Human Rights. It follows that the public policy exception impedes the enforcement of a foreign judgment in Italy only if such judgment is incompatible with the fundamental principles derived from the Constitution and, more in general, with the values aimed to protect the fundamental rights of individuals resulting from the supranational order.[27]

The Italian Supreme Court highlighted the significant evolution of the concept of public policy over the last few years. The Court also stressed that its application should take the international legal order, of which the Italian law system is also a part, into account. In particular, it stated that the main effect of the transposition of supranational law is the promotion of European protected values, not the progressive loosening of traditional control by national law limiting the entry of foreign rules and judgments.

In sum, a common trend appears to emerge from the decisions under review: the application of the public policy exception requires a very thoughtful consideration of the specific circumstances of the case. There is lesser support for an "all or nothing approach" where the recognition and enforcement of a foreign judgment is automatically refused because punitive damages are contrary to the forum's public policy. Instead, a case-by-case analysis is carried out, where the compatibility or incompatibility with the public policy exception remains the quintessential factor. Whether the pendulum oscillates in one direction or the other is difficult to assess: as an addendum, we can refer here to a judgment rendered by the Court of Appeal of 's-Hertogenbosch (the Netherlands) in 2021. The Court refused the recognition and enforcement of a US judgment that had awarded punitive damages for the same amount as the compensatory part of the damages, after a thoughtful consideration of the specifics of the case, the transcription of the judgment *a quo* and an extensive motivation of the elements that argued against the enforcement. Despite no explicit reference, the Dutch court seems to have taken into account whether and to what extent the damages awarded by the court of origin serve to cover costs and expenses relating to the proceedings, in line with the second element of the HCCH blueprint. The Court concluded that it is unclear whether this element influenced the amount of the damages granted.[28]

---

27 See G. Corsi, 'Le Sezioni Unite: via libera al riconoscimento di sentenze comminatorie di punitive damages', *Danno e responsabilità*, 4, 2017, p. 431, according to whom the judge will deny the *exequatur* only when there is a permanent contrast of the foreign norm to the entire regulatory framework. Moreover, see G. Ponzanelli, 'Polifunzionalità tra diritto internazionale privato e diritto privato', *Danno e responsabilità*, 4, 2017, pp. 435-439, according to whom "*questa ristretta nozione di ordine pubblico rende evidentemente meno severo il riconoscimento di sentenze straniere, e questo costituisce il primo tassello del revirement giurisprudenziale del luglio 2017*".

28 Court of Appeal 's-Hertogenbosch, 31 August 2021, ECLI:NL:GHSHE:2021:2699, paras. 3.7.3 and 3.7.4 (after an extensive consideration of the U.S. Transcript of Proceedings).

4 Concluding remarks

Our schematic *tour d'horizon* of some European jurisdictions has yielded discrete results. We think that, for the time being, the HCCH blueprint on the recognition and enforcement of punitive damages is either unknown or insufficiently considered. To recall, the three characterising elements of the HCCH blueprint are the possibility of a partial enforcement despite the punitive component, the quantitative assessment (in terms of amount) of damages, and the holistic approach to procedural costs and expenses and damages. The practical effects of the HCCH rules will of course gain traction once the relevant conventions enter into force and/or secure more ratifications.

While such processes may take time, we see merit in the use of the HCCH blueprint as non-binding guidance for domestic courts faced with such particular cases. After all, this HCCH legal framework was specifically designed for the assessment of punitive damages in the specific context of the recognition and enforcement of foreign judgments and adopted by consensus.

Maastricht Law Series

The Maastricht Law Series is created in 2018 by Boom juridisch and Eleven International Publishing in association with the Maastricht University Faculty of Law. The Maastricht Law Series publishes books on comparative, European and International law. The series builds upon the tradition of excellence in research at the Maastricht Faculty of Law, its research centers and the Ius Commune Research School. The Maastricht Law Series is a peer reviewed book series that allows researchers an excellent opportunity to showcase their work.

Series editors
Prof dr. Bram Akkermans (editor-in-chief)
Prof. dr. Monica Claes
Prof. dr. Fons Coomans
Prof. dr. Mariolina Eliantonio
Prof. dr. Michael Faure
Prof. dr. Bram van Hofstraeten
Prof. dr. Saskia Klosse
Dr. Denise Prevost
Prof. dr. David Roef
Dr. Marcel Schaper
Prof. dr. Jan M. Smits

Published in this series:

Volume 1: Reinhard Zimmermann, Does the Law of Succession Reflect Cultural Differences?, ISBN 978-94-6236-856-9

Volume 2: Anna Berlee, Access to personal data in public land registers, ISBN 978-94-6236-841-5

Volume 3: Marcus Meyer, The Position of Dutch Works Councils in Multinational Corporations, ISBN 978-94-6236-848-4

Volume 4: Jaap Hage, Foundations and Building Blocks of Law, ISBN 978-94-6236-860-6

Volume 5: Bastiaan van Zelst, The End of Justice(s)?, ISBN 978-94-6236-881-1

Volume 6: Agustín Parise & Lars van Vliet (eds.), Re- De- Co-dification? New Insights on the Codification of Private Law, ISBN 978-94-6236-900-9

Volume 7: Caroline Rupp, Rafael Ibarra Garza & Bram Akkermans, Property Law Perspectives VI, ISBN 978-94-6236-904-7

Volume 8: Aalt Willem Heringa, Europees Nederlands Staatsrecht, ISBN 978-94-6290-604-4

Volume 9: Symeon C. Symeonides, The "Private" in Private International Law, ISBN 978-94-6236-949-8
Volume 10: Jaap Hage, European Integration: A Theme, ISBN 978-94-6236-981-8
Volume 11: Jan M. Smits, Five Uneasy Pieces. Essays on Law and Evolution, ISBN 978-94-6236-982-5
Volume 12: Hannah Brodersen, Vincent Glerum, & André Klip, The European Arrest Warrant and In Absentia Judgements, ISBN 978-94-6236-985-6
Volume 13: Bram Akkermans & Gijs van Dijck, Sustainability and Private Law, ISBN 978-94-6236-986-3
Volume 14: Antonia Waltermann, David Roef, Jaap Hage & Marko Jelicic, Law, Science, Rationality, ISBN 978-94-6236-989-4
Volume 15: Frans L. Leeuw, Van Legal Realism naar Legal Big Data, ISBN 978-94-6290-781-2
Volume 16: Josua Sitompul, Cross-border Access to Electronic Evidence, ISBN 978-94-6236-133-1
Volume 17: Bram Akkermans & Jill Robbie, Property Law Perspectives VII, ISBN 978-946236-181-2
Volume 18: Bram Akkermans & Anna Berlee, 'Sjef-Sache', ISBN 978-94-6236-197-3
Volume 19: Froukje van den Borne, Luca Cox, Youri Cremers, Daan Groenewoud, Sven Schaghen & Tom Stijns, Het stopzetten van KEI-civiel nader bezien, ISBN 978-94-6290-955-7
Volume 20: Nicholas Mouttotos, The Impact of Europeanization in Cyprus Contract Law and the Spill-Over to Matters of Civil Procedure, ISBN 978-94-6236-206-2
Volume 21: Katja Zimmermann, Facilitating Cross-Border Real Estate Transactions in Europe, ISBN 978-94-6236-220-8
Volume 22: Alexis E. Antoniades, Remedies for human rights violations by the European Union, ISBN 978-94-6236-275-8
Volume 23: André Klip, European Arrest Warrant, ISBN 978-94-6236-284-0
Volume 24: Bram Akkermans, Sustainable Property Law, ISBN 978-94-6236-289-5
Volume 25: Sarah Schoenmaekers & Pauline Melin, The Art of Moving Borders, ISBN 978-94-6236-296-3
Volume 26: Agustín Parise & Olivier Moréteau, Comparative Perspectives on Law and Language, ISBN 978-94-6236-328-1
Volume 27: Renata Barbosa, Vincent Glerum, Hans Kijlstra, André Klip & Christina Peristeridou, Improving the European Arrest Warrant, ISBN 978-94-6236-327-4
Volume 28: Cedric Vanleenhove & Lotte Meurkens, The Recognition and Enforcement of Punitive Damages Judgments Across the Globe, ISBN 978-90-4730-162-2

www.ingramcontent.com/pod-product-compliance
Lightning Source LLC
Chambersburg PA
CBHW061355240926
51846CB00007B/1414